WALKING THE ENGLISH COAST

A Beginner's Guide

D1730734

RUTH LIVINGSTONE

🐦 @iamselfpub
www.iamselfpublishing.com

Preface

Once I dreamt of running marathons, climbing Everest, swimming the Channel, skydiving out of aeroplanes... but when I hit my mid-50s, I realised I was too unfit and too timid to do any of these things. So I started walking instead.

Since then, I've completed over 3,000 miles on my feet, most of it around the coastline of Britain, and I run a successful walking blog, describing my adventures, at coastalwalker.co.uk.

If I can turn from a couch potato into an experienced coastal walker, anybody can.

This book is intended for those of you who want to set out on a coastal walking adventure of your own, and is particularly designed for newcomers to the world of long-distance walking.

I can't provide a detailed description of the England Coast Path, which is still under development and with a definitive route yet to be finalised at the time of writing. And I'm not going to instruct you on exactly which interesting sights you really should visit, because there are plenty of guidebooks that do that already. Instead, I will give you the skills and knowledge you need to plan your own walks. I will discuss some of the decisions you need to make before you start, share with you the lessons I learnt from my mistakes, and offer plenty of practical advice.

My aim is to fill you with enthusiasm for the days ahead, while making your life easier and your planning simpler.

Each of us, whether we walk alone or with a group, has to find our own path, our own way of walking. This book should give you the confidence to do that.

It's the sort of book I wish I'd read before I started out.

Please drop in and visit my blog: coastalwalker.co.uk. You can find out how I coped with various sections of my coastal walk and, most importantly, I would love to hear about your own walking adventures. Contact me in the comments sections, or catch up with me on Twitter: @RuthlessTweets.

Contents

SECTION 4: LOGISTICS, CLOTHING, EQUIPMENT

SECTION 5: SAFETY MATTERS

SECTION 6: ADDITIONAL INFORMATION

Section 1

The Benefits of Walking

'Walking helps you stay healthy, live longer and keep happy.'

(*The Ramblers*, an organisation for walkers)[1]

In this section, I'm going to explain why I decided to start my own coastal walk, outline the health benefits of walking in general – based on medical evidence – and share some of the many wonderful things you'll experience as you trek around the coastline of England.

Walking has changed me. I've become fitter, tougher, more adventurous, and developed skills I never had before, such as map reading and navigation. Yes, walking has changed my life and it will change yours too.

If at this point, you would simply prefer to get on with planning your walk, and want to skip forward to the next section, please go ahead. You can always come back later.

Chapter One

Why I Walk

My mother loved walking and her walks were part of her daily routine, along with afternoon naps and a morning cup of tea. But, when I was younger, I thought my mother was crazy because I just didn't see the point in doing all that walking. 'If humans were meant to walk everywhere, we wouldn't have invented the motorcar,' I told her.

'Anywhere is walking distance, if you've got the time,' says Steven Wright, the American comedian.[2] But if you are a busy person, the one thing you haven't got is time. There are so many other things to do.

Life passes by, and at a faster and faster speed as you get older. By the time I reached my 50s, I was well-established in my career, working as a GP in partnership with my husband within the NHS, and we had a happy family life. I was experienced and confident at work, and had reached that point of competence where nothing seemed a challenge any more. In fact, every day seemed much the same – mundane, routine – rather boring in fact. I had the strong sense of time slipping past, of my life slipping away.

I decided I needed a real challenge. An epic challenge.

In my daydreams, I thought of climbing Kilimanjaro, or taking long train journeys across Asia, or backpacking through the Himalayas – but none of these madcap ideas seemed to fit in with my professional commitments as a busy doctor, not to mention my domestic commitments with a husband, three teenage daughters, and a couple of aged parents. It's a sign of my desperation that I even considered training to run marathons.

'Are you crazy?' my husband said. 'You hate running.'

He was right. I do.

Then, little by little, a plan began to form. I realised I wasn't going to become a triathlete, swim the Channel, or take up rock climbing. But anybody with two working legs can walk, can't they? You just put one foot in front of the other and keep going, and keep going, and keep going.

Walking. Yes. I could go walking.

The more I thought about it, the more attractive it seemed. But I wasn't going to go on aimless rambles, the sort I had hated going on as a child. No, a pointless ramble is... well, it's pointless. I needed a purpose to my walking, a challenge with an ultimate goal. But a trek that thousands of others had done before me didn't appeal either, so that ruled out popular routes such as The Pennine Way or Land's End to John O'Groats. I wanted to do something different. If not unique, at least something that was unusual.

We prefer to create stories to explain our decisions, rather than admit they are entirely irrational and arbitrary. And so I might tell you how I was born in a hospital overlooking the ocean, or how I love the sea because it connects the earth with the sky and makes me feel close to the mysteries of the universe. I might explain that I now live in the centre of the country, far from the shore, and miss the tang of salt, the heave of the waves, and the vast, empty seascapes of the coast.

But the truth is this: I can't remember exactly why I stumbled on the idea of walking around the coast.

In 1986, a lady called Helen Krasner set off to walk the entire coast of mainland Britain. She had the added advantage of being a writer, as well as a walker and, after she finished her walk, she sat down and wrote a book about her exploits, entitled *Midges, Maps and Muesli*. 'I invented dozens of reasons for the walk for the benefit of reporters and TV interviewers,' Helen explains, before going on to say she wanted to walk around Britain simply because 'it seemed like a nice thing to do'.[3]

Once the idea had formed, I started researching.

Britain is full of walkers. We're obsessed with walking, which is commonly cited as one of our favourite national pastimes.[4] We talk about it, write about it, and blog about it. We go for rambles in our National Parks and follow the long-distance trails that crisscross our countryside. We tramp over moors and bag Munros.[5] We walk through forests, fields and peat bogs. Thousands of us have marched from Land's End to John O'Groats. Yes, we go walking everywhere.

'Walking the coast,' I typed into Google, thinking surely everybody was doing it, because nobody in England lives more than 75 miles from the coast.[6] And I discovered something startling: very few people have actually walked around the entire British coastline. In fact, more people have climbed to the summit of Everest (7,000, according to Wikipedia)[7] than have walked around the coast of Britain (possibly around 50, according to David Cotton's website).[8] Which seemed astonishing.

Immediately, I knew *this was it*. Walking around the coast was both unusual and a challenge, but it involved only one skill, and that skill was something I already possessed – the ability to put one foot in front of another.

Walking the coast. It was well within my capabilities and exactly the right thing to do.

My mother-in-law became suspicious of my new obsession. She reminded me: 'You can go to faraway places, but no matter how far you travel, you can never leave yourself behind.' In a way, she was right. In a way, she was wrong. Yes, you can never leave yourself behind. But walking will change you. It has changed me. It has turned me into a more thoughtful person, a more rounded person, and has made me aware of the great beauty and fragility of the wonderful country I live in. So, you see, I really have left myself behind. The old me.

I was 54 years old when I set off to walk the section of coastline within easiest reach of my home, which happened to be the Norfolk Coast Path. My husband thought I was suffering from a temporary, and possibly menopause-related, insanity and would soon give up. But I didn't, and when I reached the end of Norfolk, I kept on going.

Six years later, with over three thousand miles beneath my feet, I'm still walking. And I've never looked back.

Your reasons for walking will be different from mine. And your ambition may be very different too. You might want to walk in order to get fitter, or slimmer, or for companionship, or to find happiness. You might be contemplating a very long, continuous walk, or you might be thinking of a series of short walks around sections of the coastline.

Whatever reason you have for walking and whatever type of walk you decide to do, remember, it's *your* walk. Only you can walk it.

TOP TIP: It might be a good idea, at this point, to grab a piece of paper and just jot down a few reasons why you want to walk the coast. And then, read on... you'll probably think of some more to add to your list in a moment.

Chapter Two

Health Benefits of Walking

There are many health benefits to walking, and as a doctor, it's a form of exercise I've recommended to numerous patients of all ages, shapes and sizes during my years as a GP. But it wasn't until I started walking regularly myself that I realised how much walking can improve both your energy and your happiness levels.

During difficult moments out on the trail – and you will have a few difficult moments, I'm afraid – you can remember how good walking is for both your body and your mind. It's a great way to cheer yourself up.

In this chapter, I will briefly outline some of the scientific reasons why walkers are healthier and happier than the rest of the world.

Aids Weight Loss

It is staggering to think that nearly a third of children in the UK are overweight or obese, and when it comes to adults, nearly two-thirds of us weigh too much. This is shocking. But diets are miserable and most of us rarely stick to a reducing diet long enough to make a lasting weight change. So while diets are important, physical activity is your number one weapon in the fight against obesity.[9]

The Chief Medical Officer recommends we indulge in at least 2.5 hours of moderate physical activity every week.[10]

Sadly, only around a third of us actually achieve our recommended level of activity. Remember, adults have it relatively easy. The advice for children is at least 60 minutes every day and preferably more.[11]

When we think of exercise, we often think of joining a gym or going jogging. This seems appealing from the comfort of our armchairs, but less appealing when facing the sweaty reality of physical exertion. How many of us start off an exercise campaign with good intentions but soon give up?

But there is an easier way to achieve your 2.5 hours of exercise a week. Yes, by walking. Walking isn't just a way to get from A to B. Walking can be exercise too. Even walking slowly will help with weight loss, but *brisk* walking is the best way to lose weight, and beats many other forms of exercise.[12,13]

How fast is brisk? It's fast enough to get your breathing going a little quicker and your heart rate pumping a little harder than normal, while allowing you to continue a sensible conversation with a companion.

How much brisk walking do you need to do? Let's think about the maths. If the Chief Medical Officer recommends 2.5 hours of exercise a week, this equates to a brisk 30-minute walk on 5 days of the week. For most of us, walking for half an hour a day is entirely achievable within our busy working lives. Long-distance walkers, of course, will easily reach the 2.5-hour target in one session.

Reduces the Risk of Serious Disease

There are many ways in which walking will improve your health, and we have a wealth of convincing scientific evidence to prove it.[14,15,16] Walking will:

- Improve the strength and performance of your heart muscle.
- Increase your lung capacity and improve your breathing.
- Improve your circulation.
- Lower your blood pressure.
- Increase your level of 'good' cholesterol.

The combination of the above benefits has a miraculous effect on your body. It reduces your risk of developing some of the major diseases that afflict the 'civilised' world. By making walking a regular part of your life, you can:

- Cut in half your risk of suffering from either heart disease or stroke.
- Decrease your risk of developing dementia.
- Reduce your risk of Type 2 diabetes or, if you already have Type 2 diabetes, reduce your need for medication.

Improves Joints, Muscles & Bones

Walking is gentle on your body, but can still have a powerful effect. Regular walking will improve the flexibility and strength of your joints, muscles and bones, making you less prone to falls and injuries as you grow older. It will also reduce the rate at which your bones become thinner – something that happens to all of us as we age – and will help protect you against fractures.

Even people who are already unwell can take up regular walking.[17] If you have already had a heart attack or suffered a stroke, for example, walking can help you manage and recover from the experience. Walking will help people with angina by strengthening their heart muscle, and people with long-term lung problems, such as emphysema, asthma, and other pulmonary diseases, can improve their breathing with regular walking.

If you suffer from a long-term condition and are wondering if walking might help you, and if it is safe for you to take this form of exercise, you should discuss your plans with your nurse or doctor.

Protects Against Cancer

Everybody worries about developing cancer and sadly, around one in two of us will be faced with this diagnosis at some time in our lives.[18] Although most cancers are easily treatable and completely curable, it still remains a devastating diagnosis in many cases.

But did you know that exercise helps protect you against some common forms of cancer?[19] In fact, it is one of the most important cancer-avoiding things you can do.

Exercise doesn't protect against all cancers, but it does reduce your risk of developing some of the most serious and life-threatening tumours, such as bowel, breast and lung cancer. And, in some treated cases, we know that regular exercise – such as walking – will help reduce the risk of recurrence of cancer.[20]

Makes You Happy

I'm sure you've discovered that walking improves mental health and mental well-being.[21] This is because walking, like other physical activities, releases endorphins, which are nature's equivalent of 'happy pills'. Endorphins make us feel better, and reduce many aspects of mental distress.

In fact, walking has a very powerful relaxing and anti-depressive effect.[22] Yes, walking can help you reduce your feelings of stress and anxiety, and even if you are not affected by depression at present, walking can reduce the risk of you ever suffering from this horrible condition in the future.

Endorphins are also your body's natural painkillers, which means if you are suffering from long-term (or chronic) pain then walking may help.

There are other psychological benefits too. Feeling fitter makes you feel better. And realising you can control your weight will help improve your confidence and give you a great boost.

TOP TIP: Go walking regularly. Two and a half hours a week is all it takes to change your life for the better.

Walking is Safe, Free and Easy!

And here are three additional, and really important reasons, to build walking into your life.

Walking is safe. Yes, of course it's possible to injure yourself while out on a hike. You might trip or slip over, and you can face hazards of other sorts – some of which I will deal with later in this book under the section *Safety Matters*. But walkers have an extremely low risk of injuries and accidents, compared to other forms of exercise.

Walking is free! You don't have to buy any special equipment; all you need are a set of comfortable clothes and a good pair of shoes or trainers. You don't have to join or pay for gym or club memberships. You don't have to worry about travel costs, as anybody can step out their front door and go for a walk.

And walking is easy. Most of us walk a little every day, even if all we do is stagger from our couch to the kitchen. And walking is one of the easiest activities to fit into your everyday life. Unlike jogging or cycling, we can walk almost everywhere and anywhere. You don't need to concentrate or force your body. While you're walking, you have the time and energy to look around and enjoy your surroundings, chat to friends and family, listen to music, or just relax and think your own thoughts.

So why exactly did *you* decide to go walking? Remember the list you made earlier? Now might be a good time to grab that piece of paper again and add a few more reasons.

Chapter Three

Seven Great Reasons to Walk the Coast

There are thousands of footpaths in Britain and a huge selection of long-distance routes. There are shorter walks, more famous routes, and easier challenges than tramping round the coastline.

So why choose to walk the coast?

Like Helen Krasner, I decided to walk along the shore because it seemed a nice thing to do,[23] and it was an unusual route that few other people had completed. But I didn't really understand what a good choice I'd made until much later. Now, looking back, I'm amazed at all the wonderful new things I've seen and experienced.

So, here are seven great reasons why *you* should choose to walk around the coast.

1) Discovering nature

On my walking odyssey, I've learnt a tremendous amount about the wonderful flora and fauna of the English countryside, and come across hundreds of plants and animals I previously knew nothing about.

There are birds everywhere. The coastal strip is populated by an incredible mixture of species, both seabirds and others: kestrels, kites, cormorants, egrets, herons, gulls, oyster catchers, Cornish choughs, jays, peregrine falcons, wrens, stonechats, wheatears, sandpipers, larks... and I could go on and on. I've watched a seagull steal a fish right off a fisherman's line in Devon, seen blackbirds mobbing a kestrel to protect their young, and been repeated dive-bombed by ferocious, little gulls who were guarding their nests.

TOP TIP: The Royal Society for the Protection of Birds (RSPB) has an excellent bird identification resource on its website.[24]

I've walked along beaches covered in thousands of jellyfish, watched seals ducking in the waves, and followed the looping wake of dolphins. On magical days in isolated sections, I've stumbled across sleeping rabbits in the bracken, and been startled by deer running across my path. We may not have many predators in England, but I've met stoats out hunting, smelt the stink of fox-marked territory, and come across a fair number of snakes, including adders. (I will talk about dangerous animals in the *Safety Matters* section of this book.)

And, of course, the coast is covered in hundreds of types of plants and wild flowers, most of whose names I will never remember. My favourite coastal scent is the wonderfully evocative perfume given off by flowering gorse in springtime, with its blend of coconut and honey. I've enjoyed the fluttering beauty of butterflies and moths in summer, and been pelted by falling acorns as I walked through oak forests in the autumn.

There is much natural beauty to see and enjoy along the coast. But the biggest tranche of learning hasn't been about the here and now. It's been about the past.

2) Learning about history

It seems that every inch of shoreline has been invaded, fought over, defended or protected. There are ancient fortifications everywhere. Irregularities in the grass disguise the earthworks of ancient Iron-Age forts, while a pile of tumbled stones may turn out to be the remains of a medieval castle. You can stand at Tilbury Docks and imagine the first Queen Elizabeth giving courage to her troops as they prepared to repel Spanish invaders.

'I know I have the body of a weak, feeble woman; but I have the heart and stomach of a king,' the Queen said in her famous speech.[25]

And you can't escape stumbling across her father, King Henry VIII's, forts – at Deal, Netley, Southsea, Poole, Portland – to name a few.

Other redoubts and fortifications seem to sit on every vantage point. The southeast coast, from East Anglia round to Eastbourne, is punctuated at regular intervals by the Martello Towers, designed to protect the English from the French during the Napoleonic Wars. Later, the Victorians added to the paraphernalia of defence by building a series of Palmerston Forts. And you will find plenty of reminders of the wars of the twentieth century, including hundreds of decaying brick pillboxes from the Second World War, with their horizontal gun slits tilted at odd angles, as the structures slowly succumb to shifting ground.

If you are interested in military history, the shoreline is a living museum.

3) Witnessing the power of the sea

The one invader we have found hardest to repel is not a human enemy, but the sea itself. And all along our ravaged coast, you will find evidence that we are on the losing side in this unequal battle.

In Norfolk, the doomed village of Happisburgh is slowly slipping into the sea. When I walked along its beach in 2010, I saw lines of rusting metal supports standing like rows of decaying teeth. The wooden barriers they once held had completely disappeared. In a further desperate attempt to stop erosion, a mass of boulders were piled up under the crumbling cliffs. But the waves continue their relentless assault and, since I walked that section of the coast, more Happisburgh residents have seen their houses slide away.

In Suffolk, I've seen houses standing on the edge of the cliff with their back walls tumbled onto the beach below, and garden sheds lying as smashed piles of timber among the pebbles. It's common to find an old pillbox settled into the sand at a rakish angle and covered by sea as the tide comes in, or to discover a section of road, hanging vertically on the side of a precipice, with its white line still marking the route for traffic to take.

We try to hold the sea at bay with a variety of constructions. You will see them all as you walk the coast:

- wooden groynes stretched across the beach,
- huge rocks piled up to create rip-rap barricades,
- and massive sea walls with high esplanades.

But these barriers only temporarily impede the relentless power of the ocean, and you can almost hear the waves laughing at us as they smash through our wooden fences, toss aside the rocks, and pulverise our carefully-laid concrete.

There is nothing new about coastal erosion. St Peter's Chapel in Essex was built from stones reclaimed from the nearby Roman fort of Othonae, which now lies hidden under the waves. Further up the coast, the thriving medieval port of Dunwich, in Suffolk, was swallowed up – not in one large gulp, but in a series of slurps and sips and licks. All that remains are a few houses and a solitary church, still clinging stubbornly to the shoreline. The town's other churches have long since disappeared into the sea, and they say, if you listen carefully, you can hear the sound of old church bells tolling under the waves.

In other parts of the coast, the opposite problem occurs. Silt, shingle and sand dunes pile up, rendering harbours impassable, while meandering dune systems turn once bustling seaports into land-based villages.

- In East Anglia, I was surprised to find the tiny town of Orford appearing on numerous signposts throughout Suffolk. 'All roads lead to Orford,' I joked with my husband. But, although the town now has less than 1,000 permanent inhabitants, it used to be an important seaport. What caused its downfall? A long spit of shingle formed just off the shore, effectively cutting the connection between the town and the open waves.
- In Sussex, Rye Harbour is kept functioning only by continual dredging to remove 55,000 tons of shingle a year, and the attempt to create a new port, two miles further along the coast, failed when the mouth of the new harbour silted up within a few months of its construction, an act of defiant vandalism by the sea.

Our shoreline is fragile and constantly changing. As you walk the coast, you will come to understand that when humans try to battle against the sea, it's the sea that usually wins in the end.

4) Developing navigation skills

Finding your way along the coast is easy. All you need to do is keep the sea close on your left or your right-hand side. You can't possibly get lost, can you?

'Then why do you need a map?' people ask.

Yes, as a beginner to the world of the walking, following a coastal route seems a great idea and enticingly simple. But, in reality, the shoreline doesn't follow one easy unbroken line. One day, when the England Coast Path is completed, perhaps the route will be properly signed and the path will be clear. Until then, it is not always straightforward, and that makes it both challenging and fun to navigate.

You will find your way continually interrupted: by steep cliffs, by deep rivers and by treacherous marshes. Sometimes, even where there is a proper coastal footpath, the route deviates inland for various reasons, such as to navigate around an estuary, or to avoid disturbing bird life, or sometimes just to provide you with a more scenic route. At other times, local landowners conspire to keep you away from 'their' section of the coast, and you might find yourself separated from the sea by private gardens, residential housing, commercial premises, industrial zones, marinas, farmland, private woodland, country estates, holiday camps, and – something I found surprising – by numerous army firing ranges.

I will talk about maps in another section, but for the moment, I just want to say that maps are essential once you get off the beaten track, and not only to help you find your way. A good map adds considerably to your enjoyment of a walk by identifying features you come across, such as ancient ruins, Roman roads, old castles, etc.

During my trek around the coast, I've learnt a tremendous amount about map reading, navigation, public transport, and about the laws governing public rights of way. I know what types of cattle are legally allowed in a field with a footpath, understand who owns which sections of coastline, and much, much more.

Later in this book, I will share some of that information with you. For the moment, I just want to say how much I enjoyed facing the challenges and acquiring new knowledge and skills. I'm sure you will too.

TOP TIP: Always carry a good map with you.

5) Dealing with varied and challenging terrain

Before I started walking the coast, I equated coast walking with beach walking, and anticipated I would be strolling across vast expanses of flat sand. For a novice walker, it seemed easy walking and the perfect choice, with no hills to climb and no mountains to worry about. I was in for a rude shock.

Most of the English coast does not consist of beaches, and not all beaches are made of sand.

I found even the flat beaches of Norfolk surprisingly tiring. Deep sand is hard on the muscles and slowed me down, and then I came to an endless shingle beach, and discovered how difficult it is to walk along a path of shifting pebbles. And there were unexpected hills. In fact, the official Norfolk Coast Path deliberately deviates inland at one point, rising up over high ground, as if the route planners decided it was rather too boring simply to follow the coast. (You will find a surprising number of coast paths make inland detours.)

Norfolk is flat. Suffolk is flat. Essex is flat. The northern bit of Kent is flattish. But when you get to white cliffs of the south coast, you can't escape the hills. If you start your walk on the cliffs in the north of England, you will have ups and downs to contend with from the very start. And some sections of the South West Coast Path are as difficult as anything the Pennine Way can throw at you.

So walking the coast isn't the easiest option for long-distance walkers, although there are plenty of flat stretches, and you can build up your cliff-legs gradually. But that's the great thing about the shoreline. It has a mix of everything: sand and shingle, rocks and marshes, lowlands and cliffs.

6) Easy access to amenities and facilities

Like me, you probably want to spend some time walking through wild areas; places that are quiet and remote. But, unless you are a masochist, you will appreciate a few creature comforts on your expeditions. You will need to find places to stay along the way, and you'll be grateful for the odd cup of tea or cold drink, not to mention something tasty to eat at the end of a long day.

Luckily, you'll find more cafés, pubs, cheap hotels along the shore than in many other areas of the countryside. That's one of the bonuses of coastal walking.

Of course, there are long stretches where you will find nothing much – in fact, nothing at all in some of the more remote places. You should also be aware that while a seaside resort can be bustling in the summer months, it may turn into a barren wasteland during the winter.

TOP TIP: Finding food and accommodation is more difficult outside of the holiday season, but you will usually find somewhere open if you are prepared to search around and make the odd trip inland to find a village or town

I have visited an amazing array of local cafés, tea shops, chippies, and wonderful pubs. And I've enjoyed tasting local delicacies. Of course, I've also visited places that were cold and uncomfortable, serving overpriced and tasteless food, with weird opening times and unfriendly staff. But, in general, I've been impressed. Gone are the days where you should expect nothing more from English food than overdone meat and over-boiled vegetables, and even the smallest of pubs may surprise you with the quality of its menu.

7) Beating the bounds

Humans have always settled beside the coast, and even those of us who live inland continue to be drawn back. We come for holidays, for daytrips, to sail, to swim, to lie on the sands and, of course, to walk along the shore.

Have you wondered why the sea exerts such a magnetic effect?

Maybe there is an evolutionary thread, like an umbilical cord, connecting us to the ocean. Mankind has always built settlements along the shore and for thousands of years, the sea has nurtured us. It's provided us with food – fish, seaweed and shellfish – and has thrown up driftwood and flotsam, providing us with building materials, whilst also demonstrating that exotic lands lurk just beyond the horizon.

Once we learnt to build ships, the sea became a leaping-off point for overseas exploration, and a convenient route for transporting goods both around and between continents.

In fact, the whole coastline is dotted with the history of our human development: from ancient castles to modern military fortifications, from tiny fishing villages with pirate coves and smugglers caves, to commercial ports with deep-sea harbours and ranks of automated cranes.

When I walk along the shoreline, I don't feel alone, even when the landscape seems empty of human beings. I know that this is where people have lived and thrived for millennia. And I feel connected with the whole of humankind, both past, present and future.

I remember moving to a new village when I was about four or five years old, and feeling very unsettled by the move. I had the strong compulsion to walk around the perimeter of our new house and, somewhat to my mother's irritation, insisted on touring the property in a systematic way. I went into each room, walked along every corridor, and tramped right around the outside wall. When I'd finished my tour, I felt a sense of completion, a sense of connection to this new place, and it was no longer a strange house. It had become my home.

My childhood experience is not unique. There is an old English custom called 'beating the bounds', which dates from medieval times or possibly earlier. Although nowadays, 'beating the bounds' has simply become a quaint custom, it was once an important method of both sharing and maintaining a local knowledge of each parish's geography and boundaries. At certain times of the year, groups of young people were escorted around the perimeter of their parish by the elders of the community. During the tour, the boys were encouraged to use sticks to, quite literally, *beat* any boundary stones and other features they came across, thus fixing these features in their memories.[26]

In 1995, Shally Hunt walked around the entire coast of mainland Britain with her husband, and later published an account of her walk. In her book, *The Sea on our Left*, Shally wrote: 'Every place we had walked through now meant something to me. I was seized with an overwhelming sense of achievement and, more surprisingly, possession. Somehow all those long miles were now my property, all those places exclusively personalised.'[27]

Shally's words sum up, far more eloquently than I could, my own feelings about the places I have walked. Yorkshire and Lincolnshire, Norfolk and Suffolk, Essex and Kent, the glorious South West Coast Path – all these places were now attached, in some way, to my person. I have been there and seen them. They are part of my experience and their fabric is embedded in my memory. No longer abstract places on the map, they belong to me.

Section 2

Right Around the Coast

'It had been a tremendous adventure, something I would never forget, and I was very glad I had done it. I had learned a lot, both about myself and about Britain and its people. [...] And most of all, it had been fun.'

(*Helen Krasner*, who walked around the coast of Britain in 1986)[28]

This section contains vital information for those who want to follow the entire coastal route around the whole of the English shoreline, and for those ambitious walkers who might want to go even further and complete the circuit around mainland Britain, including Wales and Scotland too.

Even if you are planning on walking just a segment of the coast, you will still find these chapters worth reading, as they will help you to decide how to tackle your own walking expeditions.

During the course of this section, I'll also introduce you to some of the famous coastal walkers who have gone before us, and talk about their experiences.

Chapter Four

The Five Types of Coastal Walking

There are some walkers who choose to walk around the whole coast, and others who only tackle sections. How you choose to walk the coast is up to you, but there are five different approaches you could take.

1. All-in-one-go continuous walking: day after day until you've covered the whole distance.
2. Continuous walking in stages: walking in short bursts along a continuous line, while returning home at regular intervals.
3. Segment walking: covering non-sequential sections of coastline along only those parts of the coast that interest you.
4. Joining-up-the-dots walking: segment walking with the intention of completing the whole coast eventually.
5. Flip-flop walking: an approach used by walkers who prefer not to be tied to walking in a single direction; for example, heading from the north towards the south one day, and then walking from south to north the next.

Any of these approaches are fine. But let's go into each option in a little more detail.

1) All-in-one-go continuous walking:

What it Entails

The Americans call this **thru-hiking**, and it's not for the faint hearted. It means walking day after day after day after day until you've covered the whole distance. It involves carrying a large pack on your back. It means never returning home and staying in whatever accommodation you can find along the route.

Completing the whole coast in this way would be a tremendous achievement, but it is also an incredible challenge.

Things to Think About

This sort of continuous walking demands a certain single-mindedness. It requires many months of dedicated time and, before embarking on it, you would need to consider the effects on your family, your job and your finances.

There is a lot of detailed planning to do.

Where are you going to stay, and how far ahead are you going to book your accommodation? If you are walking for charity, you may find well-wishers willing to put you up for free or for reduced rates, but you can't rely on this. And it will all need to be planned according to a schedule drawn up in advance.

You must also plan how you will collect new maps and clothing along the way, and how to deal with your dirty laundry. Will you carry food? Spare boots? Or a tent? These will all add to the weight of your backpack. Along some parts of the coast, you can hire services to transport your luggage for you, cutting down on the days you would need to travel with a full load. Such baggage transfer services will add to the expense of your trip and there will be many sections where this is impractical.

If you're really, really lucky, you might persuade a friend, or a series of friends, to provide transport and backup for you. If you're a member of a society, such as the Rotary Club, or walking on behalf of a charity, that organisation might assist with some of the planning, accommodation and transport. But they are unlikely to cover your whole venture and you will have to beware of stretching the goodwill of others too far. If they pull out, you will be stumped.

In any case, somebody needs to coordinate all this activity. Will you be doing this yourself, using your mobile phone as you go along? Will you have the time and energy to organise logistics after a full day of walking? And you should be aware there are many areas on the coast where you will be unable to get a mobile signal.

If you want to walk the coast all-in-one-go, you must spend time on planning and preparation. And you must be able to put your normal life on hold for many months.

Learning from Others' Experiences

It's no coincidence that most of the successful all-in-one-go coastal walkers have been unmarried, and most have walked alone.

Let me introduce you to a few of them.

- **John Merrill** was the first person to document a walk around the entire coastline of mainland Britain, back in 1978. In his book, *Turn Right at Land's End*,[29] John describes himself as a marathon walker, although that name doesn't really do justice to his feats, as he regularly walks more than 30 miles a day and has covered more than 200,000 miles over the course of his lifetime.
- **Vera Andrews** was the first woman to walk around the British coast, in 1984.[30] She called herself 'Granny Vera', despite being only 42 years old. Vera undertook the trek as a way of coming to terms with the early death of her husband from cancer and to raise money for charity.
- **Helen Krasner** was the second woman to complete the British coastal circuit, a few years after Vera, in 1987. Helen is both an excellent writer and has a great sense of humour. I recommend her book, *Midges, Maps and Muesli*, in which she describes her walk.[31]
- **David Cotton** was the first coastal walker I discovered on the Internet. He maintains an excellent website where he describes his walks in meticulous detail,[32] and I found this information incredibly helpful when planning my own, much shorter, expeditions, especially in the early days of my walking adventure. David has patiently answered my questions during several email conversations, and has become a mentor as well as an inspiration.

It *is* possible to successfully complete the coast all-in-one-go with a companion, and I know of two sets of couples who have walked together.

- In 1995, on New Year's Day, **Richard and Shally Hunt** set off from Eastbourne and completed their walk around the coastline of Britain, arriving back in Eastbourne 10 months later. They found the reality of walking together testing, with Richard striding ahead and Shally struggling along in his wake. Luckily, their marriage survived. If you're thinking of walking with your partner, it is worth reading Shally's book, *The Sea on our Left*.[33]
- Five years later, also on New Year's Day, **Alison Shaw and Martyn King** set out from Liverpool. It was the year 2000, the dawn of the new millennia, and the couple became engaged on the first day of their expedition. A year into their walk, Alison became ill with a brain tumour. She underwent treatment and, incredibly, the couple managed to finish their trek in 2001, getting married a few months later. Sadly, Alison died the following year.[34]

The wonderfully-named **Spud Talbot-Ponsonby** walked the coast with a companion, but that companion was a dog called Tess, not a human being,[35] while **Jannina Tredwell** walked the coast with the intermittent company of *two* dogs.[36]

Words of Advice

If you are thinking of completing the coastal path all-in-one-go, I will give you three specific pieces of advice.

Firstly, read the chapters below: 'How Far?' and 'How Long?' before you decide. Walking the coast takes time.

Secondly, read the accounts of others who have done it. In the final section of this book, I list coastal walkers who have written books about their experiences. Some of it may not be the greatest literature ever written, but it's well worth reading at least one of these books.

Thirdly, make sure you've done a continuous walking expedition, lasting at least a week and carrying a pack, before you make your mind up. You need to get a feel for how you will cope. Be warned and be prepared. All-in-one-go is not for walking novices.

TOP TIP: I recommend David Cotton's website, where he describes the route of his 2002 round-Britain coastal walk in detail: www.britishwalks.org.

2) Continuous walking in stages:

What it Entails

Walking in stages means walking in stretches of one or two days, or perhaps several weeks at a time, before returning home. Each new walk starts from the point on the coast where the previous one ended, and so your walks added together make up one long, continuous line. (The Americans call this **sectional walking**, but I think that's a misleading term as it implies you only walk certain sections and leave gaps in between.)

Things to Think About

If you plan to walk the whole coast then walking in stages is the easiest way to tackle this mammoth challenge and has plenty of advantages.

- Firstly, you can fit walking into your normal life, while continuing to hold down a job and maintaining your social or family commitments. You don't have to take several months out from the real world.
- Secondly, it's easier to find the small amount of funding for each expedition, as you don't have the single, large financial commitment of an all-in-one-go walker. Each expedition will still cost you money, of course, for travel, food and accommodation expenses. And, because you have to pay for several journeys

to and from home, the whole trek may end up being more expensive in the long run, but at least you can continue earning money as you make progress.

- Thirdly, you can avoid walking in bad weather, or when you're feeling ill. And, in between walking stints, you can go home for a good rest and give any injuries or blisters time to heal. Read the accounts written by all-in-one-go walkers and you will notice the large amount of pain they seem to suffer. It *is* gruelling to walk day after day and the trek often turns into an endurance test. If you're going to expend money and effort on this project, you should aim to make each day as enjoyable as possible. That's my view, anyway.

The downside is that the whole enterprise will be spread out over several years. In some cases, many years. The problem with taking so long is that you may lose enthusiasm for the project, become downhearted because the end is never in sight, develop health problems, or have to put your walking ambitions on hold because of changes in your personal circumstances.

Of course, you really don't have to walk the whole of the English coastline. You might be planning a more modest expedition. Perhaps you want to tackle the 63 miles (101 km) of the Norfolk Coast Path, or undertake the substantial challenge of the 630-mile (1,014 km) South West Coast Path. Even if you're tackling a relatively short stretch of coastline, you will still need to decide whether you do this all-in-one-go, or in separate stages.

TOP TIP: For most of us, walking in stages is a good way to tackle the challenge of long-distance coastal walking.

Learning From Others' Experiences

Ted Richards took 20 years to complete his 3,500-mile walk around the coasts of England and Wales. He keeps a retrospective blog of his experiences: http://walesenglandcoastalwalk.blogspot.co.uk/.

Andy Phillips is walking the coast of England, Wales and Scotland. So far, his trek has lasted over 20 years, and he might beat Ted as the longest ever coastal walker, because Andy hasn't finished yet.[37]

3) Segment walking:

What it Entails

This is the commonest type of coastal walking. It means you only walk those parts of the coast that suit you, and forget about the rest.

Most people in Britain have been segment coast walkers at some stage; perhaps a stroll along the promenade in Scarborough, a walk up Beachy Head, or a visit to Blackpool's Golden Mile.

Things to Think About

Segment walkers may not have the same lofty ambitions as continuous walkers, but that doesn't matter. Life doesn't have to involve a stream of difficult challenges. Walking segments of the coast is a great way to spend your weekends and holidays, while enjoying some splendid scenery.

When I trudged through dreary marshland, or plodded along endless roads, I must say, I envied segment walkers. Some parts of the coast are decidedly unattractive, and other sections are just plain boring.

It doesn't all have to be daytrips and short walks. You could choose, for example, to explore the beaches of Northumberland, or you could tackle the Somerset Coast Path, or the Cleveland Way. You could walk continuously for a week, or take several shorter weekend breaks.

If looking for ideas of where you might go on a brief coastal-walking trip, do take a look at the chapter *Places to Start Walking*, towards the end of this book.

TOP TIP: Segment walking is a great way of exploring the best parts of the English coastline.

4) Joining-the-dots walking:

What it Entails

Some segment walkers have grander ambitions. They begin by walking separate stretches of the coastline, but have the intended aim of returning to join up their walks to form a continuous line at some point in the future.

In other words, they plan to *join-the-dots* one day.

Once complete, the walker will be able to claim they have walked the entire coastline, just not necessarily in sequential order. Although it may feel less satisfying than completing a continuous stretch, this is a perfectly acceptable way of walking the coast.

Things to Think About

Joining-the-dots gives you wonderful flexibility because you can choose to start each walk in a different place. For example, you might have set aside a week for a walking trip in Cornwall, but now the weather forecast shows rain and gales in the southwest. No problem. You head up to Northumberland instead, where they are enjoying brilliant sunshine. Or you may realise the tide is too high to walk the beach safely on a particular day, or the footpath has been closed for repairs, or the army are using the coastal strip as a temporary firing range. No problem. You return and walk that section on another day.

Perhaps the downside of joining-the-dots as a method of walking is this: you have to remember to go back and complete the sections you missed out. I suspect a lot of people set off with the intention of linking up all their separate walks, but never get around to it. There is usually a good reason, after all, why you missed out a particular stretch in the first place; perhaps because it wasn't very appealing.

Learning From Others' Experiences

I know of someone who walked the coast of Scotland in this way, and of several people who are currently using this method to walk the coast of England. These include **Alan Palin**, who is also a flip-flopper (see below).[38] In fact, I must thank **Patricia Richards-Skensved**, another coastal walker, for giving me the joining-the-dots phrase.[39]

5) Flip-flop walking:

What it Entails

Flip-floppers will walk the coast in one direction, and then the next day, may turn around and walk the coast in the opposite direction. Flip-floppers may be segment walkers, happy to tackle small stretches of coast as the mood takes them, or they may be planning to walk the whole coastline.

Things to Think About

Flip-flopping has some wonderful advantages. You can, for example, on a windy day, choose to walk in the same direction as the prevailing wind, instead of battling against the gale. Or you can flip-flop in order to fit in with public transport. Or you may change direction to avoid walking directly into the bright sun, as it's always easier to walk with the sun behind you, which is why walking northwards is usually preferred to walking southwards.

The disadvantages for flip-flop walkers are the same as for joining-the-dots. The danger is that you will miss out sections and never return to complete them. And for some people, changing direction is far less satisfying than walking in a continuous line.

Walkers who don't mind flip-flopping are more flexible, and can take advantage of opportunities to make the most of the weather and to simplify their travel arrangements.

My Own Experiences

When I first started on my coastal trek, I had no fixed ideas about what sections I would walk, nor in what order or direction.

There were practical reasons for my vagueness. My husband, believing I was suffering from temporary madness, left me to get on with my crazy plans on my own. This meant I had to rely on public transport. My preliminary research of bus routes confirmed that parts of the coast are pretty inaccessible. I was, therefore, quite prepared to walk intermittent sections, in either direction, returning later to fill in the gaps when I could work out a method of transportation. In other words, I was happy to be both a flip-flop and joining-the-dots walker.

I drove to the section of coastline closest to my home and started walking along the North Norfolk coast. Finding transportation back to my car was surprisingly easy at first, due to the wonderful Norfolk Coasthopper bus. Once I reached the end of the bus's limits, I entered much trickier territory because the coastal roads, if they ever existed, had disappeared with the eroding shoreline. It was impossible to travel by public transport from point A on the coast to point B, without taking a serious and time-consuming inland detour. It was at this point that my husband realised I was serious about this walking malarkey and offered to be my chauffeur.

Once I got into the habit of walking sequentially, I found it impossible to contemplate missing out a stretch, and now I can't even bring myself to walk the 'wrong way' along a piece of coast, so I don't flip-flop either.

But YOU don't have to walk the coast in this obsessional manner. The best way to walk the coast is the way that suits you.

Deciding on Your Own Way of Walking

I hope the discussions above have helped you finalise your own plans for walking the coast, and have helped you understand the advantages and disadvantages of each method.

If you find all this too abstract and hard to visualise, don't worry. In general, it's a good idea to think through how you want to set about tackling your walks, but detailed planning may not be the right approach for you. The most important part of coastal walking is enjoyment. In fact, perhaps the best way to determine whether you want to be a continuous walker, a segment walker or a dot-to-dotter is just to set off and see how you get on.

In the final part of this book (in the section *Additional Information*), I suggest some places on the coast where you might like to start walking. These are lovely areas, accessible by public transport; the sort of place you could visit for a day or two and dip your toe into the water, so to speak.

TOP TIP: Don't get too bogged down with planning, or make this an excuse for not walking. Just get out and do it.

Before you set off, there are a few more choices you have to make. Are you going to walk alone or in the company of others? And how far should you walk on your first day? We will deal with these, and many other planning matters, in a later section, *Planning Before You Start*.

Chapter Five

How Far is it?

Your walk can be as long or as short as you choose, but in this chapter, let's talk about the distances involved if you plan to walk the entire length of the English coast. I'll also describe the distances involved if you decide to continue your walk to include the whole of mainland Britain.

How Long is the English Coast?

It depends who you ask.

The British Cartographic Society has estimated the actual length of the coastline of England to be 5,581 miles (8,982 km). The Society calculated this distance from maps, by measuring along the mean high water mark.[40] Of course, it's simply not possible to walk around the coast following the high tide mark. Rocks and cliffs intervene. Some areas are inaccessible, due to steep cliffs or marshland, or because of private ownership, and commercial or military activity. For all these reasons, the cartographic measurement is not a realistic indicator of the miles you will actually walk. In addition, any path you take will smooth out some of the contours of the coast, and so the real number of miles you walk will be considerably less than the cartographers' figure.

The England Coast Path, when completed, should measure approximately 2,800 miles (4,500 km).[41]

Even when it's finished, the official coast path will undergo constant adjustments and amendments to its route because we know the coastline is constantly changing. Chunks of Norfolk are lost every year, the white cliffs of Dover are gently crumbling, while along the north coast of Cornwall, dunes pile up as more land is added.

- John Merrill estimated the English section of his walk to be 3,363 miles (5,412 km).[42]
- David Cotton's mileage for England appears less, at 2,872 (4,622 km).[43]
- Helen Krasner records a lower figure, 2,520 miles (4,055 km).[44]
- Tom Isaacs, who finished his coastal walk in 2003, gives an even shorter distance of 2,280 miles (3,670 km) for his English section.[45]

You might be wondering why there is so much variation in these distances, with more than a 1,000-mile difference between the walks of John Merrill and Tom Isaacs. It partly depends on which route the walkers took – whether they used ferries, bypassed estuaries – and how many diversions they made along the way. It also depends on how they measured their distances. John Merrill, for example, used a pedometer and an estimate of his average stride length. Others used map measurements. Only in recent years has modern technology been able to provide us with a far more accurate assessment of walking distances, using global positioning satellites (GPS).

TOP TIP: Despite all this variation, from the point of view of planning your trip, the official 2,800 miles (4,500 km) of the proposed England Coast Path gives you a reasonable starting point.

How Long is the Coastline of Mainland Britain?

Remember, when we talk about walking around the coast of mainland Britain, we mean the coastline of England, Wales and Scotland. We don't usually include Ireland, nor the many smaller islands that lie off the coast – such as the Scillies, Isle of Wight, Isle of Man, etc.

If we go back to the British Cartographic Society, following the mean high water mark, the length of the mainland coastline is as follows:

England = 5,581 miles (8,982 km)

Wales = 1,317 miles (2,120 km)

Scotland = 4,174 miles (6,718 km)

Total distance = 11,000 miles (17,700 km)[46]

But, of course, we know nobody can actually walk around Britain following the mean high water mark, and so 11,000 miles is a gross overestimate.

A more realistic assessment might be using official paths, as follows:

The official England Coast Path = 2,800 miles (4,500 km)

The official Wales Coast Path = 870 miles (1,400 km)

But Scotland has no official path, and a very indented coastline. How do we factor in the Scottish coast?

Learning from Other Coastal Walkers

We know the first man to document a round-Britain coastal walk was John Merrill in 1978. Before he set off, John contacted the Ordnance Survey and asked for an estimate of the total length of the British coast. As the Ordnance Survey is the premier mapmaker of Britain, they should know. They suggested the following distances:

England and Wales: 3,240 miles (5,214 km)
Scotland: 2,855 miles (4,595 km)
Total distance around Britain: 6,095 miles (9,809 km)

After he had finished his walk, John Merrill estimated he had actually walked the following:

England: 3,363 miles (5,412 km)
Wales: 766 miles (1,233 km)
Scotland: 2,695 miles (4,337 km)
Total distance: 6,824 miles (10,982 km)[47]

Why was John's walk 700 miles longer than the mapmakers' estimate? It's partly because of the sneaky extra miles that creep into any walk (I'll deal with these in a later chapter), and partly because John made some inland diversions. Simply walking the coast wasn't challenging enough. He decided to climb the highest peaks in England, Wales and Scotland – Scafell Pike, Snowdon and Ben Nevis respectively – while he was at it.

Years later, when David Cotton walked the British coast, he repeated John Merrill's feat, scaling the three highest peaks along the way. David estimated his walk would be 5,500 miles (8,850 km) in length. In fact, his completed distance came to significantly more, at 6,294 miles (10,129 km).[48] That is similar to John Merrill's figure, but still gives a difference of 530 miles (853 km) between them, for what was, essentially, the same walk.

The Kings set off to walk the entire coast in order to raise money for the Royal National Lifeboat Institution (RNLI). Despite their trip being dramatically interrupted when Alison King developed a brain tumour, they completed their walk in 2001 after covering a total of 5,200 miles (8,370 km). Although they didn't divert to climb any mountain peaks, they did visit every lifeboat station along the way.[49]

Other walkers have been more consistent in their walking routes and avoided detours.

In 1987, Helen Krasner estimated her round-Britain walk as 4,922 miles (7,921 km) in length.[50] Twenty years later, Jannina Tredwell repeated the same feat, but her estimated walking distance was shorter: at 4,500 miles (7,242 km).[51] More recently, Pete Hill finished his coastal walk in 2014 and claimed a distance very similar to Helen's: 5,045 miles (8,120 km).[52]

We mustn't forget the first woman to walk the coast, Vera Andrews (Granny Vera), who covered 3,524 miles (5,670 km) in 1984. This is the lowest figure I've seen and comes to just over half John Merrill's mileage. Vera's distance may have been unusually short because she followed roads, not coastal paths, and missed out several sections of the coastline as a result. She did, however, make it into *The Guinness Book of Records* for what was, at the time, the longest continuous walk by a woman.[53]

Each of us will have to find our own route and our own way of walking the coast. But, if you do decide to walk the whole way around mainland Britain, you can expect to be covering somewhere between 4,500 and 6,500 miles (7,250 to 10,500 km), depending on the route you take.

Chapter Six

How Long Will it Take?

This chapter considers how long it would take you to walk around the English coast, and then we'll discuss how long it might take you to walk around the coast of the entire British mainland.

How long depends on a combination of the following factors:

(a) The total distance
(b) How fast you walk
(c) How many hours you plan to walk per day

We've already talked about the problems in estimating total distances. Later, I will talk about how to decide on a sensible daily mileage, in the chapter, *Building up Your Walking Distances*. For the moment, I just want to talk through some of the timescales you might be dealing with.

To Complete the England Coast Path (2,800 Miles)

Depending on the miles you intend to cover every day, it will take you anywhere between four months and the best part of a year to walk the English coast.

Averaging 25 miles (40 km) a day = 112 days or 16 weeks
Averaging 20 miles (32 km) a day = 140 days or 20 weeks
Averaging 15 miles (24 km) a day = 187 days or 27 weeks
Averaging 10 miles (16 km) a day = 280 days or 40 weeks

To Complete Mainland Britain (Est. 5,500 Miles)

Most of the all-in-one-go walkers have managed to complete a circuit of mainland Britain within 12 months. But, if you're walking in stages, you're going to take considerably longer.

Averaging 25 miles (40 km) a day = 220 days or 8 months
Averaging 20 miles (32 km) a day = 275 days or 9 months
Averaging 15 miles (24 km) a day = 367 days or one year
Averaging 10 miles (16 km) a day = 550 days or 18 months

Please note, all the above figures are related to actual walking days, and don't include rest days, trips home, time in between when you're sightseeing or doing other things. It's reasonable to suppose a fit and healthy young person might average 25 miles or 40 kilometres a day. For most of us, somewhere between 10 and 20 miles is a reasonable figure.

The Reality of Walking

I've already mentioned Ted Richards, who took 20 years to complete his 3,500-mile walk around the coasts of England and Wales.[54]

Andy Phillips is in the process of walking the whole of mainland Britain (at the time of writing this). He started walking from Gravesend, on the Thames, in the 1980s, heading clockwise, and three decades later, he reached Scotland. That's a long time on one walking expedition! To be fair, Andy took a decade off for personal reasons and doesn't walk during the winter. Since retiring from work, his pace has increased considerably.

When I first started walking the coast of mainland Britain, I reckoned it would take me between three to four years to complete the full circuit of mainland Britain.

This was a completely unrealistic dream. I overestimated both the distance I could walk on any one day, and the number of days I would be able to spend walking in any given year. In fact, the further I walked along the coast, the harder it was to fit in my walking trips because of the extended travelling involved. I managed to get away walking, on average, one weekend per month, and in the summer season, I could spend a whole fortnight of holiday walking.

All this works out at less than 50 walking days in a year and, on each walking day, I covered around 12 miles, on average.

50 days at 12 miles a day gives a grand total of 600 miles a year. With an estimated route of 5,500 miles, and covering less than 600 miles a year, it would have taken me nearly 10 years to finish my walk. 10 years? Wow!

If I simply walked the coastline of England, I would only need to cover 2,800 miles in total. At 600 miles a year, that would still take me four and a half years. Wow, again.

Life and Distractions

Even my recalculation turned out to be wildly optimistic.

Six years after setting out, I should have covered 3,600 miles, but I had actually achieved around 2,400 miles of coast walking. That's a measly 400 miles a year, only two-thirds of what I envisaged.

What went wrong?

Nothing.

I've enjoyed every (well, *nearly* every) minute of my walking adventure. But other things happen in life. Here is a list of the events that interfered with my walking trips, and they range from the trivial to the serious: visits from family and friends, study weekends, winter storms, summer floods, my father's illnesses and eventual death, university assignments, work commitments, my support team (aka my husband) having alternative plans, my daughter's wedding… and I could go on.

We start out with the best of intentions, but life gets in the way.

Despite my slow progress, I've walked hundreds more miles more than I would have dreamt possible a few years ago. And I've turned from a couch potato into a seasoned long-distance walker. I've been to some amazing places and seen wonderful sights. I've pushed my body through tough times, enjoyed some glorious high points as my fitness levels improved, and I've learnt many new skills.

I'm still walking the coast. Even if I never finish my coastal odyssey, I'll never regret the miles I've done. In fact, I'm enjoying it so much, I never want the adventure to stop. At the rate I'm going, it doesn't feel as if it ever will.

Chapter Seven

Rules for Walking the Coast

'There are in fact no "rules" to long-distance walking, and people set about it in different ways,' says John Merrill in his book, *Walking My Way*.[55]

The first rule to remember while walking the coast is that there are no rules.

The above statement is not strictly true. There is one set of rules that all walkers should always obey, no matter where they are: The Countryside Code.[56]

In this chapter, I will give you an outline of The Countryside Code, and then talk about my own invented rules for walking the coast, as well as introducing you to a number of other coastal walkers and the rules they have used. You don't have to follow any of these (except for The Countryside Code), but it will help you to organise and plan your expeditions if you have some guidelines in mind.

The Countryside Code: (Respect, Protect, Enjoy)

This code is statutory guidance, issued by Natural England, a government agency, and backed by walking organisations such as The Ramblers. The latest version of The Countryside Code (2014) is reproduced in summary below.

Respect other people: be considerate towards others. Leave gates and property as you find them, and stick to paths unless wider access is permitted.

Protect the natural environment: leave no trace of your visit and take your litter home. Keep dogs under control.

Enjoy the outdoors: plan ahead and be prepared. Follow advice and local signs.

The full version of the Code is published here: https://www.gov.uk/government/publications/the-countryside-code

My Rules

When it comes to walking the coast, I only have six rules, some of which I break occasionally. My number one rule is probably both the hardest to keep and the most important rule of all.

1. Enjoy each and every walk.
2. Keep as close to the coast as is safe, legal and reasonable.
3. Start each walk at the point where I stopped the coastal section of my previous walk.
4. I don't have to walk around islands (but I can if I want to).
5. I don't have to walk around peninsulas where the only link to the mainland is a narrow isthmus or causeway (but I can if I want to).
6. When I encounter a river or estuary, I cross at the nearest public crossing point; stepping-stones, bridge or ferry.

And I have an additional guideline – not a rule, but a philosophical statement. While I'm walking, I concentrate on **being present** in the place I am walking through. This means: I don't listen to music or the radio while I walk, I don't read up on history or check which sights I should view in advance of my walk, and I avoid looking beyond my current map, except for planning my start, lunch stops, and end point.

There is nothing special about my rules. They are just MY rules. Many other coastal walkers have similar rules and I've included a selection below so that you can see what others have decided on.

John Merrill's Rules

John Merrill is the great granddaddy of long-distance walking and a legend among coastal walkers.

When John walked the British coast back in 1978, the England Coastal path was not yet even a dream, and John followed public rights-of-way that ran closest to the coast. When he came to an estuary, he did not use ferries, but crossed at the first bridge passable by foot, as long as it wasn't a motorway bridge. Islands were not included but peninsulas were.[57]

Other Walkers, More Rules

Pete Hill walked the coast continuously in 2014, and his rules are laid out on his website in some detail.[58] I have summarised them below.

Pete followed National Trails where they existed. Otherwise, he walked along public paths or roads, or walked along the beach or the seawall. Unlike John Merrill, Pete decided he would use short-hop ferries, as long as the crossing was part of a recognised trail. He didn't walk around islands or around peninsulas.

When collected by transport at the end of his walk, Pete returned to the place of collection in order to resume his walk the next day. He used the Viewranger app to record his distances (I will talk more about apps later in the Chapter 12, *Maps and Stuff*).

Pete's blog pages (http://gbcoastwalk.com/) might be useful when planning your own walk, and he has recently published a book about his trek.

Nat Severs walked the coast of Britain in 2010. His rules are short and sweet:

> 'The entire journey will be completed using leg power and if there is a bridge, I will be crossing it (so Anglesey and the Isle of Skye will both be on the agenda). I will stay true to the coastline at all times, so if there is a ferry across a river (the River Dart, for example) that is not classed as coastline, then I will allow myself to take a ferry if one is available. But a ferry cannot be used at any other time. I aim to be home by Christmas!'

Nat completed his walk, of around 7,000 miles, on the 5th of November, well in time for Christmas.[59]

Ted Richards was the man who spent 20 years walking the England and Wales coastline in stages, eventually finishing in 2004 after covering over 3,500 miles. His rules were remarkably similar to mine. He always set off from the exactly the place where he had finished his previous walk, and he kept as close to the coast as was legally possible, without falling into the sea. But he didn't use any form of transport to travel over water.

This meant he walked up estuaries to cross at the nearest bridge, rather than take a ferry. Like Nat Severs, Ted also walked around any peninsula or island that was connected to the mainland.[60]

Some readers will have spotted that all the walkers whose rules I've referred to so far happen to be men. The only female coastal walkers I've discovered who have spelt out their rules, other than myself, are Babs and Nancy.

Babs and Nancy are two friends who set off from Beachy Head in early 2014 and intend to walk the entire coast of Britain in stages. They run an entertaining blog called *B & N's Ridiculous Journey* (https://babsandnancy.wordpress.com/) and describe their rules as 'loose'. They also plan to take ferries when they want to and have decided not to stick too slavishly to the coast.

'The starting point for each walk needs to be the end of the last, creating a continuous loop around our island home. The sea stays to the left.'[61]

Chapter Eight

Technical Questions

Via my coastal walking website (www.coastalwalker.co.uk), total strangers will contact me to ask questions of a technical nature, such as:

1. Where is the official round-the-coast route?
2. Is there an award for completing the whole of the coast successfully?
3. Can you get into *The Guinness Book of Records* for completing it?
4. How close to the coast do you have to stick and what about shortcuts?
5. What do you do when you come to a river?
6. What about islands?
7. Why didn't you walk around the Isle of Grain?

One of the reasons for writing this book is to answer those queries as best as I can. So, let's begin with the first question...

1) Where is the official route?

The England Coast Path is due to be completed in the year 2020. When finished, it will provide a waymarked route along a protected strip around the whole of the English coastline. And it will be a fantastic amenity. At nearly 2,800 miles (4,500 km) in length, the path is set to become the longest of England's National Trails, and one of the greatest coastal walks in the world.[62]

Wales has already completed its own Coast Path, which opened in May 2012 and covers the entire 870 miles (1,400 km) of the Welsh coast.[63] I have walked most of it, and it's a glorious trail.

Scotland has sections of coastal path in place, including the Fife Coastal Path and the Moray Coastal Trail. Sadly, there are no official plans for a complete around-Scotland coastal walk.[64,65]

Progress on the England Coast Path

2020 isn't far away – only four years in the future at the time of writing this book – and yet progress on the Path remains excruciatingly slow. In fact, I will be amazed if the whole of the route is completed on time, and sometimes I wonder if it will ever be finished at all.[66]

On the positive side, the project didn't start from scratch. Many areas in England already had a coastal path of some sort, although not necessarily meeting the strict criteria demanded by the England Coast Path plan.

Here are some of the recognised coastal trails that already exist:

- Norfolk Coast Path: 63 miles (101 km) from Hunstanton to Sea Palling[67]
- Suffolk Coast Path: 50 miles (80 km) between Lowestoft and Felixstowe[68]
- South West Coast Path: 630 miles (1,014 km) from Minehead to Poole, via Land's End[69]
- Somerset Coast Path: 25 miles (40 km) from Minehead to the River Parrett[70]
- Cleveland Way (coastal part): 50 miles (80 km) from Saltburn to Filey Brigg[71]

Meanwhile, in other areas of the country, a few shorter sections of the official England Coast Path have been established. For example, there are new pathways in the northwest, linking Whitehaven and Allonby, and in the northeast, between Hartlepool and South Bents.[72]

At the time of writing, only 30% of the coast has a recognised coastal trail. Along the remaining 70% of the route, you have to find your own way. Luckily, England is covered in a network of tracks, footpaths, bridleways and public rights of way, and most of the coast can be walked using these routes.

Even where an official coast path exists, you may decide not to stick to it because many of the existing trails deviate inland for sections of their course, for a number of reasons. You will find, for example, significant deviations away from the coast in various sections of the Norfolk Coast Path, the Somerset Coast Path and the South West Coast Path. And in Wales, if you're interested, around 20% of their new coast path follows routes that are nowhere near the shore at all.[73]

Some existing footpaths have misleading names. The Saxon Shore Way runs around the southeast corner of England, between Gravesend and Hastings. But, as its name suggests, the trail follows the line of the original Saxon shoreline, not the coastline as it exists today, and so it misses out the pretty beach at Broadstairs, and bypasses the incredible shingle landscape of Dungeness.[74]

It is up to you, I suppose, whether you follow an official trail when it deviates inland. I try to stick as close to the shoreline as I can, and if there's an alternative footpath, or quiet road, that takes me closer to the coast, I will follow this route rather than the official one. Similarly, I try to walk along the beach whenever this is possible.

TOP TIP: Whatever you decide to do, you'll need a decent map that shows footpaths. I'll explain in detail about public rights of way and maps in other sections of this book, but my strong advice is to use the Ordnance Survey maps (OS maps),[75] which are the best maps in the world.

2) Is there an award for completing the coast path successfully?

There is no official body for round-England coastal walkers, nor for round-Britain walkers, and at the moment, you can't apply for an award. When the definitive England Coast Path is completed, it will become one of England's official National Trails. Some of the existing National Trails provide certificates to walkers who complete their routes, although I don't know if this will be the case for the England Coast Path.

A certificate is only a piece of paper. If you have successfully completed your walk, YOU will know you've done it and you'll know how much effort it took. You will also have all the memories of the good (and maybe some of the bad) times you had along the way, and the immense feeling of satisfaction that comes from completing a long trail.

Remember this astonishing fact: **more people have climbed Mount Everest than have completed a circuit of Britain's coastline.** But if you do attempt to complete the circuit, either of Britain or just the English coast, you won't be alone, because at any one moment, there will be two or three people undertaking a continuous round-the-coast walk, and maybe 20 or so other people doing it in stages.

Not all coastal walkers will finish the entire route. Not all of them want to. But the thing to remember is this: as you set out on this journey, and if you have Internet access, you will not be without virtual company, even if you walk on your own.

David Cotton has an excellent website at www.britishwalks.org. Not only does David supply routes and narratives describing the very many walks he has done, he also maintains a list of those who are attempting, as well as those who have completed a round-Britain coastal walk.[76]

There is no list, as far as I know, for those who have only completed the English part of the coastline, and I'm wondering if I should start one. If there is enough demand, I could even issue badges and certificates!

3) Can you get into The Guinness Book of Records?

I could find nothing about walking the coast of Britain in the latest version of *The Guinness Book of Records*. Neither could I find any statistics about British coastal walkers on their website. When I contacted the official Guinness World Records Twitter account (@ GWR), I received this reply: 'Unfortunately, that's not a category we monitor, though we do have numerous Land's End to John O'Groats records.'[77]

I do know that two round-Britain coastal walkers, John Merrill and Vera Andrews, both achieved an entry in *The Guinness Book of Records*, although their records may well have been overwritten by now.[78,79]

TOP TIP: If you are interested in trying to achieve a Guinness Record, you first need to register with their website at www.guinnessworldrecords.com and discuss it with them. You need to do this long before you set off on your expedition.

4) How close to the coast do you have to stick and what about shortcuts?

It would be unreasonable to insist on walking around every tiny spur of land or clump of rocks that stick out into the sea. But, if you are claiming to walk the coast, it seems reasonable to expect that you won't miss out significant sections of the coastline.

For example, you could cut right across Cornwall by following the Cornish Coast to Coast trail. It sounds like a wonderful walk, but you would miss out the 'foot' of England, including the stunning Lizard Peninsula and the famous landmark of Land's End. Not only would you be shortening your route considerably, but you would also be depriving yourself of some of the best coastal walking in the world!

I would suggest one of my rules is a sensible guideline for you to follow: 'I will keep as close to the coast as is safe, legal and reasonable.'

5) What do you do when you come to a river?

Twenty major rivers interrupt the coast of England as they empty into the sea, and so do hundreds of smaller streams. You are going to need a plan for crossing them.

It's not just rivers that break up the coastline. You will come across marshes, estuaries, mud flats, and lakes. Luckily, mankind has been ingenious in finding ways to get across these watery barriers. And one of the joys of coastal walking is the fun of crossing – whether it's via bridge or ferry, by clambering over stepping-stones, or wading through a ford.

Some people set off to walk the coast with the intention of following rivers back to the limit of the sea's influx at high tide. This limit is marked on Ordnance Survey maps with the letters NTL, meaning the Normal Tidal Limit.

If you insist on walking up every river to its tidal limit, you will find your walking distance considerably extended. The NTL of the River Thames is 55 miles upstream, at a place called Teddington Lock.[80] That's a 110-mile round trip away from the coast. An added complication is that access along riverbanks may be restricted because the land is private, and following the exact course of the river may be difficult or impossible.

Yes, you *can* walk up to the NTL of every river if you want to, but most of us don't.

So where should you cross?

My own rule is as follows: 'When I encounter a river or estuary, I cross at the nearest public crossing point; stepping-stones, bridge or ferry.'

I know of one coastal walker (Helen Krasner) who was given a lift in a boat across an estuary.[81] According to my rules, since this wasn't a 'public crossing point', that would be cheating. But I don't begrudge Helen her lift, and you are perfectly entitled to make up your own rules.

Many ferries were started as commercial enterprises back in the days of horses and carts, and one of the joys of crossing at a traditional ferry point is the sense of continuing along an ancient and historic route. With the invention of the motorcar, road bridges were built and, inevitably, many of our ferry services disappeared. Where a ferry still exists, it may primarily serve visiting tourists and may close out of season.

One of the oldest ferry crossings in England is the Butley Ferry near Orford in Suffolk, which dates from the 16th century, and cuts out a five-mile (eight km) trek up the Butley River to the nearest bridge. The ferry ceased as a commercial operation a long time ago, but the crossing is kept going by enthusiasts, who operate at weekends from Easter through to September. The ferry claims to be the smallest ferry for hire in Europe, which I can well believe. Basically, it's a small rowing boat.[82]

Other coastal walkers have stuck to bridges, but most of us love crossing by ferry. It is up to you.

6) What about islands?

There are hundreds of islands dotted around off the English coast, only 20 of which are inhabited. Some are large, such as the Isle of Wight. Other islands are nothing more than lumps of rock.

Islands are fun and it seems a shame to miss them off your itinerary, but where do you stop? For example, the Scilly Isles are 28 miles from Cornwall and everyone who has visited them says how wonderful they are – quiet, friendly and tropical-looking. But do you really want to include them in your coastal walk?

Some islands are tantalising accessible because they are connected to the mainland by a causeway, such as Hayling Island in Hampshire and Portland near Weymouth. Others are only accessible on foot at low tide, such as St Michael's Mount in Cornwall and Lindisfarne in Northumberland.

Will you walk around islands as part of your coastal walk? You can if you want to. Most of us don't walk around all the islands we come across, but some of us choose to walk around some of them.

My own rule is as follows: 'I don't have to walk around islands (but I can if I want to).'

7) Why didn't you walk around the Isle of Grain?

The Isle of Grain is a knob of land sticking into the English Channel on the south side of the Thames Estuary, opposite Southend-on-Sea.

The Isle of Grain isn't really an island because the waterway, which once separated it from the mainland, has silted up. Neither does it grow much grain, as a considerable part is taken over by industrial structures, including a power station and the dockland of London Thamesport. From Southend, you can look across the mouth of the Thames and see the Isle's conglomeration of chimneys, tanks, storage bins and cranes. At night, when it's all lit up, it looks quite pretty.

Now, I like walking through industrial areas. I find them interesting and full of photo opportunities. I love the shape of huge tanks, chimneys, and gantries. These structures represent some of our greatest achievements as human beings. So, it wasn't the industrial nature of the Isle of Grain that put me off.

It was the fear of dying

There is only one way to get on and off the Isle of Grain, and that is along the busy A228. There is no pavement alongside the road, no footpaths to provide an alternative route and the land is too marshy to consider a trespassing expedition. Walking on the verge of the road is your only choice and this road heaves with container lorries and juggernauts. To walk along it is to dice with death.

In fact, between October 2000 and September 2003, there were thirty-three road traffic injuries, including three fatalities and seven serious injuries, recorded on the A228.[83] Since then, speed limits have been reduced and speed cameras installed, but the road is not an enticing prospect for pedestrians.

Nic is walking the coast with his wife and children, and Nic's family was brave enough to walk around the Isle of Grain. The journey along the busy road wasn't pleasant. In fact, one workman tried to insist on giving the family a lift, a kind offer, but one that would have broken the rules of coastal walking to accept.[84] The Isle of Grain repaid the family for its bravery by providing a wonderful shell-covered beach and many exciting ruins from the Second World War to explore.

I treated the Isle of Grain as a peninsula, because of its single entry and exit point. And my rules for peninsulas are the same as my rules for islands. I don't have to walk around them, although I can if I want to. In this case, I chose not to.

So, you can gamble with death and walk around the Isle of Grain if you want to, or you can choose not to. It's up to you.

These questions illustrate some of the difficult decisions you face when walking the coast. Must you include this part? Can you skip that section? How do you cross this river? Each individual quandary has to be considered and resolved, and it really helps if you have some rules to guide you.

TOP TIP: Decide on some rules (or guidelines) in advance, because this will help you make decisions when you plan your walking routes.

Section 3

Planning Before You Start

'I had started planning the coast walk on paper much earlier. Before I could begin to work out a daily schedule, I had first to decide how closely I could keep to the coastline, what I should do at river estuaries, whether to include islands, whether to walk around every single peninsula, and what bridges I should use.'

(John Merrill, the first person to walk around the coastline of Britain)[85]

Any walking expedition, however long or short, requires a little planning.

In the next few chapters, we'll discuss the decisions and choices that apply to all coastal walkers, including those who want to travel a vast distance and those who only want to walk shorter segments of the coast.

We'll talk about how to build up your walking muscles, and why the miles you actually walk are more than the miles measured on the map. After that, I'll explain everything you need to know about public rights of way, talk about maps, apps and GPS systems, and end with a host of practical advice on how to plot your route.

Chapter Nine

Decisions and Choices

In this chapter, you're going to look at some of the broader decisions you need to make when planning to walk a significant section of the English coastline.

- Which direction will you head in?
- How will you deal with the gaps in the coast?
- Are you going to walk alone or with companions?
- How much will the expedition cost you?
- And should you be raising money for charity?

Direction: Clockwise or Anticlockwise?

Which way should you go? Do you keep the sea on your left or on your right? If you are a flip-flopper, you can walk in either direction, alternating as you wish, but if you are planning to walk in a continuous line, you're going to have to make an early decision.

I'm walking clockwise, with the sea on my left, as are most (but not all) of the coastal walkers I know. But the guides for the South West Coast Path are written with the assumption you will be walking anticlockwise, as are the guides for the Wales Coast Path.

There are good reasons, apparently, for suggesting the anticlockwise direction.

1. Firstly, the prevailing winds blow in from the west, making your walk along the south coast of England easier because the wind is behind you.
2. Secondly, some people claim that we naturally turn to our left when faced with a junction, leaving our right arm – our sword arm – free to defend ourselves against enemies. It's this inclination to turn to our left that results in an anticlockwise circuit.

If you follow these arguments, we would all be walking anticlockwise. So it's strange that so many coastal walkers choose to walk in the opposite direction.

John Merrill says, 'To walk anticlockwise is the Devil's Way.' And that's why he chose to walk clockwise.[86]

I don't believe in the Devil, neither do I carry a sword, and you're always going to have the wind against you at some point in your walk.

Clockwise or anticlockwise? It doesn't matter really. Your choice.

Bridging the Gaps

If you plan to walk the whole of the English coast, you will be faced with another dilemma. You can't walk in a complete circle following the shoreline of England because of the two interruptions caused by our neighbouring countries – Scotland in the north and Wales in the west.

Here are the various options available to you.

1. You could walk the whole coastline of mainland Britain, including Scotland and Wales. This would extend your walk considerably, roughly doubling the distance.
2. You can simply jump across the intervening countries, and pick up the English coast on the other side.
3. You could combine the coastal walk with inland walking to bridge the gaps. For example, the Offa's Dyke National Trail would take you along the English-Welsh border, but would add 177 miles (285 km) to your walk.[87] The Hadrian's Wall National Trail would take you across the north of England, and would add 84 miles (135 km) to your walk.[88]

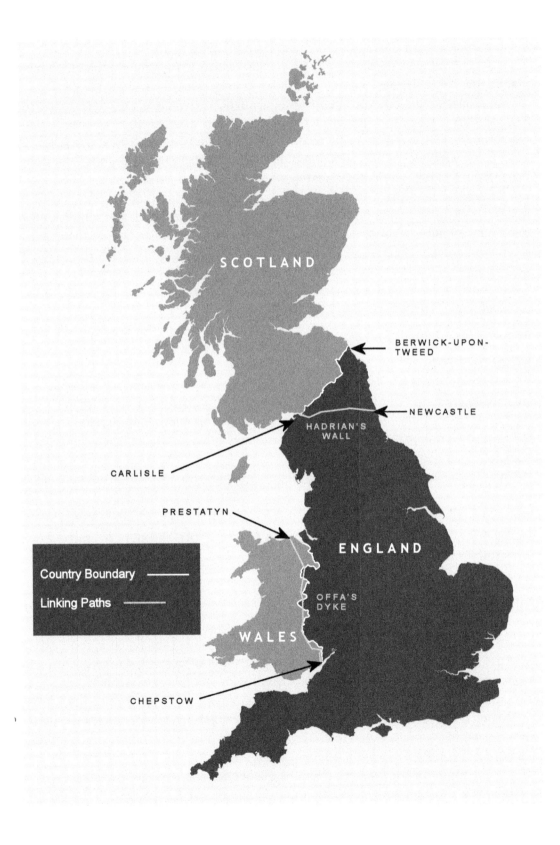

The main problem with the Hadrian's Wall path is that it doesn't follow the line of the Scottish border exactly. Although the western end begins on the border in Carlisle, the eastern end of the walk terminates in Newcastle, which is roughly 100 miles (160 km) too far south.

If you want a continuous and linear walk that covers the whole of the coast of England, my suggestion would be to begin in the north, at the eastern edge of the England-Scotland border. From the beautiful town of Berwick-upon-Tweed, you would follow the English coast southwards and continue around the coastline until you reach the border between Wales and England at Chepstow.

In Chepstow, take the Offa's Dyke Trail northwards, which follows the line of the border, roughly, until it ends on the coast in Prestatyn, in north Wales. From Prestatyn, you are only 20 miles west of the English border and will soon be able to resume your walk up the northwest section of the English coast. Your trek ends when you reach the Scottish border at Carlisle.

The above route is only a suggestion. There are no rules governing your decision. Choose whatever you feel comfortable doing.

Alone or Not

I have already pointed out that many of the successful round-the-coast walkers have done it on their own. It is your decision whether you walk with other people but, if your ambition is to complete the coastal route, then I suggest you are statistically more likely to complete your quest if you walk alone.

Why are solo walkers more successful than people who walk with companions?

'The man who goes alone can start today; but he who travels with another must wait till that other is ready,' said Henry David Thoreau (1817 – 1862), a great walker, thinker and writer.[89]

Walking with Companions

I usually walk on my own, but on a recent trip to the Peak District with friends, I found myself trying to organise a large group walk. Hearing that rain was forecast at midday, I decided we needed to be up on the hills by 9.00a.m. I hadn't realised how hard it is to get a group of people coordinated and out of the house together. Somebody had lost their walking boots, someone else wanted to take their elderly dog for a quick walk first, a couple decided they really ought to eat breakfast, and one keen sportsman had already been out for a run and needed a shower. We were nearly out the front door when we realised one of our friends was missing and discovered she was still in bed.

The whole process was exhausting and frustrating and I resolved never again to walk with a large group. But, at breakfast the next morning, everyone was asking where we were going today. It was only by choosing a long walk (12 miles) that I managed to weed the walking party down to a manageable number.

It's not just setting off that's the problem. Different walkers may want different things from their expeditions. My husband, for example, believes a good walk involves walking a long distance at a fast speed.

'Why are you stopping?' he asks. 'Do you really need to take another photo?'

But for me, the point of a walk is not to get from A to B, but to enjoy the views, to linger in interesting places and – yes – to take photographs. It was with sadness that I realised my husband and I are not compatible walking companions.

We all know when a group of people embark on an enterprise, some will be keener to make progress and will want to walk faster and further than others.

Walking the coast is going to take many months – or years – to complete, no matter how fast you walk or how many hours you put in. So your companion(s) need to be committed for the long haul. Even the most enthusiastic walker can change their minds, or, as the months go by, may find their priorities have shifted.

There are several people who have successfully walked long distances around the coast with companions. Interestingly, the most reliable companions appear to be dogs, but two sets of couples have completed the whole coastline of mainland Britain, the Kings and the Hunts. I am not sure how the Kings got on, but Shally Hunt wrote an excellent book, *The Sea on our Left*, about walking the coast with her husband.[90] Interestingly, the couple would start each day walking together, but by the end of the afternoon, Shally would be lagging behind, frustrated by the fact *he* showed little consideration for her slower pace. Her husband seemed equally frustrated, by *her* lack of progress and constant moaning. Their marriage survived, but their relationship was tested.

John Merrill, with his vast experience of marathon walking, advises you to 'adopt a steady pace that you feel happy with'.[91] If you do this, he says, you can walk vast distances without tiring. I'm not sure I believe him on this last point, but I do think it can be exhausting or frustrating to walk at somebody else's pace and rhythm.

I prefer to walk on my own, but have every sympathy for those who don't want to go it alone. If walking with a friend or partner is what you want to do, that is absolutely fine.

TOP TIP: Choose your walking companion wisely. Remember, this is someone in whose company you are going to spend a great deal of time. It might be best to go for a few trial walks first, just to make sure you are compatible and to work out the ground rules.

Walking Alone

Do you feel happy about walking alone? If not, why not?

I'll deal with the fear of assault in the section *Safety Matters*. For now, I just want to say that statistically, the most dangerous part of your walk is your journey to and from your starting and end points, not the walk itself. But statistics are statistics, and emotions are different things altogether. I believe the fear of assault might be the number one reason why there are so few solo women walkers, although this fact may also be connected to family commitments.

Another fear is the thought of being on your own and suffering from an injury or illness. Again, I deal with some practical steps you can take to reduce your anxiety in the section *Safety Matters*.

Perhaps what deters people from walking alone is the fear of loneliness. If you come across a staggering view, or have just noticed an unusual bird, or are enjoying a tasty lunch, you miss having someone to share it with. Other people's pleasure amplifies our own.

Or maybe you lack confidence in your own abilities to read a map or to find your way around obstacles. I would suggest you are braver and more capable than you think, and the only way to find out is to walk solo and see how you get on.

Companions and Setting Rules

It is possible to have the best of both worlds. You can keep this expedition your very own, while still enjoying the company of others. One way of organising this is to make it clear this is YOUR walk, but invite companions to join you for some of the trail. You can call them companions or, better still, call them guests.

- This means the walk remains your adventure, and you get to set the pace, itinerary, lunch breaks and distance each day, etc., while still enjoying the company of friends along the way.
- And it makes it more likely you will find willing walking companions, as friends and family may be unable to commit to the long haul, but might be happy to join you for one day or a single weekend.

Money Matters

Walking is free. Yes, you will need to buy some kit, and I'll discuss this in a later section, but walking gear isn't particularly expensive and you don't need much to start off with. There are, however, a number of other expenses to consider. I will deal with food, transport and accommodation in more detail later on. For now, I just want to point out that although walking itself is free, you will still need to find funds for your walking expeditions.

Food and Drink

You may prefer, as I do, to stop at pubs or cafés, although the cheaper option is to carry picnics, snacks and drinks in your rucksack. There is still a cost involved, not to mention the added weight of hauling these provisions around with you.

Accommodation

If you are planning on walking continuously for prolonged sessions, you will also have to consider the cost of accommodation. If you're a beginner walker, I would rule out the free options of sleeping rough and wild camping (by which I mean camping outside of official campsites). I'll talk more about accommodation in the section on logistics. For the moment, I just want to point out that whatever accommodation you choose to use, you will need to put aside funding for your overnight stops.

Travel

Don't underestimate the costs of travel to and from the coastal path. Even if you're undertaking a continuous walk, there will be times you have to travel away from the path to find food or accommodation. If you're a stage or segment walker, you will have to factor in train fares and bus fares every day, unless you find a friend willing to drive you to your start points or pick you up from your finishing points, and even then, it's only fair to reimburse their petrol money.

There are a variety of national railcards, which reduce travel costs by train, and can be purchased if you are under 25, over 60, travelling as a couple, or travelling as a family.[92] And, depending on the local rules of your home area, older walkers might qualify for a free bus pass.[93]

Earning While Walking

If you are a working person, how are you going walk the coast while continuing to earn a living?

All-in-one-go continuous walking is only practical for the unwaged – students, the retired and the unemployed – unless you're lucky enough to have an employer willing to grant you a paid sabbatical. Most of us cannot afford to give up our day jobs, and so we fit our walking expeditions into weekend breaks and our holiday weeks. For this reason, most coastal walkers are stage or segment walkers.

It's possible, of course, to make some money from your walking trips. You could write travel articles as you go along, sell photographs, or publish a book at the end of the project, as many others have done before you. I've already mentioned the excellent book by Helen Krasner, *Midges, Maps and Muesli*.[94] Other writers are less successful. It takes a real enthusiast to plod through Vera Andrews' listless account of her walking trip, *I've seen Granny Vera*.[95]

Writing up your account of your walk is an excellent idea, but yours won't be the first book written about coastal walking and publishers will be lukewarm unless you can think of a really unique angle. Unfortunately, therefore, writing about your exploits is unlikely to generate much income.

You might consider looking for sponsorship to cover your personal expenses. Although walking the coast is unusual, outdoor challenges are common, and there are hundreds of people seeking sponsors for various exotic treks, cycle rides, paddling adventures, etc. For something as mundane as *walking*, you are unlikely to find any organisation willing to hand over hard cash. You might find companies willing to supply you with equipment or clothing, providing you have a track record of some sort, and an active presence on social media, and if you can demonstrate something very unique about your planned expedition.

I've been lucky enough to have several offers of free accommodation by people who have read my walking blog, but nobody has ever offered me money.

Although you are unlikely to have people falling over themselves to fund the basic costs of your expedition, you are more likely to find people willing to sponsor you if you are walking to raise money for charity.

Walking for Charity

On one of my walking trips, when staying in a cheap B&B in Kent, I made the mistake of striking up a conversation over breakfast with a man on a nearby table. He was wearing heavy walking boots, but rather oddly, he was also wearing a wrinkled white shirt of the sort you might wear under a business suit. I started talking to him because I wanted to check if he was walker or not.

'Do you like Ken Dodd?' he asked me.

I nodded cautiously.

'My namesake,' he said. 'But I did Ken Dodd last year. Now I'm doing Peter Cushing. He retired to Whitstable.'

'So you're going to visit Peter Cushing?' I asked.

'No, of course not. He's dead.'

The conversation, so far, was baffling, but all became a little clearer when the man, whose name really was Ken, explained he was a great fan of music hall acts, stand-up comics and horror movies, and he planned his walks around a theme. Earlier in the year, he had been on a Ken Dodd walk, visiting the theatres where his namesake had appeared. But this week, he was doing a Peter Cushing walk, and was walking from London to Whitstable.

And the purpose of all these themed walks? He was collecting money for charity.

He asked me who I was walking for.

'Myself,' I said.

He looked horrified.

'No, no. You really must walk for a charity. Carry a bucket. You'll raise thousands of pounds.'

I told him, as politely as I could, that I wasn't interested in raising money.

'But if you're walking for charity, you can negotiate discounts.'

'Discounts?'

'I got a room here for half price, and asked them to throw in breakfast for free.' He leant forward earnestly. 'I did a Burns walk once, and a specialist shop lent me a magnificent kilt.'

'You did a walk in a kilt?'

'It's the only way to walk in Scotland.' His eyes glazed over as he remembered the joys of striding with bare legs through the Highlands.

Despite my new friend Ken's claims that raising money for charity is easy, that doesn't seem to be everyone's experience.

Vera Andrews (Granny Vera) decided to walk around the British coast after her husband died at an early age from cancer. Vera's aim, unsurprisingly, was to raise money for a cancer charity. You would have thought she was in a good position to raise funds because, back in 1984, she was the first woman to attempt to walk right around the coast. She had the support of the Lions Clubs and her late husband's employer, British Gas. In addition, Vera wrote hundreds of letters to potential donors, and handed out donation forms as she went along.

Sadly, Vera never managed to call in all the promised money and although she did eventually raise £2,200, that represents a tiny amount compared to the time and effort she put into her walking expedition.

'As an unknown quantity in the walking field, I was unable to find a financial backer… I was also let down by many promises of small and large amounts of sponsor money that did not come forth upon completion.' – Vera Andrews[96]

So, are you going to walk to raise money for charity or not?

Many of the all-in-one-go walkers did ask for donations and were successful in raising moderate amounts for their chosen charities.

- David Cotton, who completed his walk in 2002, raised money for the Riding for Disabled charity.
- Nat Severs completed the British coastline in 2010 and raised money for three different charities.
- Pete Hill raised £16,000 for multiple sclerosis and spinal injuries.
- Jannina Tredwell raised £33,000 for her four charities, although her original aim was to raise £100,000.
- Martyn and Alison King managed to raise £7,500 for their lifeboat charity.

Sponsorship by the Mile, Sponsorship on Completion, or No-strings Donations?

If you do decide to raise money for charity, you have several options.
- Either you ask for sponsorship per mile, or per hundred miles.
- Alternatively, you ask for the promise of payment on completion.
- Or you simply ask for donations as you go along.

Sponsorship according to distance walked is a risky business. Remember what happened to Alison King who developed a brain tumour? Despite careful planning, life gets in the way. Bad weather may defeat you, illness might intervene, the rigours of being away from home could become too much. And what do you do if there is an early termination to your walk? I suppose you hope that people won't mind paying up anyway.

Because of the uncertainties of any long-term walking project, and the hassle of collecting money at the end, I strongly suggest you don't go for a 'sponsor a mile' or 'sponsor me if I finish' approach. Ask for donations upfront instead.

Funding Your Trip

In my view, it isn't really acceptable to use collected charity money to fund your personal expenses on the trip, because when people give a donation to a charity walker, they expect all their money to go directly to the charity. If you want to raise money to cover your personal expenses, you need to make this absolutely clear to your potential donors.

Vera Andrews wanted to fund the expenses of her trip through patronage and sponsorship. She was given some free accommodation and equipment along the way, had the support of a cancer research charity and the Lions Clubs, and the benefit of being part of the Citizens Band radio community. Despite all this help, at the end of her walk, Vera was left with a personal debt of £1,800.[97] That's around £5,500 in today's money.

You may be able to negotiate generous discounts (like my friend Ken with his themed walks) but if you are setting out on a charity walk, you must be prepared to fund much of your day-to-day expenses out of your own pocket.

Tips for Raising Money

Having watched the progress of other long-distance hikers, I'm convinced that you need a significant amount of backup if your aim is to raise money for charity and minimise your own costs. Walking is tiring. You won't have an office and much of the time, you may not have a phone signal or an Internet connection. You can't do it on your own. You'll need help.

This is what you need to arrange:

- Decide your charity in advance. Some people advocate choosing a range of charities, in the hope of pleasing everyone, but I would pick a single cause, because it helps donors to visualise where their money is going. Contact the charity and see what support it can offer, such as T-shirts or other equipment. Importantly, the charity might have a network of local volunteers who could offer you accommodation or transport. A decent-sized charity should be able to arrange extensive publicity for your walk.

- Create a small support group of reliable people, picked from your friends and family. The group needs to be in place before you start, and each person must understand their role (see below) in helping you achieve your aims.
- From your group, designate a single main contact person. This is who you will phone if you need help. They must know how to contact everyone else in the group, and they should have a deputy.
- If your walk is going to involve many weeks away from home, you need to plan your itinerary and set a realistic schedule for the first few weeks of your walk. I suggest you book several nights of accommodation in advance. It's one less thing to worry about. After that, a planning officer in your support group should take over and maintain a rolling itinerary as your walk progresses, booking you into suitable accommodation, and letting you know the details as you need them.
- Designate someone in the support group to be your publicity officer. Their task is to liaise with the media. The national media won't be interested in your expedition unless you have a strong gimmick of some sort, so don't be disappointed by their lack of enthusiasm. Local reporters will be far more likely to run a story, but they need to know when you are passing through their area. Your publicity officer must identify and contact the local media – newspapers, TV and radio stations – one step ahead of your progress. You should be prepared to do interviews while walking.
- You must have an active social media presence. This means an account on Facebook and Twitter, as a minimum. You will be tired in the evenings, and your Internet connection may be intermittent, so someone in your support group will need to be your social media officer and do most of the work for you. It's a good idea to post an occasional update yourself, because people following you will expect a little personal contact.
- Create a fundraising web page, using a reputable site such as Just Giving.[98] This will encourage spur of the moment donations. Your Facebook page and Twitter account must link to your fundraising page. Don't ask people to pay at the completion of your walk, but ask them to make immediate donations.
- Do you want to carry a collecting box while you walk? Ken carried a bucket. Granny Vera carried a small cash box. Remember, Ken and Vera walked on roads, while you will be walking along footpaths and will have less opportunities to meet people, but you might be able to collect a substantial amount while walking through a busy seaside resort.
- If you plan on collecting cash or cheques, you should speak to your bank about opening a special bank account for donations. This helps to keep your charity money separate from your personal money. One of your support team should know how to deposit donations into the account on your behalf. An alternative is to use a notebook and keep a record of gifts as you go along. Or you could insist on only accepting web-based donations.
- Remember, people will become more interested in your exploits after you've actually achieved some mileage. For this reason, your support team should

continue their attempts to find sponsorship, in the shape of free accommodation, equipment or food, as you continue to make progress around the coast. And your fundraising attempts should ratchet up as the weeks go by, rather than winding down.

- And, finally, follow Ken's example and create a memorable name for your walk. It helps with the social media, with networking, and gives local journalists something to latch onto. 'Colin goes Coastal', 'Annabel's Amble', 'Henry's Hearty Hike', are theoretical examples.

Crowdfunding

Some of the crowdfunding websites support charitable collection and some of the charitable collecting sites have a section called crowdfunding. (I provide a list of a few crowdfunding and charity sites in the *Helpful Resources* chapter at the end of this book.) However, the whole point of a crowdfunding site is to ask people to invest in the production of an end product.

What is your end product? This could be a specific project – such as the purchase of a piece of equipment or the establishment of a new staff post in your chosen charity. If you are looking to fund your own expenses, it's best to have a definite goal for your expedition, such as publishing a book or making a film about your walk.

I've come across one walker who tried to fund the expense of writing a book about her walk in advance through a crowdfunding site.[99] She failed to raise the necessary cash, but you might have better luck.

In summary, walking is free, but any long-distance walking expedition, even one designed to raise money for charity, will create a number of personal expenses you must be prepared to cover.

Chapter Ten

Building Up Your Walking Distances

The biggest mistake people make when they begin their trek is to overestimate the distance they can comfortably walk. In this chapter, I will show you how to plan your walking and build up your distances through a training plan.

How to Judge a Comfortable Distance

Most of us overestimate our abilities, because walking is something we do every day and we regard it as 'easy'. Perhaps we remember a long walk we completed years ago. Or we pick a distance and double it. Or we take a look at the blogs of experienced long-distance walkers and think we can manage something similar.

When I planned my first coastal walk, I used David Cotton's website as a guide (http://www.britishwalks.org/). When David walked the same 17 miles from Kings Lynn to Hunstanton, he made the following note: 'Could easily have walked further if the need had arisen. I still have no blisters and I did not have any aches or pains all day.'[100] But, I wasn't an experienced long-distance walker like David Cotton, and a comfortable walk for him turned into a major challenge for me.

I finished my first walk with my feet covered in blisters and my muscles tense with cramp, and was forced to spend the next day in bed.

How far should you walk on your first day? That depends on how accustomed you are to walking and your current physical condition. In a moment, I'll explain how you can work out a sensible distance.

If you participate in regular sport, you will have a head start when it comes to walking. But, let me give you a word of warning. Don't think your experience in other sports will give you a precise indication of your walking fitness. My youngest daughter, who is a runner, was surprised at how physically different walking feels compared to running. Similarly, my husband is a keen cyclist who regularly accomplishes 50 miles or more on his bike. But after keeping me company on a leisurely stroll, of only 10 miles or so, he ended up with stiff muscles and aching knees.

Working Out Your Walking Distance

Think back over the past two or three weeks, a month at most.

How far have you been walking?

You might be on your feet all day at work, but this is a misleading guide to your walking ability, because it doesn't involve keeping up a consistent pace, step after step. Only some occupations involve continuous walking, e.g. postal rounds, security patrols, etc. But perhaps you walk to work, or go out with the dog, or go for strolls at the weekends. How far are your normal walks when you are walking deliberately and at a steady pace? If you don't know, or rarely walk any real distance, set off and find out.

There are a number of ways to measure your walks.

1. Get an app for your smartphone. There are several to choose from, and I give a selection under *Helpful Resources* at the end of this book, but Map My Walk is a good one and is available in different versions for iPhone and Android.[101]
2. Or, you could plot your course on a map. This could be on a screen, using My Maps in Google Maps,[102] but I think it's a good idea to get a good, old-fashioned paper map. You will need an OS map from the *Explorer* series, scale 1:25,000. (The *Landranger* series has a scale of 1:50,000 and is fine for cyclists and road users, but not detailed enough for footpath walking.) I will explain how to estimate distances using a map in a moment.
3. Some modern sports devices and watches can estimate the distance you have travelled.
4. If you don't want to use the above methods then you could buy a pedometer and use it to calculate your steps and multiply by your stride length. It is not ideal, but it's the way John Merrill estimated his distances.[103]

The 30% Rule

Once you know how far you can comfortably walk, add 30% to this, and you will have a reasonably challenging length to aim for on your coastal walks.

- If you can comfortably walk 5 miles (8 km), aim for a coastal walk of 6.5 miles (10 km) to begin with.
- If you can comfortably manage 10 miles (16 km), aim for 13 miles (21 km).
- If you are regularly walking 20 miles or 30 km or more, I don't know why you need my advice at all. Just get on with it!

When planning your walk, don't forget the terrain. If most of your walking has been on the flat, a big dipper, rollercoaster of a walk might not be the best place to start. Ten miles in Norfolk might seem easy walking, but ten miles along the cliffs of north Cornwall will feel completely different.

If most of your walking has been done on pavements, roads or tarmac paths, don't underestimate the additional strain on your body when you switch to rough tracks and trails. A path that involves a scramble over slippery rocks, or wading through energy-sapping shingle, will require far more effort than the same distance covered on a smooth surface.

TOP TIP: If in doubt, less is best. You can always increase your distances as you become fitter and more experienced. Remember, your prime aim is to enjoy yourself, not kill yourself.

I finished my first day of coastal walking, along 17 miles of some of the flattest coastline in the UK, covered in blisters and feeling as if I had been run over by a steamroller. It was a couple of weeks before I could walk comfortably again. If I had pre-planned a two-week walking holiday, I would have wasted both my money and my time, as I would have been unable to continue.

So remember, if you are planning on walking for several days in a row, you need to pace yourself and build up to it. Less is best.

Planning Distances on the Map

I plot my route using a paper map (the Ordnance Survey *Explorer Series*) and a very special length of string.

My special string? It's just an ordinary piece of white string that I have marked into segments using a black felt tip pen to show each mile. Since nowadays, my preferred walking distance is between 10 and 15 miles (16 to 24 km), I make a red mark at 10 miles along my string. This is the distance that I aim to walk as a minimum, but it is also the point at which I would be thinking of winding down.

People seem to think my string is a revolutionary concept. It seems common sense to me – convenient to use, cheap to make, and easy to carry around in your pocket.

I suggest you make yourself a special piece of string too.

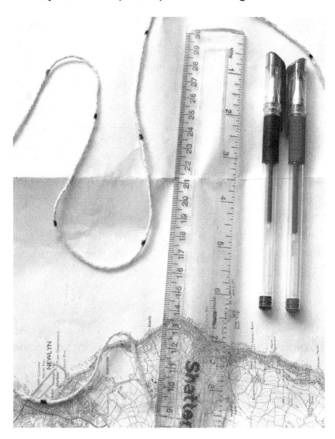

When using the Ordnance Survey *Explorer* map:

- A mile is represented by 2.5 inches on your piece of string.
- Or, one kilometre is represented by 4 centimetres of string.

Don't forget, if you switch to a differently-scaled map, you will need to use a different piece string and make a different set of markings.

Once you've made your string, here is how you use it to plan your distances.

1. Study the map and pick the footpaths, tracks or roads that you want to follow. (I'll talk more about choosing your route in Chapter Thirteen, *How to Plot a Route*.)
2. Having chosen your route on the map, lay your string on the paper, winding it along so that it exactly follows the course you are planning to walk.
3. Count off the marked segments to get your distance in miles or kilometres.

As an alternative to a special string, you can simply use a plain piece of string on the map to measure the course of your walk, and lay it out against the scale to calculate the mileage – but a marked string is so much easier to use.

There are other ways of measuring distances on the map, including a gadget that you wheel across the paper, but my string method is more accurate.

If you make yourself a version of my special string, please do contact me via my blog (coastalwalker.co.uk) or on Twitter (@RuthlessTweets). I would love to hear from you and to post up photos of your string in action.

If you prefer to use online maps, you may be able to plot your route by creating a 'line' or 'path' on the screen. This is certainly possible in the My Map section of Google Maps, but not in Bing Maps. In OS Maps, you can only mark your track online if you are a subscriber. (I'll talk more about online maps in Chapter Twelve, *Maps and Stuff*.)

Whatever method you use, don't forget to take into account the steepness of the terrain. If your path crosses over lots of contour lines, it will probably have to zigzag in order to cope with the slope. This adds an additional length to your walk.

Of course, it's not just the length of the walk that's important in planning your day. You also need to calculate the time it's going to take you. At the end of this section, I will outline several rules to help you in your planning.

But one last thing to remember. **Every walk will be longer than you expect, due to those sneaky extra miles that mysteriously appear.**

The Sneaky Extra Miles – Add 10% or 20%

I am not sure there is any walker alive today who has put more miles beneath his boots than John Merrill. Yet, despite his vast experience, John always finds a discrepancy between his measured route on the map and the actual distance he ends up walking. His walks are 20% longer in real life.[104]

My own experience is that I too usually walk further than I have calculated, but I have found John's figure is an overestimate. I usually walk around 10% further than my plotted route.

The important thing to remember is that the distance you measure on the map will not be the same as the distance you actually walk. Map miles are not the same as real miles.

TOP TIP: Your walk will usually turn out to be around 10–20% longer and you need to factor those sneaky extra miles into your planning.

Estimating Your Walking Time

Once you've decided your comfortable walking distance, and planned your route, all you need to do is work out how long your walk is going to take you. This is important if you are relying on public transport and don't want to miss the last bus of the day. It's particularly important if you are walking in the winter and don't want to be caught out after sunset.

To work out your walking time, you take your walking distance and divide it by your walking speed.

Don't mix your units up. If you are working in miles, stick to miles per hour. If you are working in kilometres, stick to kilometres per hour.

Example in miles

If your walk is 10 miles long and you walk at 2.5 mph.
10 divided by 2.5 = 4
You will take 4 hours to complete the walk, not including rests and stops.

Example in kilometres

If your walk is 20 kilometres long and you walk at 4 km/hr.
20 divided by 4 = 5
You will take 5 hours to complete this walk, not including rests and stops.

In these sections, I will give you three different rules for estimating your walking speed. The first two are official rules by respected mountaineers. The third is much easier to follow and is my own rule of thumb; Ruth's Rule.

Naismith's Rule

In 1892 a Scottish mountaineer called William Naismith devised a rule for estimating the length in time of a walk.[105]

Allow 1 hour for every 3 miles (4.8 km) along a flat path, and adjust for hills by adding an extra ½-hour for every 1,000 feet (300 metres) of climb.

Most walkers take Naismith's rule with a pinch of salt. It is best to think of it as an estimation of the shortest likely time in which a fit and experienced walker would complete the route. In practice, you and I will take much longer.

Remember, Naismith's rule assumes you will be able to walk at an average speed of 3 mph (5 km/hr). This might be easy on a pavement, but you are unlikely to be able to maintain the same pace over uneven or muddy ground, if you meet obstacles such as rocks or fallen branches, or have to battle your way along a path overgrown with brambles.

I remember taking part in an organised 21-mile hike, called the Five Valley Walk, around the town of Stroud in the Cotswolds. (Another, and possibly more accurate, name for the walk could be the Five Hills Walk!) It took me 8 hours of walking time to complete, at a walking speed of around 2.5 mph, and I was quite pleased with this because I am a slow walker. What really slowed me down, however, was not the steepness of the hill climbs, but the stiles – there seemed literally hundreds of the wretched things to climb over.

In addition to stiles and other obstructions, you will want to stop and admire the views, or to take photographs, and you will certainly need the occasional refreshment or comfort stop. These breaks are what make a walk pleasant, but they add to the time you spend out on your trek.

Langmuir's Modification

Eric Langmuir was another famous Scottish mountaineer[106] and he suggested some modifications to Naismith's rule. Unless walking on a flat road or track, he suggests you assume a slower speed of 2.5 mph (4 km/hr), not the 3 mph (4.8 km/hr) suggested by Naismith. Langmuir also adds extra time if walking uphill. When it comes to going downhill, he suggests we go faster down a gentle slope, but more slowly if the slope is steep.

Here is Langmuir's modification to the Naismith rule:

Allow 1 hour for every 2.5 miles (4 km).

Add an extra ½ hour for every 1,000 feet (300 m) of climb.

Subtract 10 minutes for every 1,000 feet (300 m) of gentle downhill slope, between 5 and 12 degrees.

Add an extra 10 minutes for every 1,000 feet (300 m) of steep downward slope, greater than 12 degrees.[107]

To use Langmuir's modification, you will need to work out the degree of the slopes by using the contour lines on the map. On an Ordnance Survey *Explorer* map, you will notice every fifth contour line is darker than the others. This dark line is called an index contour. If you measure 2 cm along your proposed path, and can count two or more of the darker, index contour lines crossing this 2 cm segment, then the steepness of your path is likely to be greater than 12 degrees. Roughly.

All the above might seem horribly complicated, and you might like a much simpler rule to follow. See below.

Ruth's Rule

Here is my rule of thumb, based on my experience of over 3,000 miles of walking, and my transition from a beginner to a moderately competent walker.

For beginners and the unfit:

- A sensible estimate of pace for a beginner is around 2 mph or 3 km/hr.
- If your path crosses lots of contours on the map, or if the walk has been graded as difficult, reduce this estimate to 1.5 mph or 2.5 km/hr.
- This time includes short breaks to check your map or to catch your breath, but you will need regular breaks for rest and refreshments. So add an extra twenty-minute break for every two hours of walking.
- If planning to stop for lunch at a pub or café, you will need to include time for finding a table and being served. So turn that 20-minute break into 40 minutes.

For experienced walkers and the fit:

- If the walk is very easy, mainly on the flat or with plenty of pavement walking, you should achieve 3 mph (5 km/hr) without too much effort.
- On rough terrain, it's safer to estimate an average pace of 2.5 mph (4 km/hr).
- Add a twenty-minute break every four hours.
- If planning to stop for lunch at a pub or café, remember to factor in a 40-minute break.

The trick is to become familiar with your own walking speed and then you will be able to judge the time needed to complete a walk with a reasonable degree of accuracy.

> **TOP TIP: Remember, if walking in a group, you must base your calculations on the speed of the slowest person.**

Training for Walking

I'm a great believer in *'just doing it'*.

But, I also know you'll get much more out of your walking trips if you put some thought into improving your fitness before you start. If you walk regularly, week after week, you will find you can trek further and faster, will suffer less muscle and joint pains afterwards, and you'll reduce your risk of developing blisters or other injuries.

Even after you've become an experienced walker, leaving long periods between your walking trips can make each new expedition seem like starting afresh.

So training is useful both before you any start serious walking and to maintain your 'walking muscles' between your trekking trips.

I've produced a walking plan, based on the same principles runners use when training for half or full marathons. You can use this to train for your very first walk, to improve your walking stamina, or to keep your 'walking muscles' in shape between walks.

Long-distance runners only train to 70%-80% of the distance of their final race.[108,109,110,111,112] Likewise, I suggest you should train until you can easily cover three-quarters, or 75%, of the distance you're aiming for, after which excitement and enthusiasm will propel you over the final few miles of your walks.

I assume that you work or have other commitments during the week, and so the plan is based on shorter, faster walks on weekdays, with a longer, slower trek at the weekend.

The plan comes in two parts. **Part One** is designed for the beginner walker and for those content to cover shorter distances. You don't have to proceed beyond this if you don't want to. **Part Two** is for a walker who wants to walk further and faster.

Part One: to Build Up to Coastal Walks of 10–12 Miles (16-20 km) in Length

DURING THE WEEK: two or three short walks, each of 2 or 3 miles (3-5 km), at a reasonably fast rate, so that each walk takes less than an hour to complete.

WEEKENDS: A single long trek at the weekend, at a slower pace. Start with a comfortable distance, and build up slowly by increasing by a mile every few weeks, until you can easily walk between 8 or 10 miles (13-16 km). Don't forget to stop for drinks and snacks when you feel like it.

Part Two: to Build Up to 20 Miles (32 km) of Coastal Walking

Start with Part One until you can easily walk 8 miles (13 km) at a stretch, without stopping for significant breaks.

DURING THE WEEK: increase the length of your short walks, aiming for 5 miles (8 km) of brisk walking at least twice a week, at a speed of at least 3 mph (5 km/hr), faster if you can.

WEEKENDS: At the same time, start increasing your long-walk distances, aiming for an increase of 2 miles (3 km) every few weeks. Build up gradually from 8 miles (13 km) until you can achieve a leisurely 16-mile (26 km) walk without discomfort.

TOP TIP: Don't forget, when building up your walking routine, to include hills and some walks over uneven ground. This will ensure that your muscles are not taken by surprise when you find yourself on a bumpy path or faced with a steep climb.

Training Breaks

You will be forced to break your training occasionally, due to interruptions caused by work commitments, family circumstances, illness, or bad weather.

- If the training gap is one week or less, continue as if you haven't had a break.
- If the gap has been two or three weeks, resume your plan but don't increase your distances during your first week back.
- If you've had to stop walking regularly for longer than three weeks, start with some gentler and shorter walks, before building up to your long walks again.

If you wish to, you can add in other exercises on your non-walking days.

Suitable additional exercises on weekdays include using light weights, circuit training, gentle jogging, short bike rides, Pilates for core strength, and swimming as a general all-round exercise.

Avoid building heavy muscles with weight training, as you want to be lean, not bulky. And I would avoid adding in too many prolonged running or cycling sessions, because you run the risk of overtraining. If time is short at the weekend, and you can't afford to take time out for your long walk, you could swap that walk for a long-distance run or cycle ride. Only do this occasionally, because cycling and running involve different muscles.

You can, of course, walk longer and further than 20 miles (32 km) if you wish to, and the younger and fitter among us may easily outpace the plans I've provided. But, for most of us, these guidelines provide a safe and effective way to build up your walking stamina and maintain your fitness between walking trips.

And, if all this seems too much like hard work, you can do what I did when I first started: just get out there and walk!

Chapter Eleven

Understanding Rights of Way

In this chapter, I will talk through the different categories of public pathways and give a brief overview of their legal status in England and Wales.[113] In the next chapter, I will describe how to find these paths on your map.

First, let's talk about footpaths. We're lucky in England and Wales to have a wonderful network of paths that are legally protected and open to the general public. These are called Public Rights of Way, or PROWs.

No other nation in the world provides such an extensive system for walkers.

Many of our public paths have been travelled for centuries, and sometimes for millennia, by our ancestors. They include drover tracks, pilgrim routes, Roman roads, funeral or coffin routes, and smugglers' paths.

With the coming of the motorcar, asphalt spread across the countryside and most of our paths became converted into the hard-surfaced, traffic-laden roads we know today. But some escaped.

If you are following a public right of way, you have a legal entitlement to walk along the route, no matter where it runs; across private land, through a farmyard, or through somebody's garden. Just as we are allowed to travel freely by car along any of our public roads, you have an absolute right to travel on foot along a public footpath or public bridleway.

Scotland has a different system, with more extensive rights for walkers. This sounds wonderful, but I will touch on the problems of walking in Scotland later. For the moment, I just want to talk about England, and Wales, and our amazing system of public rights of way.

Official Public Rights of Way (PROWs)

Public Rights of Way come in four types.[114]

1. **Public footpaths** can be used by anybody on foot, and are usually marked by yellow arrows or yellow signposts.
2. **Public bridleways** can be used by walkers, by horse riders, and by cyclists, and are conventionally marked by blue arrows or signposts.
3. **Unrestricted public byways** are unsurfaced roads or tracks that may be used by anybody, including walkers, horse riders, cyclists, and in theory, by any form of motorised transport such as motorcycles, quad bikes and cars. Most of these tracks, however, are unsuitable for vehicles because they are too narrow, rutted or muddy, although they might serve local farm traffic or provide access to the odd isolated cottage. They are marked by red arrows or signposts.
4. **Restricted public byways** have had their use 'restricted' by the local authority. This usually means you can walk, cycle or ride a horse, but are legally prohibited from driving mechanised vehicles, such as motorbikes or cars. They are usually marked by purple or plum-coloured signage.

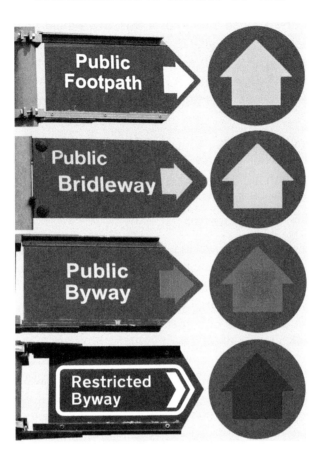

From now on, if I'm referring to any of these four types of rights of way, I'll talk about **PROWs**. If what I am saying relates to one particular type, I'll call it by its name.

Your Legal Right to Enjoy a PROW

If a route is designated as a PROW, you have an absolute right to walk along it, unless the landowner has applied to the local authority for a temporary closure for some reason, in which case there should be a clearly-marked diversion in place for you to follow.

There should be signs telling you which type of PROW it is: footpath, bridleway, or byway. At the beginning of a restricted byway, a sign should tell you what the restrictions are. You can also look for the coloured signs.

Remember, yellow indicates a footpath, blue a bridleway, red a byway, and a plum or purple colour is used for restricted byways.

The person responsible for maintaining a PROW is the landowner. For a public footpath, this means keeping the route clear of crops or undergrowth, but it doesn't mean the landowner has to pave the path, or keep it free of stones, grass or mud. A footpath should be at least a metre wide and a bridleway should be two metres wide. Where the PROW is crossed by a fence, hedge or a wall, there must be a safe way of getting through the obstruction, such as a stile or a gate.

If a landowner ploughs up a path as part of their agricultural business, they should restore a walkable route, although they are allowed 14 days in which to do this. That's a long time, and little help to a walker staring at a roughly-ploughed field of gloopy mud.

It's a criminal offence for a landowner to deliberately obstruct a PROW. It is also an offence for a landowner to keep dangerous animals in a field that has a public footpath running through it. This includes solitary adult bulls, certain breeds of dairy bulls, and any horse known to be dangerous.

The authority responsible for making sure the landowner keeps the path clear of obstructions is the designated local Highway Authority, usually either the County Council or Unitary Authority covering the area.

Just because a footpath is a public right of way, and protected by English law, doesn't mean you won't come across the odd obstruction. Despite their legal obligations, some landowners may neglect to maintain their footpaths or make them deliberately difficult to use. They plough up the route, plant crops across the path, allow their stiles to rot, tie up their gates, or try to restrict the walker to a narrow, ankle-twisting strip along the boundaries of their fields. Others may erect signs telling you it is 'Private Land', while failing to point out it is also crossed by a PROW. Some may provide a handy path so that you can walk around the edge of their enormous field, when the proper footpath actually takes a more direct, and much shorter, route across the middle.

Diversions, Obstructions and Other Barriers

Temporary Diversions

Sometimes, a footpath will be temporarily diverted. Diversions might be necessary for a variety of reasons: for example, if construction work is being carried out on the path, or if the route becomes impassable due to landslides or flooding. However, there is no guarantee that a diversion won't take you several miles out of your way.

Information about approved footpath diversions can be found on the website of the local authority responsible for that particular section of the footpath. The problem for a long-distance walker is you may pass through several different areas in the course of a single expedition, and sometimes it is difficult to know which authority is the responsible one. And even if you work out which is the correct authority and have the foresight to check their website in advance, it is not always easy to find footpath information, which might be tucked within a parks and amenities section, or within the highway section of the site.

I rarely look for possible diversions in advance of a walk. But if you prefer to meticulously plan your route, or if timing is crucial because of public transport links, you may want to check for the latest information on the Internet before you set off.

Permanent Rerouting

In some cases, you may find a PROW clearly marked on your map, but the route has been changed since the map was compiled.

I have strong views about rerouting footpaths. I don't think it should be allowed unless there are exceptional circumstances, because footpaths represent the cultural heritage of this country. We wouldn't consider moving a historic monument – such as Stonehenge – unless it was in imminent threat from some unstoppable force in the local environment. Footpaths, in my opinion, deserve the same protection.

A footpath cannot be moved without consultation and official permission. But sometimes they are. The new route should be properly signed, although there is no guarantee that any signs that once existed will still be in place when you walk along the route. This is one of the many reasons why you should always carry a map with you.

Fences, Hedges and Other Barriers

Where a PROW crosses an obstruction, such as a hedge, wall, fence, stream, ditch, etc., the landowner is required to provide some sort of crossing structure. Here are a few of them:

Stiles: These are one of the joys of the English countryside. They come in all shapes and constructions, made with a variety of different materials, and are sometimes very ingenious in their design. The commonest sort is the wooden stile set into a hedge. This is designed to provide a barrier for animals, while allowing humans to climb over. It is, essentially, a sort of stepladder. Other stiles are set into stone walls, where larger stones provide the steps. Some have an additional feature, a sliding wooden bar, to allow dogs to pass through, although not all stiles allow easy access for dogs and, if you're planning to walk with a canine friend, you may have to lift your pet over occasionally. That's something to remember if your dog is very large and you are rather small.

Gates: There is a tendency to replace stiles with gates. I guess this makes it easier for people who are less agile to walk the footpath, but I'm sad to see many traditional stiles being replaced. A common type of gate is a 'kissing gate'. This is designed to prevent the passage of animals – whilst being negotiable by humans. Most kissing gates are excellent. Some provide such a narrow space that I've sometimes had to remove my backpack to fit through.

Don't forget to leave a gate in the same condition as you found it. If it was open, leave it open. If it was shut, make sure you close it behind you.

Electric fences: If these cross a footpath, the landowner should provide a section you can open up without risking an electric shock. Look for a hook with a padded and insulated handle, often a bright blue colour. By holding the handle, you can unhook that section of electrified wire and pass safely through.

I have come across temporary electric fences where the farmer has not provided a way through. This means crawling on hands and knees – or wriggling like a snake – to get underneath the lowest wire, not a pleasant prospect when the ground is covered in animal poo!

TOP TIP: Here's a useful tip from Gayle, who runs an excellent walking blog at http://gayleybird.blogspot.co.uk/. 'If you come across a temporary electric fence, remember the supporting poles will be insulated and are designed to pull up easily,' Gayle suggests. 'Grab one of the supports and pull it out of the ground. Lay it on the ground and step over the now-lowered section of fence. Once on the other side, pick the post back up and using the horizontal protrusion a few inches from its base (which they almost always have), use your foot to stamp it back into its hole.'

Rivers: There are hundreds of rivers, streams, and watercourses flowing through the English countryside, and each one must empty into the sea at some point. So, as you walk the coast, your path will frequently be interrupted by flowing water.

Bridges: Where the path is interrupted by a tiny stream or brook, a farmer may simply lay an old railway sleeper or a couple of thin planks between the two banks. On most National Trails and well-used PROWs, you will find properly constructed footpath bridges. Enthusiastic teams of volunteers maintain some of these and some will be more stable than others!

If you come across a wide river or estuary, you may have to walk upstream to find the nearest road bridge.

Riverbanks are usually privately owned. In many cases, there is a footpath along the bank – both the River Severn and the Thames, for example, provide long-distance walking routes – but this is certainly not universal. If your planned walk includes tramping up and down river estuaries, you will need a decent map so you can find and follow PROWs. (Of course, if the riverbank has flood defences and is clearly being maintained by the taxpaying public, you might feel happy to trespass. I certainly have done so at times.)

Stepping-stones: I love stepping-stones. They provide the most ancient way ever invented of crossing water with dry feet. Remember, the river level may depend on the tides and you may only be able to use the stones at low tide. Stepping-stone crossings are usually marked on an OS *Explorer* Map and it's a good idea to check the tide tables in advance (using https://www.tidetimes.org.uk/).

TOP TIP: If you know you'll be using stepping-stones, don't forget to take a walking pole to help you balance.

Ferries: This is absolutely my favourite way of crossing water. Ferry crossings are marked on the Ordnance Survey maps, but some are seasonal and others run very infrequently. Remember to check that the ferry is running, and check the last crossing time, before you set off. You can usually find the ferry operator's contact details with an Internet search. Take spare change. Like a bus driver, the ferryman will not want to be scrabbling for coins if you offer a high-value banknote.

Wading: This is rare and usually the result of a rotten bridge or missing planks. In some cases, wading across a shallow stream can help you avoid a long detour up to the nearest bridge crossing. On the South West Coast Path, and at low tide, you can wade across the River Erme in Devon. Or, if you are a coward like me, you can walk up the river and cross at the nearest bridge – an eight-mile diversion. If you anticipate wading, you may like to take some shoes you don't mind getting wet, such as a pair of light trainers or sandals, and a travel towel.

National Trails and Long-Distance Footpaths

National Trails are official long-distance footpaths, supported by central government and maintained by local agencies. There are currently twelve National Trails in England and three in Wales, making fifteen in total. They vary in length, from the shortest at 83 miles (the Hadrian's Wall Path) to the lengthy 630 miles of the wonderful South West Coast Path.

The England Coast Path, when completed, will become the 16th National Trail and, at an estimated 2,800 miles in length, will become the longest of them all.

The relevant National Trails for coastal walkers that are currently in existence are as follows:

- The Cleveland Way (coastal part)
- The Peddars Way and Norfolk Coast Path (coastal part)
- The South West Coast Path
- And, if you walk along the Welsh coast, the Pembrokeshire Coast Path

The advantage of walking along a National Trail is that you will find the route well maintained. You will meet few obstructions, and the bridges and stiles you come across should be in good condition. Signposts are clearly marked with a yellow acorn, the official symbol of the National Trails, and the routes are chosen because they pass through great scenery.

The downside of the National Trails is their popularity, which means sections may become crowded in summer. You can buy detailed guidebooks for each trail, or find out more on the National Trails' website, at http://www.nationaltrail.co.uk/.

Other Long-Distance Footpaths

In addition to National Trails, England is crisscrossed by over a thousand other long-distance footpaths. These have been created by local authorities or by local rambling groups, usually by cobbling together a series of shorter footpaths to create a lengthy route. They are given various names, such as the Saxon Shore Way or the Viking Coastal Trail.

If a long-distance path has been created by a local authority, and given a name, it's usually an indication that the path will be well-signposted and easy to follow. Some even have guidebooks.

TOP TIP: The best source of information on long-distance paths is the Long Distance Walkers Association: https://www.ldwa.org.uk/.

Wales and Scotland

The Wales Coast Path provides an 870-mile (1,400 km) route right around the coastline of Wales. Funnily enough, this wonderful path is not a designated National Trail, except for the relatively short 186-mile section in the middle, the Pembrokeshire Coast Path.

Scotland has its own equivalent to the National Trails; a series of long-distance routes called The Great Trails. Although Scotland doesn't have a complete coastal path, and there are no official plans for one, parts of the coastline are covered by these trails.

Theoretically, Scotland doesn't need to provide official public footpaths, because the Scottish people have full access rights to their countryside, something often referred to as the 'right to roam'. That doesn't mean you can tramp anywhere you want to in Scotland. You're not allowed in people's gardens, golf courses, military areas, airports, farmyards, sports fields, places with an entrance charge, or across fields of growing crops, for example.

The downside to this wonderful scheme is that it can be an excuse for not providing proper trails. The walker, therefore, can find themselves battling through thick gorse or towering bracken, tramping through peat bogs and marshes, wading across rivers and splashing through streams. When, finally, they've almost reached their intended destination, they can find their way blocked by a barbed wire fence that stretches for miles across the landscape. Or even worse, come to a stop against a 10-foot-high deer fence.

So the famous 'right to roam' enjoyed in Scotland is not without its problems.

But let's get back to the topic of this book; walking the English coast.

In England, you don't have to confine yourself to PROWs. There are other places you can walk.

Other Permitted Walking Routes

Permissive Footpaths and Bridleways

Permissive paths or bridleways are routes that a landowner has agreed the public can use.

Unlike official Public Rights of Way (PROWs), a permissive path is not enshrined in law. This means the landowner can remove his or her permission at any time.

The landowner will often put up a sign telling you what you are and are not allowed to do along the permissive route. Usually, both camping and fires are forbidden, and you may be instructed to keep your dog on a lead. Sometimes, the list of prohibited activities is very long but, irritating though these signs might be, I am always very grateful to find a permissive path and treat the landowner's wishes with respect.

Public Roads

You are legally entitled to walk along almost any road in the country, with only a few exceptions.

Access to military establishments and commercial docks may be closed to pedestrians, and some roads are privately owned. You can't walk along a motorway or its slip road, although in a few circumstances, a walking route is provided adjacent to a motorway. (For example, a combined cycle and footpath runs beside the M5, where it crosses over the River Avon.)

Apart from these exceptions, if there is no footpath or pavement next to the road, you are legally entitled to walk in the road itself. But do you really want to walk in the gutter next to hurtling traffic? It's not only highly unpleasant but you could also be risking your life. Even a sleepy rural road can turn into a rat-run during rush hour.

So while, technically speaking, you can walk down almost any UK road (apart from the exceptions noted above), in practice, you want to find an alternative footpath route wherever possible. If you have no option but to walk in the road, you can take some sensible precautions, following the guidance rules set out in the The Highway Code, as detailed below:[115]

If there is no pavement, keep to the right-hand side of the road so that you can see oncoming traffic. You should take extra care and:
- *be prepared to walk in single file, especially on narrow roads or in poor light.*
- *keep close to the side of the road.*

It may be safer to cross the road well before a sharp right-hand bend so that oncoming traffic has a better chance of seeing you. Cross back after the bend.

Help other road users to see you. Wear or carry something light-coloured, bright or fluorescent in poor daylight conditions. When it is dark, use reflective materials (e.g. armbands, sashes, waistcoats, jackets, footwear), which can be seen by drivers using headlights up to three times as far away as non-reflective materials.

TOP TIP: My jacket has reflective strips but, if I anticipate a prolonged stretch of road walking, I wear fluorescent armbands that I carry around in my rucksack, just in case.

Cycle Ways

A comparatively new feature of the English landscape is our extensive National Cycle Network, providing safe cycling routes for both short and long-distance journeys.[116] Cycle routes should not be confused with cycle lanes.

Cycle lanes usually consist of a narrow strip along the side of the roadway, often indicated by a yellow line and a yellow bike symbol painted on the road surface. A cycle lane may run for several miles, or for only a few yards. Cyclists are encouraged to use cycle lanes for safety reasons and to improve traffic flow, but may have to share their lanes with buses and taxis.

Cycle lanes are not designed for walkers. Don't use them.

Cycle routes are different. Official cycle routes form part of a network, providing alternative routes for cyclists to travel long distances. These long-distance routes are given numbers, just like our road system

Although walkers should avoid cycle *lanes*, we can use most of the official cycle *routes*, as these are usually designated for shared use. Despite having to dodge the occasional cyclist, there is one main advantage – you will find the surface of an official cycle path is better maintained then the surface of an ordinary footpath. This means that cycle routes may be suitable for wheelchairs, pushchairs and for those wet winter walks when an ordinary footpath becomes impassably muddy.

The downside of cycle routes is that they can offer rather monotonous walking. For example, long-distance cycle routes may run along the tracks of disused railway lines.

This makes for a long, flat, straight path, excellent for cycling but very boring for the walker.

Cycle routes may also follow the routes of existing footpaths or bridleways, which have been adapted for cyclists. But many local authorities have constructed new cycle routes in popular areas, either as a way of trying to get the local population to commute by bike and leave their cars at home, or as a tourist amenity.

Cycle routes come in two types.

1. **Cycle routes that follow roads.** The routes chosen are usually country lanes or quiet routes through towns. There may or may not be an inner strip of the road marked off for cyclists and pedestrians. In any case, you will have to watch out for traffic. Their hard surface makes for rapid progress, but can be tough on your feet.
2. **Traffic-free cycle routes** are wide pathways that run separate from any road. In places, they may run alongside a road, but with a grassy verge between. Traffic-free cycle routes may have a road-like surface, but they may also have a surface of gravel or packed earth, and they can be muddy.

Both the *Landranger* and *Explorer* versions of the Ordnance Survey maps indicate cycle routes and show the two different types that make up the National Cycle Network.

Other Permitted Areas Around the Coast

There is a bewildering array of organisations that can 'own' part of the coastline, even if they are not always the true landowners, and a plethora of national organisations that control what can and cannot happen along the coast. I will outline some of them below.

Don't worry if you find this very confusing, because I do too. Although it's not essential to remember all the possible different types of land designation in Britain, having a basic understanding will help you to plan your walking routes.

Open Access Land

This has been specially designated as being open to the general public. Sometimes, these areas are known simply as Access Land or Common Land. The main set of regulations governing these arrangements is set out in the Countryside and Rights of Way Act of Parliament (or CROW Act), and so another term used for open access land is CROW land.[117]

These lands include some large areas of open countryside, moorland or hillsides, some forests and woodland, and areas that historically have been freely used by the local inhabitants in villages and towns. They can include village greens and local parks.

Some areas of open access land are owned by the local authorities or public bodies, some by charities, and some by private landowners.

When walking across open access land, you don't have to confine yourself to a path and you can generally roam as you wish. But there may be some restrictions. You cannot walk into private houses or walk through their gardens, for example. You won't normally be allowed to cycle, may be forbidden from camping or lighting fires, and there may be restrictions applying to dogs. You should find information boards setting out what you can and cannot do.

TOP TIP: Areas of open access land are marked on the official Ordnance Survey *Explorer* maps by an orange border.

National Parks

There are fifteen National Parks in the UK, ten in England, three in Wales and two in Scotland.[118] Each park has its own National Park Authority. The Authorities don't 'own' the land in the National Parks, much of which belongs to private landowners and a great deal of which is used for farming. But the National Parks are recognised as being special landscapes, and are designated areas where there are restrictions on development. The National Park Authorities oversee the use of the land and promote conservation and public access.

National Parks should not be confused with CROW or open access land. Just because you are in a National Park, does not mean you have the right to roam anywhere you want. You should, however, find some open access land within a National Park, and there is likely to be a good network of footpaths, bridleways and cycle routes.

Some of the National Parks include coastal areas. Exmoor, for instance, includes a section of the Somerset coast; the North York Moors covers a section of coast in the northeast; while the Lake District covers an adjacent section of coastline in the northwest of England.

Areas of Outstanding Natural Beauty

There are 38 areas in England and Wales that are designated as being Areas of Outstanding Natural Beauty, and each of these areas may consist of several scattered locations.[119] They are recognised as special landscapes and, although they don't have the full infrastructure of regulation as a National Park, they have some legal protection restricting the amount and type of development allowed.

Much of the coast of Cornwall, including Land's End, the Lizard, the area around St Ives, and Tintagel, for example, are designated as Areas of Outstanding Natural Beauty.

Again, don't confuse this designation with the right to roam. Much of the land will be in private ownership. If you are walking, you may need to follow one of the official Public Rights of Way or a Permissive Footpath.

Nature Reserves

Anybody can slap the title of 'Nature Reserve' on their land. It seems to be a good way of deterring walkers, many of whom are keen on nature and conservation and therefore, don't want to disturb a fragile habitat or frighten birds. I have come across stretches of private land where the landowner has stuck up crude signs, declaring his or her land a nature reserve. In some cases, if you peek through the barred gate, you will see signs saying 'Private Shooting' – so much for conserving nature! In other cases, I've seen private gardens covered in children's play equipment labelled as nature reserves.

There are, however, 224 official **National Nature Reserves** (NNRs) scattered around the UK countryside, some of which cover coastal areas.[120] There is no automatic right of access to a nature reserve, official or otherwise, although most genuine nature reserves will welcome visitors and may provide a variety of walking routes.

Other Designated Areas

Along with the National Parks, Areas of Outstanding Natural Beauty and the National Nature Reserves, mentioned above, there are certain other designations that can be applied to parts of the countryside and which, therefore, provide some legal protection. These include:

- Sites of Special Scientific Interest[121]
- Heritage Coast[122]
- Environmentally Sensitive Areas[123]
- Marine Conservation Zones[124]
- National Scenic Areas (Scotland)[125]
- Ramsar Sites (Conservation of Wetlands)[126]

Many areas around the coast will fall into one of these categories. In fact, a third of the total coastline of England is designated as Heritage Coast.[127]

Sometimes, a single section of coast will have several designations. The Lizard, England's most southerly peninsula, is an Area of Outstanding Natural Beauty, and contains a National Nature Reserve, along with three sites of Special Scientific Interest.[128] In addition, it's part of the UK's Heritage Coast too.[129]

As far as the walker is concerned, these designations do not confer any particular right of access, but they do ensure continuing protection of the landscape and its plants, birds and animals.

The important thing to remember is that we, as a nation, care passionately about our countryside in general and our coastline in particular. All the above classifications and attendant organisations should help us to protect and promote our precious coastal landscapes.

Walking Below the High Tide Mark

One day, I was walking along the shore when I came across a sign: 'Private Beach. Keep Out.' Two elderly gentlemen ambled up beside me and one of them poked the sign with his walking stick, shaking his head in disgust.

'They can't own the beach,' he said. 'It belongs to the Queen.'

'Only below the high tide mark,' said his companion.

'Right then. We'll walk below the high tide mark.'

They walked forward and I followed. Carefully, we made our way across the 'Private Beach', making sure we stuck to the sand below the line of seaweed that marked the limit of the latest high tide. When we came to the end of the beach, I rejoined a coastal footpath and continued on my way. The two elderly gentlemen, having made their protest successfully, simply turned around and walked back the way they had come. At one stage, they stopped and waved to somebody watching from one of the nearby houses. They were being deliberately provocative, of course, but making the point: 'You can't stop us walking here.'

Does the Queen really own the beach below the high tide mark? The answer is rather complicated, and if you're not British, you may find it even more complicated than I do. I shall try to explain it as simply as I can.

Who Really Does Own Our Foreshore?

Three parties share the ownership of much of our foreshore, by which I mean the area between the high and low tide marks. These are: the Crown Estate,[130] the Duchy of Cornwall,[131] and the Duchy of Lancaster.[132]

The Crown Estate owns much of the foreshore, along with many other properties. But that doesn't mean the Queen, personally, owns it. The Crown is a term we use in a general 'it belongs to the state' and 'therefore it belongs to all of us' kind of way. This implies that the Queen holds the shoreline in trust for the nation. But, in reality, the law is a bit muddy about the exact question of ownership. The Queen can't sell the shoreline, neither can she hand it over to someone else when she dies, but she does keep 15% of the income generated from the Crown Estates. The rest goes to the government via the Treasury.

A huge tranche of Cornwall, including almost its entire foreshore, belongs to the Duchy of Cornwall. The Duke of Cornwall is always the eldest living son of the ruling monarch and so, at the time of writing this book, the Duke of Cornwall is Prince Charles. The Prince doesn't, technically speaking, own the lands that belong to the Duchy of Cornwall, although again, this is a somewhat muddy area, but he gets to keep all the revenue earned by the estate. When Prince Charles becomes king, the Duchy of Cornwall will be handed over to Charles' eldest living son, Prince William.

The Duchy of Lancaster is the third party in the trio and owns a 100-mile (170 km) stretch or foreshore in northwest England, between the River Mersey and Barrow-in-Furness. The Duchy of Lancaster arrangement is distinctly odd. The British Monarch, among his or her many titles, is also the Duke of Lancaster. Today, of course, that means the Queen 'owns' the Duchy of Lancaster, although many would argue it is held by The Crown and therefore, owned by the state, or by 'all of us' British citizens. In any case, the income generated by the Duchy of Lancaster goes directly to the Queen. A Duchy Council oversees the administration of the estate, and overall responsibility for the estate is in the hands of the Chancellor of the Duchy of Lancaster. This person is appointed by the Queen, but recommended by the Prime Minister. In other words, it's a political appointment.

Who else can claim to own the foreshore? Well, usually through lease arrangements with The Crown, the following may claim to own the foreshore: the military, port authorities, local authorities, the National Trust, the Royal Society for the Protection of Birds (RSPB) and, possibly, some private individuals.

Confusing, isn't it? Clear as a muddy beach.

Like my two, protesting, elderly gentlemen, who insisted on walking across the private beach, most British citizens firmly believe that the Queen owns the beach. And, if you take 'The Crown' to mean the Queen, then I guess most of the foreshore does indeed belong to the Queen. In fact, you could argue that all the property in Britain, technically speaking, belongs to The Crown, and is only leased out to private individuals.

What should you do when faced with signs saying 'Private Beach, No Entry'?

My personal opinion is that you should respect the following:

1. Bona fide nature reserve signs if they are put up by established bodies such as the National Trust or the RSPB, and are designed to protect nesting birds or other wildlife.
2. Official government and military signs, as you don't want to be arrested as a terrorist or blown to pieces during a firing exercise.

In all other cases, you should hold your head high and walk determinedly across the beach, making sure you march below the high tide mark.

You are unlikely to be challenged. I've never been. But, if someone did question your right to walk there, you could just say, 'Don't you know that all the land below the high tide mark belongs to the Queen?' Even if it doesn't, your challenger is unlikely to be able to prove his or her case.

Reporting Problems With Public Paths

You can't make an official complaint about the weather. Neither can you complain about mud or the steepness of the terrain. But you can complain about dangers such as rotten bridges, mad cows and rabid dogs on a public path. And if you do meet an obstruction – a fallen tree, a collapsed stile or a locked gate – you should consider reporting it.

The National Trails and other popular long-distance paths are usually well cared for and looked after. It's the smaller footpaths, the unloved and neglected routes, where you are more likely to come across a problem. Remember, local authorities have a duty to ensure that all Public Rights of Way, whether a footpath, bridleway, or byway, are properly maintained and accessible.[133]

Yes, complaining takes time and effort. Yes, it can be frustrating, and nine times out of ten, you will get a bland and standard reply. But if you don't notify the authorities of a problem, they won't know it exists.

First step: Record the exact location and nature of the problem. Do this at the time you spot it, otherwise, you will forget the details.

If you're using a paper map, make a mark on it. If you're using an electronic device (an app or a Garmin) record a waypoint. You need to know which county you are in. If this isn't clear, record the name of any nearby village or town. Note the name or number of the footpath if it has one, and – if you can work it out – the grid reference. Some of the trails provide grid references on signposts or gates, so it's worth looking around to see if you can spot one.

It's also useful to record the nature of the problem by taking a photograph.

Second step: Make sure you understand the status of the path you are complaining about. Is it a public footpath or a public bridleway? Or are you in area designated as open access land? (Open access land is shown with an orange border on a standard *Explorer* map.)

Is it within a National Park? If so, there is a different reporting route you can use.

Or is it a permissive path? If it's a 'permissive' path, remember, there is no legal right of access, but you may like to contact the owner of the land and let them know about the problem, if you can work out how to do this. In some cases, the owner's name will be displayed on a signpost.

Assuming you are complaining about a genuine PROW, move on to the next step.

Third step: Once you've worked out the status of the path, you can work out who you should be complaining to.

If the problem occurs in a National Park, you can contact the National Park Authority at http://www.nationalparks.gov.uk/contact-us.

If the problem occurs on designated open access land, you may also contact the owner if you can discover who that is. Often, there will be a sign up somewhere telling you. It may be the National Trust, another charitable body, or a private landowner. Alternatively, you can contact the government agency responsible for open access land. This is Natural England: https://www.gov.uk/government/organisations/natural-england.

In all other areas, the responsible authority for PROW is the local highways authority. This is usually the county council, but might be a district council, a unitary authority or metropolitan borough. Don't worry about the distinctions between these agencies; the trick is to track down the right one.

In many cases, the relevant authority will be obvious, but if you are out in the fields on the edge of a boundary, it may be unclear. This is one of the reasons why you need to make a mark on your Ordnance Survey map or create a waypoint on your GPS system, so that later, you can work out exactly where you spotted the problem.

TOP TIP: If you need help to establish the name of the responsible authority, you can use a search facility on the official gov.uk site at https://www.gov.uk/find-your-local-council/. Unhelpfully, the site uses postcodes, and street addresses, not grid references.

Fourth step: Work out how to send your complaint in.

Once you've identified the responsible authority, you will need to visit the authority's website and track down the officer who looks after footpaths.

On the county council's site, you might find a 'footpath' section and the email address for a 'footpath officer'. If not, you should look in the 'roads and highways' section. There may be an online form for recording problems or a contact email address.

If the problem was on a designated National Trail, the Trail will have its own officer you can report problems to. You can find out who to contact by visiting the National Trail website: http://www.nationaltrail.co.uk/. I've found that some officers are more proactive than others, who may simply pass your complaint on to the responsible local authority.

Another excellent way to alert the responsible council is to use the reporting facility on FixMyStreet, at https://www.fixmystreet.com/. Although the site is designed to help people report problems with roads, it is happy to accept reports about footpaths too. This wonderful facility provides online maps so you can pinpoint the exact location of the problem. Even better, the site sends a message directly to the authority on your behalf.

Fifth step: Making your complaint.

When making a report, be as specific and as helpful as you can.

A footpath officer may be responsible for a lot of different functions inside the authority, and footpaths may come low down in their hierarchy of priorities. So your aim should be to make their life as easy as possible. Make sure they have no excuse for not following up your complaint.

Tell the officer exactly where you found the problem. You could include grid references from the OS map in your complaint – although I've discovered that not all footpath officers understand these. Some local authorities number their footpaths, so this will be useful information if you can find it. Otherwise, use local landmarks, such as roads and villages.

Here is an example:

'I would like to report a broken stile. This is to be found at grid reference [insert grid numbers here] on OS map [insert series name and map number here]. The stile is situated halfway between the villages of [XXX] and [YYY], just to the north of [insert number of road here] road. Thank you for investigating this problem.'

Where possible, I try to include a screen shot from Google Maps to help the officer understand the exact location, along with a photo to illustrate the problem.

Sixth step: Waiting for a response.

Don't hold your breath. The standard reply goes something like this: 'Thank you for reporting the problem. We will look into it when resources permit.'

This is always disappointing. Sometimes, however, I receive a much friendlier response, such as: 'Thank you. I agree this needs fixing and will be visiting tomorrow to verify the situation and will deal with it immediately.' That counts as a great result.

If nothing happens, an alternative route for action is to contact the local Ramblers group. They may know who to talk to in order to trigger a proper response, or they may even have volunteers who will go out and correct the problem, if it's something simple like fixing a broken stile. You can identify a local group via the Rambler's website: http://www.ramblers.org.uk/go-walking/group-finder.aspx

Similarly, a local group of the Long Distance Walker's Association may be able to help: https://www.ldwa.org.uk/clubs/clubs.php

Please remember, if you contact either the Ramblers or the Long Distance Walkers, these are voluntary groups whose members are unpaid. If they can help, they will, but it is not their responsibility to fix footpath problems. The responsibility lies with the local highways authority.

Chapter Twelve

Maps and Stuff

We've talked about choosing your distance and calculating your walking times, and I've given you a brief overview of public rights of way. Now all you have to do is pick your route. To do this, you will need a map.

There are different types of map you can use, paper or electronic, detailed or outline. In this chapter, I will explain how to access maps, both the paper versions and digital versions. I will also talk about GPS devices and apps that might be useful.

The Joy of Maps

Shally Hunt, who walked around the coast with her husband, describes how friends expressed surprise at the idea the couple would need maps. 'Don't you just keep the sea on your left?' they asked innocently.[134]

My non-walking friends don't understand why I need maps either. 'Why don't you just follow the coast path?'

As I hope you realise by now, coastal walking isn't that straightforward. Much of our coastline has no official path. One third is either inaccessible or difficult to access. Even when there is a clear path, you still need a map.

Without a map, you can't see what lies ahead. Without a map, you don't know if a promising footpath is going to come to an abrupt stop. Without a map, you can't work out if it's possible to walk along a beach and find a way through at the other end, or how to navigate around rivers and estuaries. You won't know how far you have to go to reach your destination, or where the nearest toilet is, or whether there is a pub nearby, or a village over that hedge, or how to shorten your route if you are feeling ill or tired.

All these things would be obvious, if only you had a proper map to look at.

To walk without a map is like walking around blindfolded.

You need a map.

John Merrill, with his vast experience of long-distance walking, always carried a map with him and held it in his hand while he walked.[135] Although, like John, I always have my paper map with me, a map only tells me *where* I should be going, but not where I actually *am* at any given moment, and so I also carry a device with GPS navigation facilities. I'll talk about GPS devices towards the end of this chapter.

Ordnance Survey Maps

In his book, *A Walk in the Woods*, Bill Bryson talks about his experience of walking the long-distance Appalachian Trail in the USA.[136] He describes how each local region produced their own maps, and how variable these maps were, with some offering little more than a few vague squiggles on a small sheet of paper.

I was surprised because I thought every civilised nation in the world had its own version of the British Ordnance Survey maps. Now I realise they don't, and we are extraordinarily lucky.

According to their website, the Ordnance Survey has 'mapped the location of every fixed physical object in Great Britain, from the ground upwards, to within one metre accuracy'. And the Ordnance Survey continues to gather information at an astonishing rate, making 10,000 updates to its database every day.[137]

So, what is the Ordnance Survey and why do they make such great maps?

History of the Ordnance Survey Maps

The idea of creating accurate and comprehensive maps was spurred by that great catalyst of innovation – war.

The word 'ordnance' refers to military supplies or military weapons, and the first serious ordnance mapping began in 1746, when King George II commissioned a military survey of the Scottish Highlands.[138] He needed information to help subdue a Jacobite uprising. It wasn't just about the positions of weapons and defensive structures, but about knowing how the land lay, where to find high ground, and what obstructions existed, such as cliffs and woods and rivers. All this was vital information that could make the difference between a successful military campaign and bloody defeat.

Comprehensive ordnance mapping really took off towards the end of the 18th century, when Napoleon and his dreaded French forces threatened to invade the south coast of Britain. As part of our defence preparations, the first comprehensive map of Kent, our most vulnerable county, was commissioned, and this was completed by 1801. Slowly, because mapmaking was a slow process in those days, other areas were mapped, until by 1820, nearly a third of the land mass of England and Wales was covered.

And once the mapping habit started, it couldn't be stopped, even after Nelson defeated the French and Spanish fleets at the Battle of Trafalgar, and the threat of invasion receded. We needed maps for other enterprises, such as the developing railway system. In fact, when it came to planning major construction projects, we needed maps that were even more detailed than the military maps produced so far.

So, yes, we can thank Napoleon for kicking off our Ordnance Survey maps. And after that, we can thank the industrial revolution, and in particular the railways, for placing the emphasis on greater detail and larger scale.

From its military beginnings, the Ordnance Survey has never looked back, and the organisation is now one of the largest map producers in the world, providing a wide variety of maps in both electronic and printed format. They even produce a map of Britain especially for use by *Minecraft* gamers.[139]

Our Ordnance Survey maps are a national treasure.

Paper Ordnance Survey Maps

There are two types of Ordnance Survey map that are suitable for walkers.

1. The *Explorer* series has an orange cover and a map scale of 1:25,000. This means that 2.5 inches on paper represents 1 mile (or 4 cm represents 1 km).
2. The *Landranger* series has a dark-pink cover, with a map scale of 1:50,000. This means that 1.25 inches on paper represents 1 mile of land (or 2 cm represents 1 km).

TOP TIP: My preferred maps are the *Explorer* series. They contain more detail than the *Landranger* and are perfect for walking.

From now on, I'll refer to Ordnance Survey maps by using the abbreviation OS. And I'll be talking about the *Explorer* series, unless I make it clear I'm talking about another type of map.

When you first start out, your OS map may appear a confusing maze of lines and colours. Don't be daunted. You'll find a key printed along one side of the paper sheet to help you decipher the information. My advice, whichever type of map you choose, is to stick to the same series. With time, and once you've become comfortable with using a particular type of map, you will be able to open it up and almost *see* the terrain by looking at the contours. I say 'almost', because I am far from perfect at doing this, although my map-reading abilities have improved considerably with practice.

Each OS map represents a large area of land. One map will fit neatly into a deep pocket but, once unfolded, is equivalent to just over 15 sheets of A4 paper. Of course, your walk may extend over the edge of a single map, and adjacent maps usually have a small overlap, but not always. Some of the *Explorer* maps are printed on both sides, which sounds good in theory, but in practice, I find a double-sided map a little confusing to use, as I always manage to open it out on the wrong side.

There is a facility on the OS website to create your own paper map. You choose the area you want, and they print it out and send it to you through the post. You can even select your own photograph to go on the cover.[140] This facility may be useful if your walk crosses over the edge of a paper map, because you can create your own version where the centre of your route is in the centre of map and, hopefully, you can fit far more of your itinerary within the single sheet. But, of course, there is a charge for creating your own custom OS maps, and a single custom map works out more expensive than buying a couple of off-the-shelf maps.

The main problem with printed OS maps is that the costs can soon mount up if you are planning an extended walk. The Hunts worked out they would need a hundred maps to cover the whole of the British coastline, including England, Wales and Scotland.[141] At today's current price of £7.99 per map, that would add up to a whopping £799 for the complete set.

Cheaper Sources of Paper OS Maps

You can buy second-hand OS maps from eBay and Amazon. Remember, many of these will be out of date, and postage and packing bumps up the price.

When buying new maps, I use an online wholesaler called Dash4it, because their maps are consistently cheaper than the recommended retail price, and postage and packing is free.

TOP TIP: Dash4it send maps via first-class post, making their service ideal for last-minute planners: http://dash4it.co.uk/

Online Ordnance Survey Maps

When planning your walks at home, and if you haven't got a relevant paper map to hand, you can view OS maps online in a number of ways. The best sites to use are either the official Ordnance Survey site, or Bing Maps.

Ordnance Survey Site – www.ordnancesurvey.co.uk

On the official OS site, you can view 'standard' maps free of charge, and toggle the aerial view if you wish. Sadly, the free standard maps aren't suitable for walkers because they don't show up public footpaths and other PROWs. You can only access their detailed OS *Explorer* and *Landranger* maps if you pay a subscription fee.

At the time of writing, a subscription to OS maps is very cheap – just under £20 for a year's access.

If you become an OS subscriber, not only can you access both *Explorer* and *Landranger* views over the whole of the UK, but you can download and print maps off from your own computer. It's a great facility, but remember, each map you print will only be A4 size, assuming you have a standard printer. A4 is fine for short walks, and has the advantage of being easy to fold up and stuff in your pocket. But, if you are planning a long expedition, you will need to print numerous sheets.

On the OS site, you can also plot routes onto the maps and download them as GPX files for loading onto a GPS device such as a Garmin. (I will talk more about GPS in a moment.)

I use the OS subscription service for planning my walks, and I also use it while daydreaming about National Trails and other routes I might follow one day. I sometimes print out their maps if I'm going on a short walk. But when it comes to long-distance coastal walking, I much prefer to buy and use the full-size paper versions of the maps.

Bing Maps – www.bing.com

Currently, Bing provides views of OS maps, both *Explorer* and *Landranger*, absolutely free of charge. Go straight to http://www.bing.com/mapspreview to access them. It is an excellent service and I have no idea why it's free.

TOP TIP: On Bing Maps, you can also toggle between OS maps and aerial views. And you can drill down to see street names and bus stops. Very handy. You can print off Bing Maps. But printing is not very satisfactory, as the area of the map will be constrained within a box inside the A4 sheet, which makes it frustratingly small. If you want to print off a Bing Map, I suggest you use a screenshot.

Other Sites for Free OS Maps Online

There are other websites that allow you to view OS maps online without subscription. Most have limits to the amount of data the Ordnance Survey service allows them to display on any given day, and that limit is soon used up. Unless you log on first thing in the morning, you may find them to be unreliable. Some ask you to register before you can view the maps.

These sites come and go, but here are some of the URLs currently offering free viewing of OS maps.

http://maps.the-hug.net/
https://www.walklakes.co.uk/
http://footpathmaps.com/
http://www.trailzilla.com/

Other Online Maps

OpenStreetMap at www.openstreetmap.org provides a set of open source maps that have been amended by contributors. It's an admirable project, but does not clearly show up every PROW and is incomplete in its coverage of other features. There is no aerial view.

Google Maps at www.google.co.uk/maps is great for aerial views and road maps, but doesn't show PROWs, and so is of limited use when planning your walking route. But I find Google Maps invaluable for finding local accommodation, pubs and cafés. And, in common with Bing Maps, you can also read road names and see the location of bus stops.

Local Maps and Guides

Many areas will produce their own tourist guides, including map leaflets. These are usually free of charge but, if they're not available online, will be of limited use in planning your walk because you can't access them in advance. Tourist maps usually show circular walks, which may not suit a coastal walker who wants to walk in a series of linear hikes.

If you are using a recognised long-distance path or National Trail then the responsible authority might provide a series of downloadable maps. Others may only provide a simple schematic map, which doesn't really give you enough detail.

In addition, there are numerous walking guides. These vary in quality, but there are some respected series such as the Cicerone guides.[142] A guidebook should provide you with useable maps, although they may be of limited scope and not detailed enough to help if you find you've wandered off the marked route for some reason, or if your chosen path is closed or diverted.

A good guidebook will also give you plenty of interesting background information about the area you are walking to. This can either distract you from your walking, or add to your enjoyment.

In summary: I don't think you can beat a proper paper OS *Explorer* map. It shows you the PROWs you can follow, and the location of car parks, pubs and toilets. It gives you a wealth of additional information, such as the names of the cliffs and islands you'll come across, and interesting features such as Iron Age forts and ancient monuments. To me, knowing this detail adds greatly to the fun of every walk.

Digital Maps and GPS Devices

Paper maps don't suit everybody. Some of my walking buddies don't like carrying them, because of the weight and cost, and prefer to use digital maps.

Good digital maps cost money. A single OS digital map may cost far more than a single OS paper map, but usually covers a much wider area. Some of this wider area will be of little interest to you, as you only want a view of the coastal strip. Even so, digital maps may work out cheaper than buying paper maps. And, on a single tiny device, you can store literally hundreds of maps without having to carry any extra weight around.

There are two ways of using digital maps while walking:

1) A special standalone GPS device such as a Garmin.
2) A GPS mapping app on a smartphone.

It is possible to use an electronic map without GPS, but the advantage of having proper GPS is the ability to see exactly where you really are at any given moment. If you don't understand what GPS means – and I didn't before I started my coastal walking adventure – don't worry, I will explain. GPS stands for Global Positioning Satellites. A GPS device is something that can communicate with those satellites.

The primary purpose of the GPS system is to pinpoint your exact position on the planet, and to tell you how your position is changing over time. That's the principle behind a simple GPS sports watch, which records a runner's speed. Bundled with a map, and with a screen to look at, the device becomes a useful navigation tool.

Most of us are familiar with satnav systems installed in modern cars. You can use a similar system on your walks.

1) Standalone GPS devices

Popular GPS devices for walkers include those made by Garmin[143] and Satmap.[144] They are roughly similar in size to a chunky smartphone, are designed to sit easily in your hand, and come with small screens on which you can see a scrolling map. You can check your position and keep a record of the route you've walked, time taken, etc. And you can download pre-planned routes from the Internet and export your own routes to share with others.

Most GPS devices are pretty reliable to within a couple of metres while you're out in the open, but they do need to be able to communicate with overhead satellites. This means they won't work in tunnels or caves, and may be less accurate on stormy days when cloud cover is unusually thick.

The main problem with these GPS systems is that they are expensive to buy. More importantly, the standard maps that come pre-installed are useless. If you want a proper OS map, either *Landranger* or *Explorer*, you will have to buy map cards to insert into the device. These are sold per area and they're not cheap.

There are alternatives to buying expensive map cards. Walking enthusiasts have created plenty of sites where you can download open-source maps, either free or at minimal cost, often with GPS routes already marked for you. Once the map is downloaded onto your PC or laptop, you can connect your GPS device to your computer and transfer the map onto the device.

> **TOP TIP: Internet sites providing downloadable digital maps may come and go, but a useful one is Talky Toaster at http://talkytoaster.co.uk/.**

Remember, the screens on any handheld GPS device will be small. The more you are prepared to pay, the bigger the screen you'll get, but if you want to follow the course of a path as it crosses the map for any distance, you will have to scroll the screen. This means you can't quickly get a good overview of your whole route while you're out on your walk.

Personally, I find scrolling maps both restricting and annoying, although it doesn't bother others. For this reason, I plan my walks using a paper OS *Explorer* map, and only use my Garmin to check my position during the walk to make sure I'm on the right track, as well as to keep a record of the route I've taken.

There is another, much cheaper way of using GPS while out walking. You can simply download a GPS app and use it on your smartphone.

2) GPS apps on a smartphone

I find these apps amazing. Your little phone sends a signal up into the sky, reaching beyond the atmosphere, and talks to tiny satellites orbiting on the fringe of space itself. And as long as your phone can access at least four satellites, the app can work out where you are to within a few yards. The greater the number of satellites your phone finds, the quicker and more accurately it will pinpoint your position. Even better, your phone doesn't need to connect to a mobile network carrier, and so the system works even when you have no mobile signal. It's wonderful.

There is a multitude of different GPS apps available for both the iPhone and the iPad, and for Android and Windows smartphones as well. We are spoilt for choice. Some are free, but even the ones you pay for are very cheap. Many GPS apps are geared towards runners and cyclists, although some cater specifically for walkers.

The app should be able to show your position on a map that is detailed enough for you to be able to work out where you are. At the end of the walk, many of us want to be able to see the route we've walked, the distance we've covered, the time we spent walking, and our speed. These aren't strictly necessary functions, but they are fun, and most apps can do this because they are designed for competitive runners or cyclists to keep tabs on their performance.

Remember, if your app works by accessing online maps, it won't work if you have no phone signal or if your data limit has been reached.

- I've used Map My Tracks.[145]
- And I've tried Runkeeper,[146] although this app is mainly geared, as the name suggests, towards runners.
- Other people I know use Map My Walk,[147] and this is my current favourite.
- WalkJogRun[148] comes very highly recommended and has a good community of users.
- ViewRanger[149] seems to have an excellent set of features too, including a 'buddy' facility, allowing another person to follow your progress in real time – potentially a very useful safety feature. In the chapter on communication, in the *Safety Matters* section, I mention some more apps that allow your friends and family to track your whereabouts.

TOP TIP: I can't tell you which smartphone app is best for you. I suggest you read the reviews, make a decision, download one and learn to use it. If you don't like it, switch to another one.

My version of the iPhone comes with an in-built app called 'Maps'. It's useful for finding my way around city streets, but is no good in the countryside because it doesn't show footpaths.

And that's the problem with most of the apps – the maps aren't wonderful.

Ordnance Survey Maps on Apps

If you want a smartphone app with a decent OS map, you will have to pay for the maps. And they're expensive. There are *two* official OS map apps, which is slightly confusing, and they do different things.

OS Maps app: The cheapest route to access digital OS maps is to become an OS subscriber. Currently, this is good value for money as it costs less than £20 for a year's subscription. After subscribing, you should download the **OS Maps** app, available for both Apple[150] and Android devices.[151] Using this app, you can access the complete range of UK *Explorer* and *Landranger* maps at no additional charge.

The OS Maps app has a second function for non-subscribers. Whenever you buy a new paper OS map, it comes with a free mobile download code, which you can redeem online using the app.

OS MapFinder app: If you don't want to become a subscriber, you can still access OS digital maps via another app. The **OS MapFinder** app allows you to buy individual maps as you need them.[152]

TOP TIP: Whether you subscribe, buy as you go, or download with a free code, make sure the OS maps are stored on your phone *before* you set off on your walk. This means they're accessible even when you have no mobile signal.

And a Warning About Smartphone Batteries:

When I first started walking, I used my smartphone to track my route, but was horrified to find how quickly the battery drains when you have a GPS tracking app working in the background. This is a particular problem with the older iPhones, but no smartphone is immune. The reason? The GPS app sends signals to the satellites at frequent and regular intervals and is, therefore, working almost constantly.

There are other reasons why your battery might get sucked dry when you are walking, and I'll deal with these in the *Staying in Contact* chapter.

As my walks have grown longer, I've become fed up with the hassle of worrying about battery charge. That's why I stopped using a GPS app on my smartphone and switched to a handheld Garmin device instead.

Now you know how to access maps and understand the added value of a GPS device or app, the next step is to start plotting your route.

Chapter Thirteen

How to Plot a Route

As you may have realised, I love paper maps. There is something delicious about opening up a brand new sheet, smelling that fresh-print smell, and seeing acres of exciting new territory laid out, just asking to be explored.

Plotting a walk is one of the joys of walking. I have fallen in love with the whole experience. I enjoy tracing the paths, worrying about the contour lines, chanting the unfamiliar names of villages and towns, sniggering over the occasional double-entendre names: Shag Island, Bottom End, etc.

How I Plan My Walks

This is how I plan my walks – with an Ordnance Survey map spread out on the floor and my special piece of string in my hand. (If you want a reminder on how to make your own special string, please go back to Chapter Ten, *Building up Your Walking Distances*.)

Sometimes, I will check out the satellite or aerial view of the route on the Internet. To do this, I usually use Google Maps from force of habit, but Bing Maps is even better because it allows you to see footpaths (www.google.co.uk/maps or www.bing.com/mapspreview).

I also check the weather forecast and my preferred forecaster is the BBC weather service, which I check via their website (www.bbc.co.uk/weather), although you can also use their weather app if you prefer.[153] The BBC weather service allows you to drill down to the level of individual villages and is surprisingly accurate. I like to know if rain is forecast, of course, but also like to know wind speed, because walking with a fierce wind in your face is far more tiring than walking with the wind behind you. And I like to know the predicted temperatures, as it helps me decide what to wear.

TOP TIP: It's always good to know how many hours of daylight you will have for a walk. Sunrise and sunset times are also available on the BBC weather site.

If it seems relevant to my route, I may consult tide tables. Tide Times provides a good service at www.tidetimes.co.uk, but you can find similar charts on the BBC site and elsewhere.

You could use a digital map, instead of a paper map, if you wish. The main thing to do when planning your walk is to decide which footpaths, tracks and roads you are going to use. What you are aiming for is a continuous route to take you from your start point to your end point, while keeping close to the coast.

Finding Public Paths on OS Maps

You should quickly learn how to recognise a Public Right of Way (or PROW) on a standard Ordnance Survey (OS) map because these are the paths you will be using most of the time.

On the OS *Explorer* and OS *Landranger* maps, the official PROWs are shown by dashed lines. Just to confuse you, the two different series of OS maps use different colour schemes. The *Explorer* map shows PROWs in green. *Landranger* shows PROWs in red.

TOP TIP: I suggest you always use an *Explorer* map, and remember, 'green' means 'go'.

The pattern of dashes tells you what sort of PROW it is.

1. Footpaths are shown by a series of close-set short dashes, so short that they look like a row of dots.
2. Bridleways are shown by a series of longer dashes, with a small gap between.
3. Byways are shown by the same long dashes as bridleways, but with a short vertical line through the centre of each dash.

4.   A restricted byway is similar to a byway, but with shorter vertical lines, which alternate above or below the long dashes.

5.   If a PROW is an official National Trail, or a recognised long-distance footpath, the symbols change from dashes to diamonds. These paths are usually better signposted and easier to follow than ordinary footpaths.

Ordinary paths and private tracks may be marked on your OS map too. An ordinary path may be shown as a series of black dots and a track by a double line or series of dots, also in black. Remember, these are not Public Rights of Way. They might be private driveways, private roads, or farm tracks with locked gates, and you may be able to walk along them, or you may not.

Symbols for Public Rights of Way
OS Explorer Map

Footpath

Bridleway

Byway

Restricted Byway

Long-distance Trails

Symbols for Paths and Tracks
OS Explorer Map

(not public rights of way)

Path

Track

On *Explorer* maps, you will find additional features that are not shown on *Landranger* maps. This is one of the reasons why I recommend you use the *Explorer* series.

- Permissive footpaths and bridleways are shown by lines of orange dashes.
- Traffic-free cycle routes can provide a good alternative to footpaths, and are shown by a line of prominent orange spots.
- Open access land is surrounded by a thick orange border.
- On future maps, coastal access areas will be shaded pink with a pink scallop border.

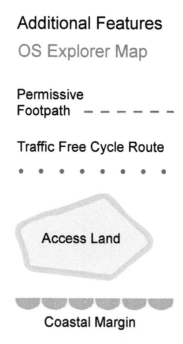

Additional Features

OS Explorer Map

Permissive
Footpath — — — — — —

Traffic Free Cycle Route

• • • • • • • •

Access Land

Coastal Margin

If all this sounds rather complicated and difficult to remember, don't worry. You can always look at the map key, which is printed as an information panel somewhere on your paper OS map. If you are going down the electronic route, or have printed off your own OS maps via a subscription service, you can find information about the OS symbols on the Ordnance Survey's website. They even provide two handy PDF files, with details of all the symbols (http://tinyurl.com/jsgucgs).

There are a host of other features to discover on the *Explorer* map, including rural pubs (a blue beer mug) and public toilets (labelled PC). You will find the railway station, the bus station, and the location of rural hotels and hostels. You can also tell if the shore consists of cliffs, rocks or a beach, and whether the beach is sand or shingle.

Walking Along Roads

Remember, you can walk along almost any public road, as long as it's not a motorway. Most walkers try to avoid roads, partly because of the dangers of traffic, but also because tarmac is tough on your feet. In some circumstances, however, roads may provide the best routes around the coast, or may provide a link between two separate sections of footpath, or will take you into a village or a town in search of either accommodation or refreshments.

Here is how to tell whether a road might be safe to walk along, using an OS *Explorer* or *Landranger* map.

Firstly, look for cycle routes. These usually follow quiet roads or tracks and should provide reasonably safe walking.

Secondly, look at the colour of the road as marked on the map.

A plain white road is not a public road and, although it may be possible to walk along it, there is no guarantee you will find a through route, unless the road is also marked as a cycleway.

A yellow road is a narrow public road and in rural areas, is usually the best route to choose. Dotted lines along the edges mean the road is more of a track than a road, which makes it even better from a walking point of view.

If you can't find a suitable yellow road, look for an orange one. These are secondary roads and are usually reasonably quiet, but not always.

In general, avoid red roads unless there is a footpath. You can use the aerial view on Google Maps or Bing Maps to see if a path runs alongside the road.

Roads Suitable for Walking
OS Explorer Map

Cycle Route on Road

Narrow Road

Minor Road (B road)

Roads to Avoid

Major Road (A road)

Although the colour of the road provides a reasonable guide, it's not a fool-proof method of assessing the safety of the route. A yellow or orange road might provide the only route between two towns or villages, in which case the traffic might be heavy.

TOP TIP: Before deciding if it's safe to walk along a minor road, check to see if there is an alternative major road that traffic could use instead.

Ferries

I've mentioned ferries briefly in the rules section. Most coastal walkers use ferries to avoid a long walk inland to the nearest bridge, but others don't. In some cases, the authorities maintaining a path will *assume* you are going to cross using the ferry.

Ferry routes are clearly marked on the OS maps by dotted lines across the water. Passenger ferries are usually donated by the words 'Ferry P', and vehicular ferries by the words 'Ferry V'. Most car ferries will also take passengers.

When thinking of ferries, don't think of the huge cross-channel monstrosities. The ferries you encounter on the coast path are likely to be small. Some crossings will have regular running times, but others will operate 'on demand'. You may have to wave a giant lollipop stick, as you do to cross over the Bawdsey ferry in Suffolk, just north of Felixstowe. Sometimes you will see a phone number you can ring. Or you may just have to wait and hope for the best.

The main problem with coastal ferries is that they often have limited running times. Vehicular ferries tend to be more reliable than passenger ferries, which are often designed for tourists and may close early in the afternoon, and often shut down over the winter months. Most ferry routes will either have their own websites or will have crossing times listed on the relevant local tourist or council website.

In November of 2012, I was walking along the South West Coast Path in Devon, heading towards Plymouth. When I reached the village of Newton Ferriers, the path came to a sudden halt on the banks of the River Yealm.

I knew there was a ferry crossing at this point across the river, but I also knew the ferry didn't run over the winter, and I was fully prepared to find an alternative route. But there was no alternative route. Instead, a sign warned of the dangers of trying to walk up the river to the nearest bridge because there were no footpaths and the road was too dangerous. Walkers were expected to catch a bus or call a taxi.

What did I do? I telephoned my husband and arranged for him to come and pick me up. That happened to be the last day of long-distance walking I did that year. In the spring, I returned and resumed my walk on the other side of the river.

TOP TIP: Check the ferry crossing times on the Internet before you set off. If you find yourself stranded on the wrong side of the river, you could be faced with a very long and difficult walk.

Satellite and Aerial Views

Sometimes, you need extra help in deciding if your proposed route is viable. Some questions to consider are below:

- Is the beach walkable or is it covered in boulders and barriers?
- There seems to be a track marked on the map, but is it passable?
- You have to walk along a road. Will there be a footpath or a pavement?

For this type of information, the satellite view on online maps, such as Google Maps[154] or Bing Maps,[155] might come in handy.

Don't forget, the aerial view only gives a snapshot taken at one particular time on one particular day. If you are planning to walk along a beach, you should check the high tide line, which is shown on the OS map, and consult a tide table.

In addition, the overhead pictures don't give a true indication of how steep the hills and valleys are. For this, you need to know how to read contour lines.

Reading the Steepness of a Slope

The OS map will also tell you how steep a path is.

Look for the contour lines. These are pale orange lines that wiggle like thin snakes across the map. Each line represents a change in height of 5 or 10 metres (it's usually 5, but look at the key on the side of the map to check). You will see some of the lines have numbers, telling you how far above sea level that particular line runs. Every fifth line is darker in colour, and is called an index line. They help you count the contours when the lines are too tightly bunched together to see clearly.

Here are some guidelines for reading contours:

- The closer together the lines are, the steeper the slope is. If you can count two index contours with a 2 cm stretch of path, the slope is definitely steep.
- To work out if a section of path is going uphill or downhill, turn your map around, as if you are facing along the path in the direction you are planning to walk, and look at the contour height numbers. If the numbers are upside down, you will be walking downhill. If they are the right way up, you will be walking uphill.
- If your path runs parallel to the contours, you will be walking along the line of the slope.

TOP TIP: In very hilly areas, where the contour lines are very close together, it can be difficult to work out all the details on the map. In these circumstances, using an online or digital OS map is helpful, because you can zoom in and magnify the view.

You want to get to know your map as if it was your best friend. If you refer to your map regularly as you walk, it won't be long before you can recognise the markings with ease. After a while, you will be able to look at your map and immediately understand how the landscape is set out and where the paths flow across it. At this stage, you will truly be able to boast, 'I know how to read a map!'

Just Do It!

Have you read this far and not started walking yet? Maybe you are feeling overwhelmed by all the choices, and paralysed by indecision. Or maybe it all sounds so horribly complicated, you don't know where to start.

If so, my suggestion is as follows:

1. Pick an area either close to home or involving reasonable travel time.
2. Buy an Ordnance Survey map (*Explorer* map) that covers that area.
3. Prepare a piece of string.
4. Using the map and string, plot out your route and make sure you choose to stop after a sensible and easy distance. (I suggest 3 miles or 5 km if you haven't done any walking before.)
5. Plot either a circular walk, or a linear walk between two separate points. If you plan a linear walk, don't forget to work out how you are going to get from the finish back to your starting point.

When you've done that, just go out and WALK.

Section 4

Logistics, Clothing, Equipment

'If you believe some of the advertisements you see in outdoor magazines, you might think that rambling is a very expensive hobby. Believe me, it isn't.'

(*John Bainbridge*, rambler, writer and freedom-to-roam campaigner)[156]

You don't need a great deal of equipment to go for a walk, but you do need some. In this section, I will discuss your various options when choosing footwear and clothing, and suggest additional equipment you may like to consider using on your walks. You also need to decide what you should carry in the way of food and drink. And that leads us onto another important comfort consideration... toilet stops.

Any long-distance walking expedition involves finding and booking accommodation and transport. I will cover these topics and offer practical advice to help you plan your trips.

Chapter Fourteen

Shoes and Boots

What is the number one rule of walking? **Look after your feet!**

I know that advice sounds obvious, but it's surprising how many people you meet out walking who are wearing ridiculous footwear.

Remember the children's fairy tale about the princess and the pea? The princess couldn't sleep because her skin was so sensitive, she could feel the tiniest pea placed underneath a tall pile of mattresses. If you are new to walking, after a few miles, your feet will become as sensitive as that princess' skin, and every little pebble on the path will feel like torture.

Later on in this book, under *Safety Matters*, I am going mention blisters and blister prevention. For the moment, I just want to talk about choosing shoes and boots.

The Seven Basic Criteria

If you are just starting out, and if you are walking five miles or less over easy ground, along hard tracks or firm beaches, then you don't really need special footwear. Any pair of comfortable shoes will do.

Here is a list of some of the types of footwear that are really NOT suitable and you should rule out: flip-flops, toe-less sandals (even the all-terrain type you see sold as suitable for walking), clogs, fashion boots, high heels, pointed toes, ballet pumps, court shoes, and soft UGG boots.

Look for footwear that fulfils the following criteria:

1. Encloses your toes, in order to keep out sand, grit and mud.
2. Has an upper that rises well over your midfoot, so that you are not forced to grip with your toes to keep the shoes on your feet.
3. Is roomy enough to allow your toes to move around a little when you set off in the morning, because your feet will swell during the course of the walk.
4. Has a thick and cushioned sole, to protect the soles of your feet.
5. Has padding inside, to keep your feet comfortable and reduce the risk of blisters.
6. Has a good tread on the bottom, to ensure a decent grip on wet or muddy surfaces.
7. Has a heel that has a gently rounded or 'rocker' shape to its back edge.

Why do I advise a heel with a slightly rounded back edge?

If you strip off your socks and look at the back of your heel, you'll see a gentle curve, not a sharp angle. Our heel is designed so that when we take a stride, the back of our heel hits the ground first and then rolls under our weight as our centre of balance shifts forwards. (You can check this out for yourself by taking a brisk walk down a hallway in your bare feet.)

A shoe with a gentle curve at the back will help you maintain a natural walking gait by allowing your heel to roll forward with each step, which is exactly the way your body was designed to walk.

In fact, most walking shoes and trainers nowadays have rocker-shaped heels, some more obviously curved than others.

But here's a word of warning: avoid very rounded heels, or heels that are rounded at the *sides*. These shoes are often marketed for the purpose of losing weight, or for strengthening your leg muscles, because they make you fight for balance with every step. They are too unstable for long-distance walking and you risk injuring yourself.

Also, beware of trainers with heels that flare outwards. These are designed to anchor your foot on the ground for instant stability, useful in playing certain sports, such as tennis, for example. There is nothing wrong with them when used within their given sport, and they would be comfortable enough for walking short distances, but you don't want to wear them for long-distance treks.

Walking Shoes or Walking Boots?

Shoes

If you're a real beginner, I would suggest you don't invest in expensive kit to start with. Just wear a comfortable set of shoes or trainers and get going. You can think about buying proper footwear later, when you have a better idea of what you need.

If you want to wear trainers, choose ones with thick and cushioned soles.

Most running shoes have thin and flexible soles, and won't give you the padding and stability you need over rough or uneven ground. But some running shoes are designed specifically for cross-country and rugged terrain. They have thicker soles, more padding, and greater degrees of water resistance. There is a growing trend for these hybrid shoes, often called trail runners or trail shoes, and you might like to give them a try.

Some of my walking friends never buy special shoes or boots, but wear ordinary shoes made by good brands such as Sketchers or Clarks.

Proper walking shoes have laces, robust soles, padded inners, and should offer much better water protection compared to trainers or ordinary shoes. They are usually made of fabric and look similar in many ways to trainers. Walking shoes tend to be cheaper than walking boots.

Walking Boots

Walking boots appear to be a British or European invention. Americans only seem to wear what they call hiking shoes or trail shoes. Even in Europe, many people choose walking shoes instead of boots.

I wear boots. Once you begin undertaking longer walks, over 10 miles or so, and once you start walking on rough terrain, you may prefer boots too. They provide more protection over rocks and stones, and more support around your ankles. (I have never yet suffered a sprain while walking, despite turning my foot several times on uneven ground.)

The soles of walking boots are thick and tough, and should last much longer than trainers, which can wear out quickly. And walking boots will grip better than trainers, with deep furrows on their soles, like car tyres, designed to prevent you slipping while walking on muddy terrain. In fact, many types of soles – both in walking boots and in walking shoes – are made from vulcanised rubber, exactly the same material as car tyres.

Leather or Not?

My first walking boots were made of leather and were the colour of glossy milk chocolate. They looked huge, as bulky as a workman's boots. I'd never tried on such a massive-looking pair of footwear before but, to my surprise, those boots fitted like bedroom slippers – and I immediately fell in love with them.

'Wow! They're so comfortable,' I said, stomping around the shop.

The shop assistant was a knowledgeable woman and a keen walker. I was a complete novice and, in my imagination, all walking boots were made of leather, came halfway up your calf, and had enormous laces tied in double bows. These boots fulfilled this description. To be fair to the assistant, she had spent some time with me discussing the merits of fabric boots, but we came to the conclusion that leather boots would be (a) more weatherproof and (b) more likely to keep out the blowing sand. I hadn't yet realised that most of the coast is composed of marsh, rocks and shingle, not sand.

Yes, my new leather boots were sublimely comfortable. For about a mile. After that came blisters and agony. I hadn't broken them in properly and this is one of the downsides of leather boots. They are unforgiving, don't mould easily to the shape of your foot, and need to be worn for several short walks before they are truly comfortable on a long one.

There are, however, many advantages.

- Leather boots look good and smell wonderful.
- They are tough and protective when stumbling over sharp rocks and stones.
- In addition, leather is waterproof. When I did get wet feet, it was either because moisture from my trousers had trickled down my legs and into my boots, or it was because water had come in over the top after I splashed through streams.
- They are easier to clean after a muddy walk.

John Merrill, who has truly earned the right to call himself a 'marathon walker', expects his boots to last around 2,000 miles and, during his 6,824-mile trek around the coast, wore out three pairs.[157] When another John, John Westley, marched around the whole of mainland Britain and the coast of Ireland too, he got through nine sets of boots during his 9,469-mile walk.[158] This works out at 1,000 miles per pair.

I had, therefore, high expectations of my new chocolate boots – 1,000 miles, at least.

Leather needs looking after. It is a natural product that requires some attention. When I came home from my walks, I was usually too tired to care about my boots, so my husband took over their maintenance. He lovingly scraped away mud and sand and anointed them with liberal helpings of dubbin, a special grease designed to keep leather soft and waterproof. Those boots shone. They gleamed. They looked glossier than ever.

My beautiful boots only lasted 200 miles. Despite the love and dubbin they were given, they developed cracks just beside the toe crease, and let in water. I walked in trainers for a while, hoping somehow my boots would magically mend themselves. Eventually, I threw them away and marched back to the shop, determined to buy a new pair of the same wonderful chocolate colour, while promising myself I would take even better care of them this time.

It was only a year since I had started my walk, but walking boot models come and go, and they weren't making the same type any more. Even worse, a spotty lad of 17 had replaced my knowledgeable walking woman.

He suggested some fabric boots.

'They don't look very waterproof,' I said.

'They're guaranteed,' he told me. 'Look at the label.'

I read the labels. There were three, attached to different parts of the boots.

'This says I must use waterproof spray before I wear them outside, to ensure they're really waterproof,' I said.

'Yep,' he said, and plonked a can of spray on the counter. 'We recommend this.'

I hesitated, and reread the labels on the boots again.

'But here it says that treatment with any product renders this waterproof guarantee invalid.'

'Yep.' He squinted at the writing. 'Of course it would.'

'But, that's confusing. Do I spray them or don't I?'

He looked at the boots, he looked at the labels, he looked at his watch and then he looked at me.

'Dunno,' he said.

I bought the fabric boots but I didn't spray them. To my surprise, they proved to be completely waterproof, through deep puddles and shallow streams, and remained watertight for 600 miles, until the stitching gave way and splits appeared around the toe seams. They were the most comfortable boots I've ever had. They still are. I haven't thrown them away yet and wear them for short walks in dry weather.

There are many advantages I've discovered to fabric boots.

- They feel softer and more comfortable than leather ones.
- They don't require a long period of 'breaking in'.
- They are easily cleaned with water and a soft cloth.
- And you can forget dubbin. The only maintenance needed is an occasional application of waterproofing spray.

My subsequent boots have nearly all been made of fabric, although I still have a pair of leather boots, which I reserve for bad weather and deep mud.

Finding the RIGHT Walking Footwear

Comfort comes first. That's obvious.

You need to spend some time trying on a variety of boots or shoes, and stomping around the shop to test how they feel. For this reason, I suggest you don't buy your first pair online.

The good news: there are plenty of high-street stores that stock walking boots and shoes. Millets, Mountain Warehouse, Trespass, Sports Direct, Cotswold Outdoor, Blacks, Go Outdoors, John Lewis, and many others. And there are a huge range of brands and types to choose from.

The bad news: having a knowledgeable sales assistant helps, but it's surprising how many sports shops employ people who clearly never walk further than the car park. And, no matter how carefully you select your footwear when in the shop, you can never really replicate the stress and strains of a long walk

Some specialist shops offer to analyse your gait and match your feet to the best footwear. There is often a charge for this service. Even if you don't pay for the analysis upfront, you will find their boots usually work out more expensive than an ordinary high-street shop. If you have weird feet, are very pigeon-toed, knock-kneed, or have over-pronation problems, a gait analysis might be helpful. But if your feet are fairly normal then it's probably not necessarily.

A few minutes of gait analysis in the shop cannot replicate the effect of hours of walking over uneven ground. But it is something to bear in mind if you are having difficulty finding comfortable footwear.

Tips When Choosing Footwear:

Tip 1: Wear the Right Socks

Try on your boots or shoes while wearing the socks you will use while out walking. I talk about socks in a moment, but remember to go shopping with your socks in your pocket. If you haven't yet bought a pair of proper walking socks, than a pair of thick sports socks, or a double pair of ordinary socks, are better than nothing. Or the shop may lend you a pair of walking socks to use while trying on their shoes.

Tip 2: Find the Right Size

Your feet swell during the course of a day's walk, and will swell further with each successive day of walking. For this reason, you should buy a size that seems a little too big for you in the shop – perhaps a full size larger than normal.

Tip 3: Check for Robustness

You don't really want to be buying a new pair of walking shoes or boots every hundred miles or so. When looking, consider how robust the shoes are and whether the sole looks as if it will last for some time over rugged ground. With my own boots, it's not the soles that have let me down, it's the seams. So check the uppers. Is the stitching solid-looking? Are the laces and eyelet holes workman-like?

Tip 4: Look for Waterproof/Water-resistant Label

There is no such thing as absolutely waterproof boots. Unless you wear wellies, of course, and they're not recommended for long-distance walking. But you should look for boots that claim to be waterproof, and buy spray (for fabric) or dubbin (for leather) to top up their water resistance.

A friend of mine spent several days waterproofing his boots in anticipation of a moorland walk. He applied multiple layers of spray and tested his boots by standing them in a shallow bath for many hours. The interiors remained as dry as a bone. Success. But on the first day out, he stepped onto a boggy piece of ground and plunged into a hole. The water came up to his knees and poured into his boots. And, of course, because his boots were so damn waterproof, the water had no way out. He walked in wet boots for days.

The lesson from this story is that if you step into a bog up to your knees, water will pour in. All you can hope for is as much water resistance as possible.

Another alternative is to wear waterproof socks. I talk about socks in the next chapter.

Tip 5: Expensive Doesn't Mean Better

Many retailers run constant 'sales', when the recommended retail price can be slashed by as much as 50%. And my best boots – in terms of comfort and durability – have been those I bought from the cheaper chains, such as Mountain Warehouse. In fact, I never buy anything at full price, and usually spend between £50 and £70 on a pair of boots. Less on shoes.

After I had walked my first 1,000 miles, I decided to treat myself to an upmarket pair of boots. They were a respected brand, had good reviews, and at full price, retailed at around £150. They fitted comfortably and I walked several miles on the flat with no problems at all. But on my first proper coastal walk, I ran into trouble. Those expensive boots suddenly turned into crippling killers. Uphill was no problem. Downhill was murder. I tried removing them and putting them on again, tying the laces tighter, then tying the laces looser – but nothing really worked.

I went back to the shop and bought a different pair. My new boots were the shops own-brand, and significantly cheaper. On their very first outing, after 12 miles of rough walking along the coast across rocky terrain and along asphalt paths, they remained really, really comfortable.

First lesson learnt: expensive doesn't necessarily mean better.

Pleased to have found a pair of perfect-fitting boots, I returned to the shop to buy a second pair. It was only six weeks later, but my perfect boots were no longer available, replaced by a newer model. I bought the latest version but found the shape of the boot had changed subtly. They weren't as comfortable.

That leads me on to the next tip…

Tip 6: Buy a Second Pair!

Once you get into serious walking, and start going on longer walking expeditions, I think it's worth having two pairs of boots (or shoes) on the go at any one time.

Why two pairs?

Firstly, if one boot falls apart, you still have a worn-in pair of boots available and can continue walking without having to modify your walking distances or risking blisters.

Secondly, if your boots become damp – whether through rain or through sweat –you will have a lovely dry pair to wear the next day.

You can never have too many comfortable boots. Even if you don't want to carry two heavy sets of boots on a walking trip, you can always take a backup pair of trail shoes or runners with you instead.

Extra tip: If you're lucky enough to find a really comfortable pair of boots, ones that continue to wear well after several long-distance walks, consider returning to the shop and buying a second pair of the same ones. Quickly, before they change the model.

Looking After Your Walking Boots

Cleaning Your Boots

I'm usually pretty good about cleaning my boots after use. But if I'm out walking for long periods on consecutive days and staying away from home, it can be difficult to find the time or energy.

With waterproof boots, you can make a habit of walking through puddles or, even better, paddle in the sea or in a shallow stream if you can find one, during the final stretch of your walk. This should get rid of much of the mud. Once the walk is over, leave any remaining mud to dry naturally and shake it off your boots in the morning. Ideally, every day, you should gently wipe your boots clean using a damp cloth.

Remember to use a cloth, or a very soft brush, for cleaning your boots. Too much vigorous scrubbing may damage the waterproof coating, crack leather, or disrupt stitched seams. That's how I ruined my second pair of fabric boots.

Drying Your Boots

There will be times when you return from a wet day with your feet soaking wet and water sloshing about the interior of your boots.

Good walking shoes and boots will have absorbent inner linings, designed to soak up your perspiration. The problem is that those same linings also soak up all the rainwater, seawater, or muddy slurry that manages to get inside. Many times, I have tipped my boot upside down, expecting to see water tricking out, and been surprised not to get a single drip. The water is there alright. It's locked inside, trapped within the inner lining.

In my early days of walking, I would sit with a hairdryer blowing into my boots. (The good thing about most B&B or cheap hotels is that you can usually find a hairdryer.) It seemed a clever solution. But the problem with using a hair dryer on boots is that it isn't very good for them. I believe that's why my first pair of chocolate leather boots developed cracks, despite my loving care and my husband's generous dollops of dubbin.

The best method of drying out boots was taught to me by a grumpy B&B host on the South West Coast Path. He was clearly an ex-walker, although by the time I met him, he was having difficulty climbing stairs, but he knew all the tricks. When I arrived on his doorstep, looking like a drowned rat, and asked for a hairdryer, he offered me newspaper instead. I muttered angrily to myself while he disappeared into some back room and emerged with old copies of the Daily Express.

He screwed the paper into balls and showed me how to stuff my boots. I thought it was a ridiculous idea but was too tired to argue with him.

The next morning, I pulled out the mass of soggy newsprint and slipped a finger inside one of my boots to test the lining. Dry. Dry as a bone.

TOP TIP: Remember this if you remember nothing else. The way to dry your soaking wet boots is to stuff them with old newspapers and leave them to work their magic overnight. It works. It really works.

One problem I've discovered is that people no longer read newspapers and you may have trouble getting your hands on them. Kitchen roll or a wad of old rags will do instead, but is not as effective.

Somebody suggested cat litter as a drying agent. Apparently, it works well, but I've never tried it.

Now let's turn our attention to you next most important item of clothing, after your boots. Socks...

Chapter Fifteen

Socks Matter Too

Socks are the second most important item of equipment, after boots or shoes.

If you're just starting out, you may not want to splash out on expensive socks and there is no need to spend much if you are only planning on walking five miles or so. But once you begin increasing your distances, you will soon realise that a good pair of socks is worth the investment.

The things to look out for when buying socks, in order of importance:

1) Sweat-wicking

It doesn't matter if you are male or female, young or old, your feet will sweat while you're walking. In fact, the skin of our feet has more sweat glands per square inch than any other area of our body, and our feet can produce around half a pint of sweat every day.[159] That's a heck of a lot of moisture.

Some people, of course, sweat far more easily than others. Adolescents and young adults sweat more than older people because of increased hormonal activity. There is even a medical condition called hyperhidrosis, where sufferers continuously ooze sweat from their hands and feet.[160]

Surprisingly, the sweat produced by our feet doesn't actually smell. It's designed to cool us down, not to give off an odour. But many of us still end up with stinking feet. Why the pong?

It is **bacteria** that make our feet smell, and they just love living among the layers of dead skin that cover the soles of our feet. But bacteria can't survive so easily if our skin is dry, because they need moisture to thrive and multiply, and so sweaty feet make ideal breeding grounds. And it's not just our skin. Bacteria will linger in wet socks and lurk in the damp lining of our footwear.[161]

Avoid cotton socks. They absorb moisture and retain it close to your skin. Perfect for breeding bacteria. Not so good for your feet. Instead, choose a breathable fabric that will both absorb sweat and wick it away from your skin. Look out for these sorts of terms on the packet: 'breathable', 'wicking', and brand-specific names such as 'IsoCool', 'Tactel', and 'Coolmax'. Buy several pairs, because you will want to change your socks frequently.

In addition, many walking socks claim to reduce odour, either as a result of their construction or because they have been impregnated with antibacterial agents.

TOP TIP: Remember, the dryer you keep your feet, and the dryer you keep your footwear, the more comfortable you will feel, and the less likely you are to be plagued with foot odour.

2) Comfortable seams

Walking socks should have flat seams to minimise friction and reduce skin damage. The crucial point, for many people, is the seam that runs across the top of the toes. You want to check this is comfortable. Feel inside the sock and see if you can detect the seam with your finger. Can you live with that rubbing across your toes for hour after hour?

I remember once, a tiny blade of grass became trapped inside my sock and cut right through the skin of my foot like a razor blade. Small irregularities can cause big damage.

A fellow walker told me that his wife solved all her blister problems when she switched to seamless socks. The brand she buys are called Teko, but there are others.

Often, the only way to know for sure is buy your socks and use them. If you find a very comfortable pair, go back to the shop and stock up with the same type.

3) Padding and thickness

This is a personal choice, but padding within the fabric of a sock fulfils two functions. It keeps your feet comfortable and it keeps your feet warm.

If you suffer from cold feet, or are planning winter hikes or hill climbs, warmth may be more important and wool socks might seem like the perfect choice. The trouble with wool is that it becomes both damp with sweat, and matted with wear, causing irregularities that create friction and lead to blisters. Some wool blends overcome these problems and may be more comfortable than wearing pure wool. Merino wool is different, in that it wears better and has natural wicking properties, while remaining very warm.[162] Merino wool is, unfortunately, pretty expensive.

For me, comfort is the most important feature and, as my feet are usually hot when I'm walking, I would look for brands that claim to be cool. I want plenty of padding around the heels and toes for comfort, but with minimal extra bulk.

Recently, I have given up buying anything other than double-layered blister socks. These have a thin inner layer and a thicker outer one, but sometimes the two layers can seem indistinguishable from each other. I ignored these types of socks at first, because I thought the double layering was intended for warmth, and I don't suffer from cold feet. Then someone recommended them and explained the inner layer was there to help protect your feet from blisters. I tried them and they're brilliant.

Instead of buying a double sock, you can buy a separate set of inner or lining socks. These can be worn under your favourite pair of hiking socks, creating a double sock effect. The advantage of this system is that the inner socks can be washed out each day and, because they are thin, they tend to dry quickly. This saves you having to wash your thicker outer socks frequently. It's a useful tip on long multiday hikes when you know you will have limited washing and drying facilities.

4) Length

As a general rule, you should choose a sock that covers your ankle and ends above the level of the top of your footwear; boot wearers need longer socks than shoe wearers.

I usually wear ankle-length socks that come a good few inches above my ankle, but if you want extra warmth then knee length socks might suit you better. Knee length socks will also protect against tick and insect bites.

TOP TIP: I suggest you avoid the short liner socks that many people wear inside trainers and which give the illusion of a barefoot look. They will almost certainly ruck down as you walk and make you very uncomfortable.

Consider Waterproof Socks

Waterproof socks are expensive, and not for everyday walking, but it might be worth investing in a pair. Many people swear by them. Others say they are good at keeping your feet dry, but wear out too quickly.

Originally designed for cyclists, some waterproof socks are too flimsy for serious walking, and you need to choose a pair that is both breathable (allows sweat out) as well as waterproof. So look for socks that claim to be hardwearing and have a comfortable inner lining – preferably ones designed for walkers. You will probably have to buy them online, as they are hard to find in high-street shops.

SealSkinz make a large range variety of waterproof walking socks, as do Dexshell. I carry a pair of Sealskinz socks in my rucksack.

Change Your Socks Regularly

I don't just mean wash your socks regularly, although that's a good idea, but change them when they start showing signs of wear and tear, or when the fabric begins to bobble. Remember, a rough area on your sock can quickly create a blister. It is best to keep your feet in good condition and good, comfortable socks are really important. Throw out the old ones.

John Merrill wore out 33 pairs of socks during his round-Britain walk. That's one pair of socks every 200 miles.[163]

Chapter Sixteen

Clothing for all Seasons

Learning from My Mistakes

I set off for my first ever coastal walk on a clear April day.

'It's always windy and cold on the coast,' my husband said.

I dressed warmly, with a cotton T-shirt, a long-sleeved sweatshirt, a warm fleece on top, and a waterproof anorak to round off the outfit. I was confident that come rain, wind, hail or storm, nothing would stop my first walk.

April the 17th, 2010, was the day all aircraft across the northern skies of Europe were grounded, due to a dangerous ash cloud spewing from an Icelandic volcano with an unpronounceable name, Eyjafjallajokull.[164,165] There may have been ash heading our way, but on that day, there was no sign of it. In fact, there wasn't a cloud in the sky, not even a vapour trail left by passing aircraft.

First to come off was my waterproof jacket. By lunchtime, the temperature had risen to 17 degrees Centigrade, and I had shrugged off my fleece, quickly followed by my long-sleeved top. I walked the rest of the afternoon in a thin cotton T-shirt, sweating like a pig.

I couldn't do much about my trousers, which I had to continue wearing for modesty, but resolved the next bit of walking kit I needed to buy was a pair of shorts.

First lesson learnt: always check the weather forecast before you set off.

On that first walk, I wore a cotton T-shirt. People my age were brought up to think that cotton is best. We wore cotton shirts for gym at school and cotton socks for games. Natural fibres were promoted as being cooler or warmer, kinder to skin, etc. When I started walking, I always wore cotton as my base layer, and I usually finished my walks damp with sweat. Walking is hot work. Even when the air is cool, we raise our core temperature as we exercise due to increased metabolic work, which generates heat.

'Mum,' my eldest daughter said, 'you should try one of those microfibre tops. I wear them when I go out for a run. They're wonderful.'

'New-fangled nonsense,' I replied.

But, eventually, I gave way to pressure and bought a running top, a short-sleeved T-shirt that promised to wick moisture away from my body, while allowing my skin to 'breathe'. I was dubious. It was made from a mix of artificial fibres, mainly acrylic. Surely it was just a marketing gimmick?

I wore my new top under my sweatshirt in May, while walking though woods on the undercliff between Lyme Regis and Seaton. It was a glorious day of walking along the South West Coast Path, an unforgettable day; a day when the only sound I could hear was bird song, when my thoughts seemed to soar on a higher plane, when I felt full of unexplainable joy. All this bliss was nothing to do with my new top; of course, I'm simply explaining why I remember the day so well.

About halfway along the walk, I sat down to rest on a patch of grass, and realised my cotton sweatshirt was soaking wet. At first, I thought I must be running a fever, but then I realised my skin felt cool and my base layer of clothing – my new T-shirt – was completely dry. It had done its job and very efficiently wicked moisture away from my skin, and straight into the cotton fibres of my sweatshirt, which had soaked it up like a sponge.

Second lesson learnt: my children were right. Wicking material might be artificial and made of acrylic, but it *is* wonderful.

Since then, I have always worn a proper wicking T-shirt next to my skin and I advise you to do the same. Look for words such as 'breathable', 'wicking', IsoCool, Lifa, Goretex, etc. (the same words you should look for when buying socks). These tops are often marketed as being suitable for runners or cyclists, but they're perfect for walkers too.

What to Wear on Top?

The secret to comfortable walking is to wear layers. Several thinner tops worn together will be warmer than a single thick one, because air remains trapped between the layers and adds to your insulation. Also, you can shed items as you get warmer, or put on extra ones if it turns cooler.

To keep you warm, you can't beat a good fleece. Again, look for brands that label the fleece as breathable or designed for sporting activities. Here, I think quality really does count and it's worth investing in a good fleece. I have a Craghopper fleece I've worn regularly for over 10 years. It seems indestructible.

If walking for several days, you can maintain reasonable hygiene while saving on washing and space by changing your thinner internal layers, while wearing the same fleece on top.

TOP TIP: Ladies, unless you are very slim, I strongly suggest you wear a sports bra while out walking.

What About Walking Trousers?

You don't need to buy anything new when you first start out. Almost any comfortable pair of loose trousers will do, or you can wear tracksuit bottoms or joggers. Leggings are fine for women, although you will probably want something with pockets.

Whatever trousers you choose to wear, make sure they have flat seams that won't chaff your legs.

TOP TIP: Avoid denim jeans, because they're made of stiff material without a lot of 'give', and the seams will rub against your skin. In addition, denim is heavy, and becomes even heavier when wet.

John Merrill loves walking in shorts and wears them even in weather when the temperature would turn my knees blue.[166] But shorts don't protect against bramble scratches or nettle stings, and I prefer to keep my legs covered.

As your walks get longer, you'll probably want to invest in a pair of proper walking trousers. Choose inexpensive ones from the chain shops, such as Mountain Warehouse or Trespass, and look for bargains in the sales. Again, you want to look for wicking or breathable material. Walking trousers come in various thicknesses, but I always wear lightweight trousers, because they are easy to pack and they dry very quickly, within 20 or 30 minutes with a bit of a breeze. The downside of thin trousers is that nettles can sting you through the material, and barbed wire or brambles can easily snag them.

You can also buy convertible trousers, where you zip off the lower legs to turn them into shorts. I have a pair. In practice, I rarely unzip while out walking, because it requires me to sit down and remove my boots in order to slip the lower legs off. These convertible trousers do, however, make an efficient travelling item in my rucksack, doubling up as both trousers and a pair of shorts, depending on my mood.

There are thicker trousers for winter walking, padded or fleece-lined to keep you warm. I have never felt the need for these, because I find walking hot work and rarely feel cold once I get going. But please remember, I am talking about walking the English coast, not climbing a Scottish mountain. If you are planning a walk on high moorland, climbing high peaks, or trekking, where the temperature plummets below zero and the wind whips the chill into your bones, you will need thicker clothing.

I'll talk about waterproof trousers for walking in the rain in a moment.

You will, I'm sure, find your own version of comfortable clothing. But I hope the above information has been helpful.

Seasonal Changes

Below follow lists of what I wear according to the season and the weather forecast, and this should help you plan your own walking kit.

Even if the forecast is for blazing sunshine, it's always sensible to carry something waterproof in your rucksack. In the summer, I take my thin Pac-a-Mac, which folds up really small and weighs virtually nothing. In winter, I wear a thick and waterproof jacket. Later I'll explain how to choose a good jacket, but we'll start with the basics for a hot day's walk.

Warm summer days:
Pants and sports bra
Base layer: sports T-shirt with wicking
Second layer: a thin, long-sleeved cycling or running shirt, also wicking
Walking trousers, made from rapid-drying material
Canvas sun hat with a shady brim
Pac-a-Mac (in my rucksack)

Cooler days in spring and autumn:
Add a fleece, either by substituting a fleece for my second long-sleeved layer, or as an additional, third layer.
If rain is forecast, I might leave my Pac-a-Mac behind and wear a lightweight, waterproof jacket instead.

Cold winter days:
Base T-shirt and thin, long-sleeved top, as before
Add a thick fleece jumper as a third layer
A padded, thigh length jacket, which is both windproof and waterproof
Beanie hat made from wicking material
A light pair of gloves

Very cold or high wind-chill expected:
I might add a second fleece under my jacket.
And wear a thick pair of skiing gloves and a woolly hat.

We all tolerate different levels of cold and heat. Remember, layers are the key to temperature control. And by setting out with a variety of tops, you can add or remove to suit the conditions.

What to Wear on Rainy Days

I try not to walk in the rain. But sometimes, you have no choice and you can't walk in England and avoid the rain altogether.

Actually, I'm happy to go out walking on a showery day, because I enjoy seeing clouds scurry across a changing sky, and I love the smell of freshly dampened earth. But, personally, I hate those dull, grey days when the rain sheets down without a break and the path is covered in puddles, or days when the sky hangs low and you walk in a grey world of continuous drizzle and can't see anything except the mud in front of your feet.

In my experience, there is no such thing as a completely waterproof walking outfit. If you walk in continuous rain for hours on end, particularly if the wind is blowing a gale, the rain will eventually find a way through. Your main aim is to stay dry for as long as possible, and hope the rain stops before you become too drenched.

There are the five defences I use against the rain: a waterproof jacket, waterproof trousers, a pair of gaiters, good footwear, and an old-fashioned umbrella.

We've already dealt with footwear, so let's start with the jacket…

Waterproof Jackets

When choosing a good jacket, here are five things to look for:

1. A jacket that's long enough to cover your bum. These provide more protection from both rain and wind than those that end at your waist.
2. A label that actually says 'waterproof'. Beware of weasel phrases such as 'shower proof' or 'water resistant', because these jackets won't keep you dry in a prolonged downpour. Waterproof ratings are measured in millimetres using something called a Hydrostatic Head test. The details of the test don't matter, but to be declared 'waterproof', a product must reach the British Standard of 1,500 mm or over. You should be looking for a rating of at least 2,000 and preferably 10,000 mm.[167]
3. Seams should be 'taped', which means the stitching is covered over by a sealed strip, to prevent water coming through the stitching holes.
4. Pockets must have flaps that fasten, and front zips should have waterproof flaps that fasten down, with Velcro or studs, to keep water from getting inside.
5. A hood with a drawstring, and preferably one that can be secured under your chin with toggles or buttons, so that you can keep the material pulled tightly

around your face. Ideally, find a hood with a slight peak at the front to keep water from dripping into your eyes. If you can't find one with a peak, it's worth investing in a waterproof cap.

Waterproof Trousers

With your top nicely covered, the next thing to worry about is your legs.

Most walking trousers are marketed as offering some degree of rain protection. I haven't found that lasts long, even if you continue to treat the material with special waterproofing spray. If you really want to protect your legs from the rain, you must wear proper waterproof over-trousers, which you simply pull on over your standard trousers.

Waterproof trousers are far from ideal. By the time I've decided I need to put them on, my trousers are usually wet anyway, and in any case, they make my legs hot and sweaty. I have to confess, I rarely wear them.

Luckily, walking clothes are made from material designed to dry out very quickly, sometimes within half an hour or so of the rain stopping. For this reason, although when you begin walking, you can wear anything you feel comfortable in, as you progress further, I strongly suggest you invest in some proper walking trousers.

Gaiters

For those who don't know, gaiters are like a thick pair of waterproof shin guards and are designed primarily to keep water from flowing in over the top of your boots.

There are many different types, but most fasten with a fiendish mixture of hooks, zips and Velcro straps. They cover your lower legs, usually from just below the knee downwards, and come over the top of your boots, ending in the front with a hook to clip into an eyelet or tuck into your laces. At the back, the gaiter has a stirrup piece that slips under the heel of your boot.

There are four problems with gaiters.

1. They are pretty difficult to put on.
2. Like waterproof trousers, they make your legs sweat.
3. The stirrup at the bottom gets caked in mud and grunge.
4. By the time you decide you really need to wear them, it's probably too late because you're already soaked.

That is my experience, anyway. And so, I rarely use gaiters.

I did watch a friend wade through a ford, where the water level came halfway up his calf. He was wearing gaiters under waterproof trousers and his legs and feet stayed completely dry. All I can say is that he has better luck with gaiters than I do.

You might like to try them out for yourself.

An Umbrella

One of the best tips I've ever been given is this: use an umbrella.

Nicholas Crane is a presenter on the BBC series, *Coast*, but he's also a great walker and, in 1992, made an epic solo journey across the mountains of Europe, starting in Spain and ending 10,000 km later in Istanbul. He wrote about his trek in his book, *Clear Waters Rising: A Mountain Walk across Europe*, where he describes how his first few weeks in Galicia were made miserable by constant rain – until he decided to buy an umbrella, which he christened 'Que Chova', meaning 'What rain?'[168]

The original Que Chova was abandoned during the trek, when rain gave way to snow, but an umbrella has become Nicholas' trademark. As he once said in an interview with *Wanderlust Magazine*, 'You can have the most expensive Gore-Tex jacket in the world, but it won't keep your notebook dry. An umbrella will.'[169]

Unfortunately, umbrellas aren't much use in a howling gale, nor in the sort of swirling mist that dampens everything it touches. But I often carry one.

I use a cheap collapsible thing that I can easily stuff into my backpack, knowing I won't worry if it blows inside out in a gale. You could also use one of those big fishermen-type umbrellas if you want to, which will double as a walking stick and is large enough when unfurled to keep both you and your rucksack dry.

Chapter Seventeen

What to Carry

The main thing to remember is to carry the *minimum* you can get away with. Most newcomer walkers, in my experience, carry far too much.

Of course, you want to take enough food and water, protection from the weather, and a few personal essentials such as a phone, keys and cash. But that's about all you really need.

Seasoned long-distance walkers are obsessional about weight, checking out the details of each object to the nearest ounce, because we know that lugging around a heavy load is tiring and will seriously hamper our enjoyment of a trip.

Day Trips

What to Take on a Day Trip

You are free to carry whatever you wish, of course, including the kitchen sink, if you really think it's necessary. To be honest, if you're only walking three miles or so, you really don't need to take anything with you at all, apart from money, tissues and possibly car keys; all things you can easily fit in your pockets.

For longer walks, here is what you might carry in your daypack.

- Warm fleece
- Waterproof top (either to wear or carry) e.g. Pac-a-Mac or jacket
- Water and snacks
- Map
- Notebook and pen/pencil
- Camera
- Binoculars
- Mobile phone
- Garmin or similar GPS device
- Spare pair of boot laces
- Wallet or purse

You don't need to carry as much as this. For example, your phone might double as your camera. You may not want binoculars, or a notebook, and you don't really need a Garmin if you have a good phone app or are using a decent OS map.

Depending on the length of the walk, and the weather, you might take the following additional items:

- A waterproof rucksack cover
- Sun hat or beanie
- Gaiters
- Waterproof trousers
- Insect spray
- Suntan lotion or sun block
- Lip ChapStick
- Torch and reflective armbands
- Strip of paracetamol tablets
- Blister plasters
- Tissue or toilet paper

To keep me on course with mileages, I always carry my special string (marked at mile intervals), which I use with my map to work out how far I have left to go and how long it will take me. Also, for some bizarre reason, I carry my Ramblers membership card. I have no use for the card, but carry it like a magic amulet or talisman, a reminder that I'm a 'proper' walker.

Backpacks and Rucksacks

You need something to carry all this stuff in, and for that, you need a backpack. There are various terms used to describe the same thing: backpack, rucksack, daypack, knapsack, kitbag, etc. In England, the term 'daypack' usually refers to a smaller-sized sack, while the word 'rucksack' is traditionally used for larger ones. The Americans simply call everything a 'backpack'.

If you've never bought a backpack before, you may be surprised to discover that the size of the sack is described in terms of litres, not in feet or centimetres. Using litres makes sense, because the external dimensions don't really matter, within reason. What's important is how much you can fit inside the sack.

TOP TIP: Don't assume your rucksack will keep the rain out, because most are showerproof but not waterproof. (I learnt this the hard way!) Either stow your clothes inside plastic bags inside your pack, or buy a waterproof rucksack cover. You can buy waterproof cases for your phone too, but I prefer to use a clear plastic sandwich bag.

Daypacks

As a general guide, you should choose a daypack between 20-30 litres in size.

On day trips, I carry a tiny green-coloured Berghaus pack, with a 20-litre capacity. Inside, it's divided into two internal compartments, each big enough for a few A4 folders, and is intended primarily to be used by schoolchildren. As a short woman, this means it's a comfortable size for me. Importantly, it has wide, padded straps for my shoulders, and mesh panels on its inner back that keep my own back cool.

There is an outside pocket for my map – something I regard as essential in a rucksack – because you want to be able to get at your map quickly and easily. (Some people wear their maps dangling in a pouch around their necks. This is OK for the Yorkshire Moors, but looks a bit weird on the promenade in Blackpool.)

Equally essential are the two mesh side pockets. These hold my Garmin, lip gloss, measuring string and Rambler's card. These side pockets are supposed to hold water bottles, but they aren't large and I prefer to carry my bottles inside my sack.

I've used the same rucksack for more than 300 days of walking, covering over 3,000 miles. It shows no sign of wearing out.

In fact, my 20-litre rucksack is a little too small for winter treks. If I want to shed my thick, waterproof jacket as I warm up, for example, it takes considerable effort to squash it into the available space. I have another 40-litre rucksack I sometimes use instead, but find it too tempting to fill it up with odds and ends – all sorts of stuff that just might come in useful, but which usually turns out to be completely unnecessary. As any lady knows, the larger your handbag, the more stuff you will cram into it. So using a small bag forces me to be disciplined.

This is what to look for in a daypack:

1) Big enough to take your jacket or thick fleece, as well as snacks and drinks.
2) Wide and padded shoulder straps, to keep your shoulders comfortable.
3) A mesh panel at the back, to keep your back cool.

On a number of occasions, I have carried enough kit in my little 20-litre bag for a two-day walk with an overnight stay in a B&B. It wasn't easy. If you want to carry enough gear for several days, you really need a larger rucksack. So, let's move on and talk about overnight packs.

Overnight Trips

There are brave and strong walkers who walk for weeks, carrying everything they need strapped to their backs.

When John Merrill walked around the coast, all-in-one-go, he carried a 50 lb pack.[170] David Cotton hefted a heavy 70-litre rucksack if he was camping overnight, but whenever he could, dropped down to a lighter 30-litre daysack. Helen Krasner dreamt of drifting around the coast, blending in with the locals, but spent the first few days of her round-the-coast walk being greeted with the words, 'That's a big pack you've got there.' Despite throwing out a few things to lighten the weight, the size of her 65-litre rucksack continued to dominate conversations with the various strangers she met along the way.[171]

Long-distance walkers develop love-hate relationships with their backpacks. Bill Bryson walked 870 miles through the wilderness of the Appalachian way, with a huge pack containing everything he needed for the trip, including camping gear and several days' worth of provisions. He likened this to dragging a wardrobe through the mountains.[172] Cheryl Strayed walked 1,000 miles along the Pacific Coast Trail, carrying a pack so heavy she could barely lift it, which she nicknamed 'The Monster'.[173]

I'm assuming you are a beginner walker, unused to long distances, and certainly unaccustomed to hiking with either a monster or a wardrobe strapped to your back and, therefore, I'm not going to cover the ins and outs of what to take for a prolonged trekking and camping trip.

In fact, wherever possible, I would advise against carrying a heavy rucksack. It can turn a pleasant walk into a day of torture. Find other ways of getting your gear from A to B.

- Pressgang a chauffeur if you can: I use my husband, David Cotton used his girlfriend. Others rely on a chain of friends.
- If you're walking for charity, ask supporters for help.
- If you can afford it, you can use a baggage transfer service, or a local taxi firm.
- In many places, a friendly B&B host might be happy to transport your bags to your next destination, in exchange for a small payment to cover petrol costs.

Sometimes, you might have no choice but to carry enough for overnight stays. In fact, some of my best walking holidays have been where I've trekked from B&B to B&B, carrying the few things I need on my back. There is nothing more intensely satisfying than the feeling of being a proper traveller, moving from destination to destination, entirely by means of your own two feet.

What if You Are Planning a Trip Lasting a Few Days, and Must Carry Everything on Your Back?

You need a rucksack of somewhere between 30 litres and 70 litres in size, depending on how long you are travelling for and how much you plan to carry. With a larger and heavier load, comfort is very important.

If you are a small woman, you won't want a rucksack that's too long for your body, or has straps in an inconvenient place across your chest. A tall man, on the other hand, may want a longer, leaner backpack with tight chest straps to take the load off his lower back. Unisex rucksacks won't suit everyone, and for this reason, you can buy rucksacks that are specifically designed either for women or for men.

Spend some time trying on rucksacks in the shop. Ask the assistant to remove the lightweight padding material inside the pack and, if possible, fill it with something heavy. This should give you some idea of whether the backpack will sit comfortably on your back during a proper hike.

As well as the clothing you wear for a walk, and the usual stuff you would carry in your daypack (see daypack section), here are extras you might need to carry if you are planning a single night's stay in a B&B or hotel.

- Clean pair of underpants
- Fresh T-shirt
- Second pair of socks
- Toothbrush and paste
- Comb or small brush
- Soap (usually supplied by your host)
- Second pair of walking trousers (optional)
- Shaving razor for men (optional)
- Pair of flip-flops or light shoes for indoors (optional)
- Night clothes (optional)

- Phone recharger (especially for those with battery-draining iPhones)
- Spare batteries for the Garmin (optional)
- Small paperback book for company (optional)

Not much, is it?

If you read the list closely, you will see the essentials boil down to a change of underclothing, teeth-cleaning stuff and hair grooming. If you have no hair (or no teeth), your list of essentials will be even shorter.

You might even query the change of underwear. John Merrill, walking the coast and camping wild along the coast of Scotland, would wear the same pair of underpants for many days. It's all a matter of how fussy you are about personal hygiene.

My own preference is to change out of my walking clothes at the end of the day and wear a fresh set of clothes for my evening meal. These clean clothes comprise my basic outfit for my next day of walking. So if walking for three days, I would carry a spare pair of walking trousers, two clean T-shirts, two fresh sets of underwear, and two pairs of socks, as well as whatever items I was wearing when I started my walk. You don't have to be as clean as this. You could, for example, wear the same clothes every day for walking and just take a clean outfit for evenings. Or wear the same things every day and evening too, if you don't mind looking a little scruffy.

I don't take anything other than walking clothes on my trips, even when I have the luxury of someone else transporting my luggage between overnight stops. If I want to be 'smart' in the evening, I wear a pair of clean walking trousers.

The great thing about walking clothes is that they are made of lightweight material, don't crease easily and dry very quickly. It's perfectly possible to wash the mud out of a pair of walking trousers, hang them on the towel rail, and they will be dry by morning. Similarly, a lightweight walking T-shirt can be rinsed through in the evening and ready to wear the next morning.

Socks are different. They can be devils to dry and begin to pong if they remain damp for any length of time. If you don't want to take any spare clothes with you, I suggest a change of socks as a minimum.

TOP TIP: Funnily enough, it's easier to dry clothes in cooler weather, because most places will have their heating turned on and you can hang damp socks etc. over the radiator. During midsummer, in the absence of warm radiators, it can be harder to dry out damp clothing, but most B&B hosts will offer a drying facility – a tumble dryer or airing cupboard – if you ask.

Walking Poles

When I was new to walking it never occurred to me to use poles. They were designed for old people who needed walking sticks, weren't they?

Then one day, I changed my mind.

I was trudging along a beach in Suffolk, just north of Southwold. Ahead, I saw a narrow gap left between the waves and the foot of the cliff, and realised I must race to beat the incoming tide. But the beach was steeply cambered and rough with shingle. To make matters worse, the cliffs were made of soft earth and numerous landslips had left fallen branches and tree trunks strewn across the shore. It was tough going.

In front of me were a couple of younger walkers with an elderly man. He was using walking poles and I noticed, with much resentment, that he was moving faster than I could. They made it around the base of the cliff just in time, but I was too late and was forced to turn back.

I went home, bought a cheap pair of poles, and tried them out. I was instantly amazed by the improvement in my walking speed and fell in love with them.

It isn't all about speed. Poles are wonderfully useful for all sorts of reasons.

- To beat down nettles.
- To push aside brambles.
- To test the depth of puddles.
- To use as vaulting poles over streams and swamps.
- To protect your aching knees when going up or down hills.
- To help keep your balance on steep steps, terrifying slopes or slippery surfaces.
- To wave threateningly when attacked by cattle or vicious terriers (see the *Dangerous Animals* chapter for more information about dealing with cattle and dogs).
- And, possibly, to help you limp back to civilisation following an injury.

Despite being the cheapest I could find, my poles lasted well and I only had to buy a replacement pair after I lost one rubber tip while walking through a field of mud. This left me with an exposed metal end that tapped alarmingly on the path and made me sound like Long John Silver.

The only downside of my cheap poles is that I am completely unable to fold them up. They are supposed to telescope in and out again so you can adjust their lengths to fit the terrain. For example, you use shorter poles when walking uphill and longer poles when walking downhill. Or one side could be longer than the other if walking horizontally across a slope. But the most useful reason for shortening your poles is to be able to tuck them into your rucksack or into your case when travelling, and I've been unable to do this.

At first, I was embarrassed carrying poles on trains and buses, because I was worried that people might assume I was a doddery, old lady. But I soon learnt not to worry. My disabled look comes with a bonus benefit. People stand up and offer me seats. It's rather wonderful.

Nowadays, I only use one pole, instead of two, because I like to walk with my camera ready in my other hand.

TOP TIP: If you've never tried them, I strongly recommend you give walking with poles a go. It's like having four feet instead of two. You'll walk faster. You'll feel stronger. You'll have more confidence.

You could use old-fashioned walking sticks instead, and some people do. But here are advantages to proper walking poles:

- You can adjust their length to suit the terrain and for storage, but make sure that (unlike me) you can actually use this feature.
- Look for poles that have a shock-absorbing mechanism, which will protect the joints in your hands and arms from constant jarring.

Chapter Eighteen

Food and Water

As a medical doctor, I'm always amazed by the amount of misleading health advice you can find on the Internet and elsewhere. There is certainly plenty of nonsense talked about nutrition and hydration. So in this chapter, I'm presenting you with the latest evidence and expert opinions. I'll give you some general advice to help you decide how much food and water you need to take with you, and I'll show how this depends on the physical needs of your own body and the nature of your walk.

Water

The two heaviest things in my backpack are my camera and my water bottle. My camera is an optional burden, while my water bottle is essential. In the previous chapter, I talked about minimising the weight you carry on your back, but the last thing you want to do is run out of water. So exactly how much should you carry on your walk?

The Dangers of Dehydration

There is nothing worse than a burning thirst, an empty bottle and no supply of drinking water around.

As well as the physical discomfort of a dry mouth, you can feel dizzy and lightheaded to the point of faintness. You will almost certainly develop a crashing headache. As you become more dehydrated, your energy levels drop and every step will become a tremendous effort. You'll not need to pee, although you might feel uncomfortable because of concentrated urine in your bladder. Your muscles can start cramping and your temperature may rise.

As you continue to dehydrate, you will become increasingly confused and, in the worst case scenario, will begin to have fits before falling into a coma. In the end... you die.[174]

The Dangers of Over Hydration

Interestingly, with amateur marathon runners, a common reason for collapsing after completing a marathon is not dehydration, but the opposite – over hydration. Amateur runners may actually drink *too much* water during a long race. This happens because they're following well-meaning advice and taking a drink at every water station along the route, while constantly sipping on a water bottle between stations. At the same time, they're losing salt through their sweat.

This combination – constant drinking and sweat loss – causes abnormally low levels of salt in the bloodstream; a condition known as hyponatraemia. It's potentially very dangerous, with symptoms ranging from nausea, faintness, and mild confusion, through to fits, coma and even death.[175]

A research study on runners in the 2002 Boston Marathon showed that 13% of them (one in eight) were hyponatraemic by the end of the race.[176]

Over-drinking fluids can be just as bad for your health as under-drinking.

The Wrong Advice

What do some misguided fitness 'experts' tell us to do? They tell us to drink *before* we get thirsty. And, they tell us that once we actually start to feel thirsty, it's too late; we've already become dehydrated.

When you think about it, this advice is pretty useless. If you have to drink *before* you become thirsty, you have no way of knowing what your current hydration state is and no way of knowing when to put the brakes on your fluid intake. Not only is the advice useless, but it can be positively dangerous because of the risk of developing hyponatraemia.

Sadly, you will see the same guidance – to drink constantly – repeated on numerous walking, hiking and exercise sites. It's both misleading and out of date. Ignore it.

The First Key to Proper Hydration

The latest advice is based on guidance from the International Marathon Medical Directors Association, whose opinion is based on research, and it's very simple: Drink when you feel thirsty.[177]

Our bodies are amazing machines that have evolved over many millennia. They are designed to self-regulate as much as they can, and to alert our brain only when things inside become disordered or out of balance. If your body needs to drink, it will tell you – you'll feel thirsty. That's your body's signal.

Trust your body. You don't have to drink all the time.

Drink when you feel thirsty.

Although this sounds simple, sometimes it's difficult to interpret your body's signals correctly.

In the summer of 2013, while walking along a tough stretch of the Cornish coast, I met a couple coming towards me. It was hot, but not overbearingly so, with an air temperature of around 24 degrees centigrade and a sea breeze. The man was striding ahead and his wife was struggling behind (a common feature among couples when out walking). She was swigging from a water bottle and was wearing a wide belt around her hips, which seemed to be stuffed with multiple weapons, so that she looked like a chunky version of Lara Croft.

As we drew closer, I realised the belt was constructed with numerous little pockets, each one holding a water container.

'It's hot,' she said, somewhat unnecessarily as we greeted each other. And then she added, 'You really should be carrying water.'

'I am,' I said. She couldn't see my bottles because I carry them inside my backpack where the water keeps cooler.

A few minutes later, I turned around to watch her progress. She had stopped again and was glugging away from one of her bottles. It struck me she wasn't really thirsty; she was hot. And she was tired because she was trying to keep up with her husband and was being pushed at a pace too fast for her level of fitness. She was misinterpreting her body's distress signals (of heat and fatigue) as thirst signals.

I finished my 10-mile walk with 500 ml still remaining from my 1-litre supply and felt fine.

The Second Key to Proper Hydration

The second key to keeping your water burden light is also very simple, and often overlooked. Make sure you **start** the day in a hydrated state.

Why? Because it's much easier to carry water stored within your body than it is to lug that same water around in heavy bottles on your back. Water is heavy. One litre of water weighs one kilogram or roughly two pounds. Walking with a backpack means you think twice about everything you carry, and every ounce of unnecessary weight is... well, it's just unnecessary.

I am amazed how some people will set off walking without eating any breakfast or while still suffering a hangover from the night before. You want your body to be topped up with both fuel and fluid before you start.

What's wrong with starting a walk with a hangover? Alcohol has a dehydrating effect and the reason you wake up the next morning with a pounding headache is because your shrivelled brain cells are screaming in agony. Yes, most of the symptoms of hangover are due to fluid deficiency in your brain, which is directly related to fluid deficiency in the rest of your body.[178] That is why some people suggest the key to avoiding a hangover is to finish off a night out by swallowing down a pint of pure water.

Always make sure you drink plenty of fluid with breakfast, and if there is a delay before you start your walk, have an additional drink of water before you set off. At this stage, you don't need to worry about hyponatraemia, as your body is relaxed and rested and will quickly correct any imbalance.

> **TOP TIP: How can you tell if you're properly hydrated? You should need to stop for a pee within the first hour or so of starting your walk. If you don't, you probably haven't drunk enough with your breakfast.**

How Much Water Should You Carry?

John Merrill walks 20-30 miles a day without water, and doesn't drink anything until the walk is over, even when trekking through deserts in blistering heat. In his opinion, 'the more you drink, the more you want'.[179]

I don't recommend going without water. I only mention John Merrill's experience to point out that we are all different. Some of us need more fluid than others.

Below, I shall give you some general guidance, based on my own experience and evidence-backed recommendations. If this guidance works for you, that's fine. If not, do whatever seems to suit the needs of your own body.

On very short walks, less than 3 miles (5 km) and less than an hour on your feet, you don't really need to carry water at all. But on a hot day, or if you might get lost and there is a risk your walk will be longer than planned, it's best to take a small (500 ml) bottle with you, just in case.

If you're a beginner, and according to the current recommendations from AIMS (the Association of International Marathons and Distance Races), you should carry 500 ml (just over a pint) for each hour of walking.[180] Assuming a walking pace of 2.5 mph, that works out at 500 ml every 2.5 miles.

- 5 mile (8 km) walk, 2 hours: take a litre
- 10 mile (16 km) walk, 4 hours: take 2 litres
- 15 mile (24 km), walk, 6 hours: take 3 litres
- 20 mile (32 km) walk, 8 hours: take 4 litres

These amounts might be far more than you need, but it's a safe guide and a starting point. As you become fitter and more experienced, you will be able to estimate how much you need to carry with you, depending on the terrain, the heat of the day, and the possibility of water stops along the way.

On a typical cool English day, and if walking across easy terrain, I only need 500 ml for every 2 hours of hiking time, or a litre for a typical half-day (4-hour) walk. If walking through a coastal area where I can buy refreshments, and if I plan to stop at a café for lunch, I might only carry a litre with me when I set off. This assumes I can stop for a drink if I want to, and I can top up my water bottle at lunchtime.

I can't tell you exactly how much water you need to drink and how much you should carry with you on your walks. It depends on the terrain, the weather, the weight of your backpack, your level of fitness, and the availability of water sources. The only way to know what you need is to walk and see. It's always best to have some water left at the end of your walk, but if you consistently end up with 1,000 ml of water left in your bottle that you haven't needed, you might like to leave with 500 ml less next time.

What to Do if You Run Out of Water

Don't be tempted to drink from streams or rivers, even if they look sparklingly clear. Remember, the water may have travelled a long way before it reaches the coast, and could include drainage from fields covered in manure, from filthy animal sheds, and from industrial sites.

You could carry water purification tablets with you. These are based on either iodine or chlorine and, once added to your water bottle, will take around 30 minutes to work. Unfortunately, the water treated by these tablets doesn't taste very nice, so you would only want to use them if you were desperate.

If you come across a café or a pub, you can ask them to refill your water bottles. Public toilets are another source of tap water, although not all such water is fit for drinking and you must check for signs saying non-potable. In a real emergency, most country folk are happy to top up your bottles if you knock on their door and ask politely.

Food

Whether or not you carry food will depend on your planned mileage and the area you are walking through. If, for example, I am walking through a built-up coastal area that caters for tourists – such as Blackpool or Bournemouth, Southend or Scarborough – I would anticipate finding plenty of snack bars, tearooms, cafes and pubs. Although I would always carry a small water bottle, I wouldn't bother packing much food for my walk because I prefer to stop to eat in a café or a pub.

British Pubs

It is my preference to eat in pubs, as long as I can find one that is open and serving food.

The great thing about pubs is that they are marked on the OS maps, either with a blue beer mug (on *Explorer* maps) or with the magical two letters, PH (on *Landranger* maps), where PH stands for Public House. The OS maps don't bother marking every pub you come across in a large town or city, but they do mark them in rural areas, in villages and smaller towns. This makes planning lunch stops relatively easy.

But let me offer a word of warning. A pub might be clearly marked on the map, but there is no guarantee it will still be there when you walk through the area. Sadly, many rural pubs have closed. They may be boarded up and derelict, or may have been converted into ordinary houses.

Once, somewhere in Suffolk, and following my map, I walked into a very pleasant pub. It had a small bar, cheerful floral wallpaper, an unusually clean carpet and comfortable armchairs. There were books scattered around and photos of the publican's family hung on the walls, instead of the usual hunting scenes.

'How cosy. It's just like someone's living room,' I thought, as I stood at the bar and wondered where the barman had got to, and why such a nice pub was empty.

Suddenly, it dawned on me. It wasn't a pub any longer. I really was standing in someone's living room.

I beat a hasty retreat, closing the door quietly behind me. As far as I know, the owners of house never realised I'd been there.

The other thing about English pubs is their weird opening times. All-day opening might be common in a large seaside resort, but is unusual in a small village. So you might find the pub exists, but is closed at lunchtime. Even if you discover an open pub, it may stop serving food at a ridiculously early hour, such as 2p.m. I don't know how many times my request for a menu has been greeted by the infamous words, 'Sorry, cook's gone home', as if it was impossible for anyone else to slap a slice of ham between two pieces of bread, or heat up a bowl of soup in the microwave.

The availability of food is better than it used to be. There was a time when most pubs didn't serve food at all. Now, any pub that wants to survive will provide a midday or evening meal. Unless it's a Monday.

At this point, I should mention Sundays. The great thing about Sundays is that pubs cater for lazy weekend lie-ins, and often serve food 'all day' on Sunday. The downside is that 'all day' may mean only until 4 or 5p.m., and Sunday food usually means Sunday roast. A roast dinner sits heavy on your stomach if you still have 10 miles to walk, and is definitely not what you want to eat on a boiling hot day in August. If you're lucky, they'll provide an alternative choice to the roast, but often they won't.

Mondays come after Sundays. There seems to be a pub rule that Mondays is a day of rest. Many pubs don't serve food on a Monday and some don't open at all. In a very rural area, they may not open on a Tuesday either. Nor on a Wednesday.

TOP TIP: If you are basing your walk around a pub lunch, you should check in advance to make sure your chosen pub still exists and provides food, as well as checking the opening hours and food serving times, so that you can plan your walk accordingly.

Thank goodness for the Internet! You can search for the pub and either get the information from their website or, even better, give them a ring.

As a backup, I usually carry a snack box with me, but in my opinion, nothing beats a good rest in a pub with a proper seat, a drink and a cooked meal, particularly when the weather is windy, cold or wet. If the pub is open but not serving food, I still enjoy a brief sit down, and I've never come across a pub that doesn't serve packet snacks, such as a bag of salted peanuts and a packet of crisps. This isn't the healthiest of lunches, but the combination is reasonably cheap, and contains sufficient fluid, protein, carbohydrates and salt replacement to keep me going.

Cafés

Cafés and restaurants are not marked on OS maps, although hotels might be. The best way to check if there is somewhere you can stop to eat is to look for local businesses using Google Maps[181] or Bing Maps.[182] Again, before relying on a café being open, it's best to check first via their website or with a phone call.

Snack Box

If you prefer picnics, or if you wanted to economise, you could carry a packed lunch with you. Also, if you require a special diet (vegan, coeliac disease, diabetes, for example), you might find it easier to carry your own food, although in many pubs and cafés, you may find vegan or gluten-free options on the menu.

I have been caught out by closed facilities, or left without options in very remote areas, and so I usually carry an emergency snack box with me. It contains a muesli bar, pressed fruit snack bars, a small packet of mixed nuts and a bar of chocolate.

If you are planning on a picnic lunch, you might want to take sandwiches with you. This is fine if you set off from home and have access to fresh ingredients, but sandwiches become more difficult to assemble if you're away from home for several days and staying in B&Bs or hotels. Some establishments will offer to make you a packed lunch, but others won't. And beware of ingredients that go 'off' quickly, particularly in summer months, including obvious fillings such as prawns, but anything with mayonnaise could provide a breeding ground for bugs.

You can buy sandwiches from local shops, but you may not want to hang around until the shops open, or waste time going in search of one. For this reason, when travelling away from home, I take long-life food with me, such as fruitcake, hard cheese, packets of nuts and pieces of dried fruit.

TOP TIP: Remember, if planning a picnic lunch, you will need to carry extra water with you, as you won't be buying additional drinks. I suggest you add 500 ml to your usual walking allowance.

Chocolate

I always carry a bar of chocolate.

John Merrill ate five or six bars every day as he walked around the coast.[183] I don't recommend you eat this amount, but a quick stop with a chocolate bar can kick-start tired legs into marching an extra two to three miles, even when you feel you can't walk another step. **Never, ever underestimate the revitalising power of chocolate.**

I've mentioned the food I carry with me, which is mainly based on fruit and nuts, plus chocolate. You must, of course, choose your own food. Ideally, you want a mix of protein and carbohydrates, and a mix of savoury and sweet things to eat.

Some keen long-distance walkers use high-energy gels – the sort that runners and cyclists carry – because they don't want to stop for food and can eat the gels while on the go. For me, a lunch break is one of the most pleasurable parts of a day's walk, and I only skip it if I am really pushed for time, or if I'm walking in the winter and can't afford to waste the limited daylight hours.

I want to end this chapter by repeating my number one tip about water. Remember, if you don't want a pee within the first hour or so of starting your walk, you're not hydrated enough. With that in mind, we need to move on to the subject of toilet stops.

Chapter Nineteen

Toilet Stops

Toilet stops are unavoidable on any long-distance walk. And when you have to go, you have to go. How and where will depend on the circumstances.

If you are walking through a seaside town during the summer months, you should have no difficulty finding public toilets. These are marked on OS maps with the letters PC (for Public Conveniences), or head for a nearby Visitor Centre, also marked on the OS maps with a blue box containing the letter V. Sometimes, you have to pay a few pence to use the facility, but most are provided free of charge. Some are clean and very pleasant, others are frankly disgusting

An alternative is to nip into a café or a pub. I usually feel duty-bound to buy something in these circumstances, even if it's just a quick orange juice or a cup of tea. I will leave that up to your conscience.

Out of season, the situation can be very difficult. Many public conveniences in tourist resorts are closed during the winter, as are many visitor centres and cafés. So you will have to resort to open-air peeing. We'll discuss this shortly.

Another difficult situation is where you are walking through a built-up residential area, which isn't a coastal resort and doesn't cater for visitors. These places are unlikely to provide public facilities, and the nearest public toilets, if any, are going to be located away from the coast and usually in the centre of the town. Industrial estates offer a similar problem and are even less likely to provide public toilets.

I have never – yet – had to knock on someone's door and beg to use their toilet, although I've felt like it at times. Usually, it's always possible to find a spare patch of land and a screen of vegetation.

Open-Air Peeing

Men have it easier than women, and are less inhibited about peeing in the open air. We ladies have to squat, which is always an odd posture at the best of times, and we also have to bare our bottoms to the world, which makes us feel very vulnerable.

I can remember my very first open-air pee while out walking on the beach, somewhere near Overstrand, in Norfolk. I could see for miles ahead, and miles behind, and miles out to sea. And there was nobody about. Still, it took a lot of screwing up of courage – and a very full bladder – before I finally resolved to squat down and drop my knickers. Illogical thoughts went through my mind. The fisherman standing two miles down the beach must be watching me through eyes with telescopic lenses drilled in the side of his head. There were men on that sailing ship, the one barely visible on the far horizon, who had their binoculars trained on my fat behind. Above, passengers on that plane cruising at 30,000 feet were staring down and tut-tutting. And on that distant pier, with its buildings merging into the afternoon haze, people must be watching, pointing, and laughing their heads off.

It was all completely ridiculous, of course. But these inhibiting thoughts can be difficult to overcome, especially when you are first starting out.

Embarrassment works both ways. On a number of occasions, I've caught sight of other walkers having a quick pee in the bushes. In such circumstances, I feel slightly embarrassed at having intruded on somebody else's private moment. And so I make the assumption that anybody who has caught sight of *me* would almost certainly feel equally embarrassed too.

Once I realised that nobody could see and, even if they could, nobody really cared, I relaxed and began to enjoy my open-air pees. It is a strangely primitive thing to do and I have to confess an almost shameful pleasure.

There is another benefit, apart from convenience. A clean patch of grass in the open air is infinitely preferable to wading through the horrors of a filthy public toilet. As I've explained before, I always start my day out fully hydrated and invariably have to stop for a pee within the first hour or so of beginning my walk. I will use a public toilet if one is available, but I much prefer a handy bush.

Toilet breaks are necessary. If you are planning on doing some serious miles in our more remote coastal areas, you will have to toughen up and lose some of your inhibitions.

Tips for Open-Air Pees

It's important not to cause offence. So peeing in somebody's garden is a definite no-no, as is squatting on the verge in a built-up area. But behind a hedge in an empty field? Or along a deserted beach? Or in the middle of a thicket of gorse bushes? Who cares!

If you are going to use toilet paper (and I always do) don't forget to dispose of it in a considerate way. Pop it in a plastic bag and put it in the nearest bin. Doggy-poop bags are ideal for this situation. An alternative is nappy bags, which come pleasantly scented, if that sort of thing is important to you.

It's natural to feel worried about getting caught in midstream, but the danger is that you rush into the process in order to get it over with, and forget the basics.

TOP TIP: Look for slopes and feel the breeze.
Women: face up the hill and into the wind.
Men: face down the hill and keep the wind at your back.
Following this simple advice will avoid a messy flow-back or blow-back situation.

Solid Stuff

Not every toilet stop involves fluid. Sometimes, you may need to pass something – ahem – a little more solid. It happens to all of us.

The standard advice is as follows:[184]

- Make sure you are at least 50 metres away from any water – streams, rivers, lakes, etc.
- Dig a hole at least six inches deep.
- When you've finished, fill in the hole and restore any surface plants you have disturbed.
- Carry away all used toilet paper in a poop bag and dispose of in the next bin you come across.

From a practical point of view, unless you walk around with a trowel in your backpack, it may not be possible to dig a hole six inches deep. You should, however, try to cover any evidence of your deposits, using anything handy in the natural environment, such as sand, earth, bracken, or leaf litter.

When you need to 'go', whether it's liquid or solid, you might be tempted to seek out a building or enclosure of some sort. But you should never use old barns, sheds, bus shelters, or ruined buildings as toilets. Don't use caves either. Deposits left on brick, concrete or stone will linger for weeks, or months, creating foul odours and causing offence to others. Please stick to soft, natural surfaces.

Chapter Twenty

Transport

It may seem strange to talk about motorised transport, because the whole point of going for a walk is to use your own two feet to get from point A to point B. But walking the coastline means you will be following a series of linear walks and this is logistically different from the circular walks you may have undertaken in the past. In a circular walk, you start and finish in the same place. Linear walks require more planning.

Here Are Your Options:

1. It is possible to walk the coast in a series of circular walks; first walking along the shore and then doubling back via an inland route to return to your starting point. I've completed a number of such circular walks, but only when I was forced to do so due to transport difficulties, because it takes a long time to make much progress.
2. Or you could walk the coast in a series of linear walks where you walk a certain distance along the shore, and then simply turn around and retrace your route. You would be effectively walking the coast twice over, once in each direction.

Again, it takes a long time and I don't know of anybody attempting to walk the coast using this method.

3. Another method avoids the need for transport altogether. Start at point A, stay overnight at point B, and the next day, continue your walk onwards to point C and another overnight stop, before walking on to point D. That is how many continuous coastal walkers do it, and it is extremely satisfying. You really feel as if you're circumnavigating the coast as a true traveller, a vagabond, a wanderer. The downside is that you must either carry all your overnight needs on your back, or you must organise a baggage transfer service. In addition, you may not find accommodation convenient to your chosen path and may have to detour inland.

4. Most of us who walk the coast in stages will use a mix of public transport or private cars to get from our chosen accommodation base to our start point, and then to get back from our finishing point. For example, you can drive and park at point A and, when you've finished your walk, catch a bus back from point B at the end of the day in order to pick up your car. An alternative – and even better idea – is to park your car at point B and then immediately catch a bus or train to point A to start your walk. This means you are walking *back to your car* and you don't have to worry about missing the last bus of the day. Or you can do it entirely by using public transport, both to get from your accommodation to point A, and public transport again to get back from point B to your accommodation. In some instances, you won't find a convenient bus or train service running anywhere near your start or finish points. In this case, you may have to use a taxi. I'll talk more about taxis towards the end of this chapter.

5. If walking with someone else, you can always use the two-car option. You drive in convoy to your finishing point B, and leave one car waiting there. You both get into the other car and drive to your starting point A. You walk from point A back to point B. You get into the waiting car and drive back to Point A, where you pick up the first car again.

I find constantly negotiating new accommodation tiring and unsettling, and I prefer staying in a fixed place for a few days, using it as my base for several coastal walks, before moving on. By staying in one place for several nights, I also avoid having to carry any overnight things with me during my walks. Whether I entirely rely on public transport, or a mixture of my car and public transport, depends on the availability and timing of bus and train services.

We are all different and you will find your own preferred method of organising your walking, but here follows some advice.

Public Transport

Never assume you can actually get to your start point, or return from your finish point, using public transport.

If you live in the country, this advice will sound blindingly obvious. If you live in the city – particularly if you live in London – it may come as a shock. I will never forget a London friend setting off to walk Hadrian's Wall and informing me, in a voice filled with horror, that he nearly missed the first stage of the walk because the 'regular' bus only ran *every two hours*. Every two hours? He was lucky.

Remember, many areas of the countryside have little or no public transport. You might find a bus stop, but read the timetable carefully and you may discover that the bus doesn't run at weekends, or it only runs during the peak summer time, or there is only a service during the school term, or the bus only runs alternate Wednesdays, as long as there isn't an 'r' in the month... etc.

Another thing you must check is the time of the first and last buses. You may not be able to start your walk, for example, until late in the morning, say 11.30a.m., which reduces your walking time considerably. And the last bus back may be ridiculously early. It is not unusual for the last bus back to be well before 6.00p.m. Sometimes, it will be even earlier, if it is timed to coincide with the school run.

It is possible to walk much of the coast using only public transport, if you are really determined. But some parts are very difficult to get to and may involve many hours and several changes of bus or train. You may also have to do a great deal of additional (or 'wasted' walking) in order to get to and from your coastal start and finish points.

As an example of what you can achieve if you really want to, Peter Caton walked the whole of the Essex coast using only public transport.[185]

So, by all means, check out public transport. But make sure, before you set off, that you can not only get a bus or train to your start point, but can also get back from your finish point too.

Train Journeys

Planning your train journey is straightforward, as long as you have access to the Internet.

I prefer to travel by train if at all possible. Although train journeys are usually more expensive than the equivalent bus journey, they tend to be quicker and shorter. And finding a railway station is easy as they are well signed and clearly marked on OS maps. If you are using a mixture of car and public transport, you can always (or nearly always) park in the station car park. There may be a charge, but rural stations will often provide free parking. Changing trains, if you have to, is an easy process too.

TOP TIP: Use the National Rail Enquiries website (http://www.nationalrail. co.uk), which covers the whole country, provides an easy search facility, works out your connections for you, and is very reliable.

Bus Journeys

Planning a bus journey is more difficult as there are a myriad of local bus providers and it's rare to find a user-friendly timetable.

If you stand at a bus stop, you will find the timetable is written in tiny print and may be faded by the weather. Even if you can see the times, you must work out what the weird little symbols mean. NSD might mean Not School Days, for example. Or TTO means Term Time Only. Or NS means Not Sunday.

Working out bus connections is even trickier, as you have to decipher two separate timetables and it helps to have a degree in decryption and advanced mathematics. The chances are your connecting bus won't arrive at the same place and you'll have to go in search of another bus stop. This makes planning doubly confusing and leads to all sorts of missing-the-bus opportunities.

TOP TIP: The easiest way to plan a bus journey is in advance by going online and using Traveline at www.traveline.info. Or you can telephone the service on 0871 200 22 33.

I usually check local bus companies on the Internet before I start. Many of them have a phone number you can ring, but that may not operate in the evening, which is just the time when you need to set about planning your next day's walk. The most helpful thing you can find on an operator's site is a proper map showing the actual bus routes, but this logical feature is surprisingly seldom supplied.

The worst experience I had was in Torquay, where you would have thought they would make it easy for tourists to use their buses, but the route map was reduced to a few lines on a chart, with no underlying map. It was impossible to identify the streets along which the buses actually ran, and there were no clues as to where they stopped.

On the other hand, some bus stops have displays showing the routes clearly, and you might find electronic boards telling you the number of the next bus and its time of arrival. Weymouth has this excellent feature.

You can also send a text to 84268, giving the code for the particular bus stop, as displayed on a sign at the stop, and you will get a text back showing you when the next bus is due. There is usually a fee for this service, and although Traveline claims these are 'live times', in reality, they are usually the scheduled times, which isn't helpful if your bus hasn't arrived and you don't know if you've just missed it or if it's running late.

In rural areas, I have always found the bus drivers helpful. Sometimes, I am the only person on the bus and many bus routes only continue to operate because they are subsidised by the local council. In such cases, the driver is often very chatty, as if glad of some company.

Car and Bike Option

I considered this at the beginning of my own coastal walk, just before my husband realised I was serious about continuing my epic trip, and stepped in to offer his help with transport. So I have never used this method in real life.

This is how you do it.

- Put your bike in the car.
- Drive to Point B and leave your bike chained up or hidden in a bush.
- Drive to Point A, park the car and start your walk.
- Walk to Point B. Find your bike, hopefully not stolen.
- Ride your bike back to Point A. Put the bike in your car. Drive home.

Helpful Friend/Partner Option

Sometimes, I use public transport to get me to and from my walks, but much of the time, I use my ever-helpful husband as a support driver. He drops me off at my walking point and picks me up at the end of the day. What does he do while I'm walking? He goes cycling on his racing bike.

The situation breaks down, of course, when he suffers a puncture or gets lost. I spend a great deal of time waiting for him to show up.

This chauffeur option is ideal, but you do need to have a patient friend or partner who is a decent navigator and can read a map.

Taxi Journeys

Taxis are expensive. Remember, if you walk for 15 miles, the taxi journey back to base may be even longer, depending on how the roads meander through the countryside. In addition, the taxi driver may charge for the inconvenience (and expense) of their drive to pick you up, so you end up paying a double fare.

Outside of major cities, you won't find taxis cruising the road looking for customers. Even worse, you might not find a taxi waiting in places where you might reasonably expect a taxi to be, such as outside the railway station, or in the clearly marked taxi rank. Rural taxi services are small outfits, sometimes consisting of just one man or one woman operating from home with a mobile phone. Often, their biggest customer is the local authority, who regularly use taxis to transport children from remote villages to and from schools.

So if you are planning on using a taxi, you really need to phone and book your journey in advance, and try to avoid the hours of the school run.

I find B&B hosts or hotel staff very helpful. They often have arrangements with particular taxi services that will do their best to fit in transport requests, and they might even be able to negotiate a good price for you.

TOP TIP: Some B&B owners in rural areas will be happy to transport you (or your luggage) themselves, asking only for a contribution to cover petrol costs, which should work out considerably cheaper than a taxi or a baggage transfer service. But never assume the B&B will be able to do this. Check in advance.

And, since I mentioned hotels and B&Bs, the next thing to think about is accommodation.

Chapter Twenty-One

Accommodation

I started out with one-day walks at the weekends. But, as I got further away, and travelling times increased, I realised I would need to set aside weekends – and later, whole weeks – to make my trips worthwhile. And this meant I had to research and arrange a complicated mix of public transport, cheap hotels, and baggage transport services.

If you plan to walk the coast for several days consecutively, the single largest expense you will face is the cost of accommodation. So let's consider your main options.

Types of Accommodation

Camping

If finances are tight, or if you are trying to raise money for charity, you will probably want to spend as little as possible on accommodation, and the cheapest option you have is camping. Luckily, there are plenty of campsites dotted around the coast, and those that accept tents are clearly marked on the OS *Explorer* maps with a blue tent symbol.

In summer, a good campsite might be fully booked, while during the winter, many sites will be closed. For these reasons, it's best to check with the site in advance.

One major downside to camping is the need to carry your tent around on your back. Even lightweight tents are heavy, especially when you include pegs, poles, a sleeping bag and a mat. A few campsites provide fixed tents that you can hire for the night. These are usually designed for the high end of the market and may work out more expensive than a cheap B&B.

A large campsite will provide a café and other facilities, but a small site in a remote location may provide nothing more than a toilet block and a couple of waste bins. You might have a problem finding an evening meal. Use the map to find out if there is a pub or other eating place within walking distance, and check to see if it opens in the evening. If not, you will have to carry food with you, along with any cooking equipment you need. This all adds to the weight of your pack.

Wild Camping

Wild camping is, of course, entirely free. Opportunities are limited because England is a crowded country and we don't have many areas of true wilderness.

In fact, in England, you have no right to camp on private land, and if this is what you intend to do, you should ask permission from the landowner. On National Trust land, special reserves, National Parks, and in most areas owned by the local authorities, you will usually find notices that specifically prohibit overnight camping. The exception is Dartmoor, where wild camping is permitted but only in certain areas.[186]

In many cases, you won't be able to identify the landowner, and in more remote areas, wild camping is tolerated as long as your tent is small and you are discreet.

If you camp wild without permission, please be considerate.

- Pitch camp late and pack up early.
- Camp out of sight of roads and paths, and away from farm buildings and residential homes.
- Bury human waste properly, in a hole between six and eight inches deep and at least fifty metres away from any water.
- Take everything away with you. Clear up your rubbish and dispose of food and toilet paper by carrying it with you until you find a waste bin.
- Restore the site to its previous state, as far as you can.[187,188]

Hostels

If you prefer a roof over your head then hostels and bunkhouses are the cheapest places to stay, as long as you don't mind sharing a room with a group of strangers. The largest chain is run by what was the Youth Hostel Association, and is now known as **YHA**,[189] although there are others. Hostels are marked on the OS *Explorer* maps by either a small red triangle (YHA) or a small red square (other hostels).

YHA hostels are no longer reserved for the young. Anybody of any age is welcome. Neither are you expected to help with housekeeping chores, which was the norm many years ago, although you will be expected to clear up after yourself. There will usually be a communal kitchen for cooking, but larger hostels may also have a café. Although the decor can be rather basic, some YHAs are sited in wonderful, listed buildings of historical interest.

In addition, many YHA hostels now offer private rooms with en-suite facilities. Unfortunately, this option is relatively expensive and, if privacy is important to you, it may work out cheaper to stay in a B&B or small hotel.

You should be aware that hostels in seaside areas will become fully booked many weeks in advance, so don't just turn up expecting a bed. And some smaller hostels in remote areas will be situated well away from shops and cafés, making it difficult to organise an evening meal unless you have a car.

Bed and Breakfast (B&Bs)

I'm lucky enough to have a consistent income and, being well past the age where I enjoy sleeping on the ground or sharing with strangers, I often stay in B&Bs.

Like hotels, the cost of a B&B is usually calculated per room, rather than per person. Although a single room will be cheaper than a double room, not all places cater for singles, and a single person in a double room will be charged almost the same as a couple sharing, with perhaps a small deduction for the extra breakfast that isn't needed.

If you don't mind sharing a bathroom, and if booking outside of the holiday season, you can find reasonable rooms for between £35 and £60 a night, including breakfast. My husband prefers rather more luxury, and if he is travelling with me, we tend to book more expensive B&Bs, at the rate of £70-£90 a night for the two of us. Some of the really expensive B&Bs cost more than £100 a night, far more than a cheap hotel, but offer luxurious surroundings and excellent breakfasts.

In popular holiday resorts, where B&Bs cater for weekend trippers, they may require you to book both the Friday and the Saturday nights together. Some establishments are closed to guests over the winter and are fully booked in the summer, so do your homework and book in advance if you can.

One downside to B&Bs is that they aren't marked on the OS maps, so you must be clear about the address before you set off. In addition, the owners like to know the exact time of your arrival – preferring late afternoon or early evening – and expect a bit of a chat when they meet you. This is fair enough; you are a guest in a private home after all. But you may not be able to predict exactly the time of your arrival, and I find the prolonged meet and greet emotionally and physically draining after a long walk, when all I want to do is collapse in a hot bath.

TOP TIP: Not all B&Bs take credit cards. In fact, many of the cheaper ones require payment in cash.

Pubs with Rooms and Hotels

When I'm travelling alone, I find the ideal place to stay is a room in a village pub. These can be noisy at weekends, and tend to be less luxurious than a modern B&B, with dated furnishings and sometimes, shared bathroom facilities, but you have the advantage of being able to buy your evening meal on site. And pubs are easy to find, being well-signposted and clearly marked on the OS maps with either a blue beer mug or the letters PH (for Public House).

Small hotels can offer very good value for money, especially if you find a small family-run hotel that offers both a friendly face and an excellent breakfast. Chains such as Premier Inn, Travelodge and Ibis Budget offer cheap rooms, as long as you don't mind the impersonal blandness of a chain, particularly if you book at the last minute. An advantage of these chain hotels is that you will be guaranteed en-suite facilities and a standard range of features, such as a working TV and Wi-Fi facilities, and hotels offer far more flexibility around the times you can check in and check out.

Accommodation Tips

Look Before You Book!

Before you make any advance booking, I recommend you check the reviews on TripAdvisor. (There are other review sites, but I find Trip Advisor to be the most extensive and comprehensive.) Some cheap hotels are awful. Luckily, I've managed to avoid any true horrors because I always check TripAdvisor and read other guests' comments before booking.[190]

A handful of bad reviews shouldn't put you off – you're on a walking trip, not the holiday of a lifetime – but if the reviews are consistently bad, you should find somewhere else, if you can

TripAdvisor covers not only hotels and B&Bs, but also hostels and camping sites.

Tips for Saving Money

- In seaside resorts, room rates are often higher at weekends and during the holiday periods. If you're prepared to book a midweek stay, and visit out of season, you can get some real bargains.
- In town and city hotels, the opposite is often true, because their main trade is business trips, and so their rates may be more expensive during the week and considerably cheaper at weekends.

- Charity rates may be available if you beg a little, and if you are raising money for a worthwhile cause. There are so many people walking, running or cycling for charity these days that you might find many landlords and landladies are not very sympathetic. They have to make a living after all.
- If you intend to stay in a number of YHA hostels, it is worth considering becoming a member. A year's membership costs a small amount (£15 at the time of writing) and many hostels offer members a small discount when you book a room.[191]
- Last-minute bookings may not be practical, depending on your lifestyle, but if you do leave it to the last minute, you can look online and snap up cheap rooms.[192,193] You may, of course, end up with nowhere to stay if it's a popular area and every place is fully booked.

Comfort Tips

Don't assume toiletries, biscuits and other luxuries will be supplied.

The cheapest hotels and B&Bs should provide clean sheets, clean towels, hand and shower soap, along with toilet paper. But that might be all you get. I always take basic toiletries with me, just in case (e.g. soap, shampoo and a supply of tissues).

Most places offer tea and coffee-making facilities. You should be able to check this before you book, and as the minimum, you should get free teabags, sachets of instant coffee and little pots of long-life milk. If you prefer hot chocolate, you might like to take your own supply. Some places are very grudging with teabags, only providing a couple and rarely refreshing supplies. For this reason, I usually take a couple of spare bags with me because I can't function without a morning cuppa.

If you pay more, you will usually get more. Expensive places will offer a range of toiletries and a free, but limited, supply of biscuits. You may even be greeted by an offer of a cup of tea and cakes when you first arrive. (If you are staying for more than a few days, make the most of this, because it's unlikely to be repeated!)

Wi-Fi facilities may or may not exist. Check in advance. For me, Wi-Fi is vital. I can live without it for a few days, but I don't like being out of touch with the world and I rely on the Internet to plan public transport and to check the weather forecast. Although you can do all this via a smartphone, there is no guarantee you'll be able to get a phone signal.

Make sure you know what time they lock the front door in the evening and, if you are given your own key, make sure it actually works in the lock!

You should offer to take off your muddy boots beside the front door. It is helpful if a seat is provided, but otherwise, you might have to sit on the doorstep. Don't forget to take a pair of comfortable shoes to change into while indoors. In the winter, I take some light trainers with me. In the summer, it's pair of flip-flops.

Your hosts may be able to tell you about public transport but don't rely on any information they give you. If they own a car, and most people do, they will base their advice on half-forgotten bus journeys and it could turn out to be wildly inaccurate.

TOP TIP: Don't be fooled by flashy websites, and always use TripAdvisor to check out the pros and cons of possible accommodation *before* you make a booking.

Section 5

Safety Matters

'Over-confidence is a terrible thing. What I had stupidly thought to be just a few wriggly miles on the map, turned out to be nearer ten. Eventually, with darkness falling around me, miles out on the seawall and not a light in sight, I grow worried.'

(*Jannina Tredwell*, who walked around the coast with her dogs in 2006)[194]

Walking must be one of the safest sports in the world. But nothing is entirely free of risks. In this section, I will cover your major safety challenges and give you practical tips to keep you free from harm.

We'll start by coping with the British weather, go on to deal with the dangers posed by strangers and cliffs, and then look at some of the physical problems that might derail your trips. I'll tell you about the three most dangerous animals you are likely to encounter, before ending with some advice on how to stay in communication.

Chapter Twenty-Two

Weather and the Elements

In England, we talk about the weather all the time. We also talk about football and other things, but the weather remains our favourite topic of conversation. Why? Because our British weather is very unpredictable and changeable. And this poses challenges for walkers.

In this section, I will talk about the various weather conditions you might encounter and give you some advice on how to cope with them.

Check the Forecast

First, I'll let you into a secret.

Yes, the weather in England is constantly changing and, yes, long-term weather predictions are notoriously unreliable. **But short-term and local forecasts are surprisingly accurate.** This means that on the morning of your walk, you should be able to get a very good idea of the kind of weather you're going to face during the day.

The site I use is the BBC Weather site at www.bbc.co.uk/weather. Here, you can select a small town or village, either on or near your chosen route, and check the local weather. You can see, hour by hour, the predicted weather conditions in astonishing detail. You can tell whether rain is likely, if the sun is going to shine, the air temperature, wind speed and wind direction, along with sunrise and sunset times.

This is golden information when it comes to deciding what to wear and what you need to carry with you, and will also help you plan your day to get the maximum benefit from the weather conditions.

I'll give you a worked example below:

> On the morning of my walk, the forecast predicts a warm and sunny start, but the sky will cloud over by midday and it will start raining heavily around 1p.m. The rain should have stopped by 3p.m., after which the sky is going to remain clear well into the evening. I note the sunset time of 8p.m.

With this information, I decide to set off early and stop at a pub for lunch. I plan to remain in the pub until the worst of the rain has passed, and so I take a book with me to read. The afternoon section of my walk will be longer than normal, to make the most of the lovely evening.

Here's another example:

> The day will be overcast but with no rain. The temperature starts at a reasonable 16 degrees centigrade, but in the afternoon, I notice it drops to 12 degrees as the wind picks up. By late afternoon, the wind will be blowing in my face at 44 mph, which is gale force.

I know the last few hours of the day will be tough walking against the wind, and so I shorten my planned route and build in an extra rest break for a snack. And I take my lightweight, windproof jacket in my backpack, because I know I'll need it later.

I hope these examples have proved how checking the forecast before you set off will help you to dress appropriately, take the right things with you, and get the most out of each and every walking day.

Walking in the Rain

I dealt with what to wear on rainy days in great detail in a previous chapter, *Clothing for all Seasons*. Here, I am just going to list the basics for easy reference.

Suggested rainy day gear:

- Waterproof cover for your rucksack
- Waterproof over trousers and/or gaiters
- Waterproof jacket with a hood
- Spare pair of socks in a plastic bag
- Plastic sandwich bags or zip-lock bags for electronic devices, such as cameras and mobile phones
- Consider an umbrella

Walking in the Heat

Walking on a hot day – a *really* hot day – creates challenges. Firstly, the heat itself will tire you more quickly than you expect. Secondly, you will lose fluid through your sweat and will risk becoming dehydrated.

Although I've dealt with what to wear on hot days in the chapter, *Clothing for all Seasons*, here is a quick checklist of what you might carry in your backpack:

- Sun hat
- Sunscreen
- Extra water, double what you usually need
- A light Pac-a-Mac waterproof top
- A long-sleeved top of thin material (such as a lightweight cycling top)
- A thin fleece

Seriously. A fleece?

Remember, when you set off in the morning, the air temperature may still be cool and you'll need one. Towards midday, as the temperature climbs, you can pack your fleece away in a rucksack. Then in the late afternoon and early evening, when the temperature in England may drop quickly, you could be glad of your fleece again, particularly if you have to wait around at a bus stop or train station.

The key to dressing for a hot day is layers.

Actually, the key to dressing for any day is always layers!

Sun Hat

This is the single most important element of your summer wardrobe. You want something that offers shade to both your face and to the back of your neck, and that is why a hat is better than a cap, because it protects both areas.

A walking friend, called Anna, wears a wide-brimmed and waterproof cowboy hat. It acts as a sun-protector and keeps the rain off her face in bad weather. My sun hat is cotton and not waterproof, so if it rains, I have to swap it for my rain hood.

When trying on hats, make sure you find one that fits snuggly to your head. You don't want it to blow away in a sudden gust. An alternative is to choose a hat that ties under your chin or is fitted with an elastic strap.

Sunscreen

I carry a small bottle of sunblock with me all year round and, because I have sensitive skin, I use unperfumed and waterproof children's cream, which I buy in small travel pack sizes – perfect for carrying in my rucksack. Even if you put on sunblock before setting off, I think it's a good idea to carry a small supply with you so that you can top up if you need to.

Of course, you will need sun protection on your face, but don't forget other exposed areas, such as the back of your neck and forearms. And, if you wear shorts, you may need to cover your lower legs too.

The main downside of sunblock is that it coats your skin and reduces the cooling effect of perspiration.

Water

Remember to start your walk in a properly hydrated state and on a hot day, you should carry more water than you think you would normally need, perhaps twice as much. (I've made the mistake of not taking enough with me, and paid for it with headaches and dizziness.)

If you haven't already done so, I suggest you read the chapter, *Food and Water*, but here is a quick recap of the signs of dehydration: strong thirst, dry mouth and throat, headache, dizziness, and not wanting to pee all day.

I prefer to carry my water inside my rucksack, where it keeps cooler than on the outside. Some people use insulated bottles. I have friends who partly refill plastic bottles with water and leave them in the freezer overnight to turn to ice, which slowly melts as they walk and gives them a regular supply of chilled water. If you're going to try this, don't forget that the bottles will drip condensation as they thaw, so keep them away from clothes and electronic equipment.

TOP TIP: Drinking *very* cold water may not be as cooling as you think. When the cold water hits your stomach, your body responds by sending a rush of blood into your abdominal area. This means blood is diverted away from your skin, reducing both external heat radiation and sweating – which are both important cooling mechanisms. Cold water may feel refreshing, but this internal diversion of blood is not a good idea.

Drinking cool water, rather than icy cold, is a good compromise.

Long Clothing

Another way of protecting your skin is to wear long-sleeved tops and full-length trousers. Funnily enough, you might feel cooler covered in material than you feel covered in sun creams, because of the perspiration-inhibiting effect I've just mentioned.

Other Tips for Keeping Cool

Wear something on your head. If you've forgotten your hat, wear a spare piece of clothing draped over your head. It will make you look weird but is better than nothing.

If you are an umbrella carrier, don't forget you can always use your umbrella as a parasol. Again, you might look rather odd, but that's better than getting heatstroke.

I've seen hot walkers glugging down water by the gallon. You do need to keep hydrated, but some people mistake feeling hot with feeling thirsty. It may be better to use some of your water to cool yourself by splashing it across your face, allowing your skin to lose heat through evaporation. Or use some to dampen the inside of your hat, helping you to lose heat through your head.

If you get *very* hot you will need to take action to cool yourself down.

- Stop walking.
- Find shade if you can.
- Sit down for a rest.
- Drink water in small sips, giving your stomach time to absorb the fluid.
- If you have plenty of water to spare, use some to dampen the pulse points at your wrist and the sides of your neck.
- It might help if you remove your boots and socks and allow your feet to cool down too.

Walking in the Wind

Of all the elements, I think wind is the most difficult for a walker to deal with, and possibly the most dangerous too. Why? Because walking in a strong wind is both energy-sapping and can cause you to lose your balance.

If you take Britain as a whole, the prevailing wind comes from the west, swooshing in from the Atlantic Ocean. This means if you are walking westwards, you should find the wind is blowing in your face, and if you are walking eastwards, you should expect to have the wind at your back. Unfortunately, the wind doesn't always play by the rules and can flip direction, sometimes during the same day. In addition, coastal areas generate their own local weather systems and on the coast, the commonest wind direction is from off the sea. In most circumstances, this means the wind is coming at you sideways.

Walking into a headwind is like swimming against a current, you have to put extra effort into each step. And so a five-mile walk against the wind can feel like a ten-mile walk on a calm day. Of course, if you have a wind behind you, you can fly along. This is fine with a linear walk, but if you are planning on turning back, remember, the return journey will be far more difficult and you'll be tired.

You might think a sideways wind would be less tiring than one blowing into your face, but I find it just as difficult. In fact, the more blustery the wind – the more stops and start and sudden gusts – the more difficult it is, because it's really hard to get into a steady rhythm of walking. You constantly have to fight for your balance, adjust your stance, alter your gait – and all this takes energy.

In addition, a very fierce wind, particularly if coming in sudden gusts, might cause you to lose your balance and fall.

Wind Speeds and What They Mean

Check the weather forecast, looking for both the direction and the speed of the wind. Here is what you will notice at various wind speeds while out walking:[195]

- Below 3 mph: air feels still.
- From 4 mph to 24 mph: increasingly breezy, but not too unpleasant.
- Above 24 mph: winds cause increased effort and stress while walking.
- Above 40 mph: strong winds and gale force, make walking difficult and dangerous.
- Above 50 mph: severe gales and storms. Don't be stupid. Stay at home.

Skincare

Wind can play havoc with your skin. Although women may be more interested in protecting their complexion than men, I think none of us want to end up with broken veins on our faces, peeling skin and chapped lips. On windy days, I apply a moisturising cream to my face and neck – not a light daytime lotion but one of the thicker night creams. And I carry lip salve with me.

The wind has a cooling effect and this may lead you to underestimate the power of the sun, so don't forget to use a sunblock on a sunny day.

How do you use both sunblock and a moisturising cream? I apply the cream first and give it a while to soak in (before breakfast is a good time) before applying my sunblock just before I set off.

Three tips for windy day walking:

1. Button down and zip up. If your jacket is billowing out behind you, it will act as a dragnet, slowing you down and making every step an effort. Streamline yourself.
2. Give yourself more time, or cut down the miles you plan to do. You will find everything takes longer in the wind.

3. Wear a beanie hat. This is really useful if the wind is chilly, because a cold wind can hurt your ears, giving you both earache and a headache. I also wear a lightweight beanie on warmer days, because I get irritated if my hair is constantly blown around. On a very cold day, of course, you might need a thick beanie or ski-hat.

Walking in the Cold and in Winter

I rarely feel cold while I'm out walking. Even in the winter. But then I'm walking the coast in stages, and so I can avoid weeks where there are blizzards forecast or freezing mornings with several inches of frost on the ground. If you are walking on exposed moorlands or across high ground then the cold will present more of a challenge. And, of course, the higher you climb, the colder the air becomes.

Rule of Thumb

On a clear day, the temperature drops by 10°C for each 1,000 metres you climb. If the high ground is covered in cloud, snow or rain, the drop in temperature is actually less, perhaps 6°C for each 1,000 metres.[196,197]

In Reality

The coast does have cliffs and areas of high ground, but you will not be required to climb mountains – unless you make inland detours to do so, like John Merrill and David Cotton. In fact, the highest cliff you will come across on the English coast is Great Hangman, in North Devon, which is 318 metres or 1,044 feet high.[198] Taking the rule of thumb above, you can work out that, even on a clear day, when the temperature difference is the greatest, the temperature fall between sea level, and the top of Great Hangman is only three degrees, barely enough to notice.

Winter Advantages

Winter walking can be great fun and the views can be staggering.

In fact, on a crisp and sunny winter day, you will enjoy better views than during the summer, when the horizon is often obscured by haze. And clear air isn't the only advantage. Bare trees mean you can see further, discovering features of the landscape that are hidden behind foliage in the summer.

As an extra bonus, you'll find that footpaths are less crowded, and accommodation is cheaper.

Winter Downsides

Many facilities are shut during the winter season, including seaside cafes, pubs and toilets. Local bus services may be reduced or non-existent.

Another bane of winter walking is mud. Heavy rainfall and slanting sunlight mean that paths never have a chance to dry out. You can overcome this by picking routes where the ground underfoot is firmer, which includes sandy beaches, esplanades, tarmac paths and quiet roads. Look for official cycle routes. Although these may be covered in a surface layer of mud, you are unlikely to come across anything deeper than a few inches.

The most difficult part of winter walking, in my opinion, is the short days. If you start at 9.00a.m., you may only have 6-7 hours of daylight. On an overcast day, the light will be dim by 3.00p.m., although you can often walk for an hour or so after sunset, because the sky takes much longer to fade to black in the winter. Some people walk in the dark wearing headlamps. This can be good fun, but is not for everyone, and of course, you miss out on the views.

Cold-Weather Clothing

In winter, as always, *layers* are the key. I've discussed what to wear in the cold in the chapter, *Clothing for all Seasons*, but I just want to mention one specific item: socks.

Winter Socks

I haven't found it necessary to buy extra thick socks for winter, as my feet quickly warm up and are usually too hot. But you need to discover your own comfort level and buy the socks that seem right for you.

On a really cold day, you can double up your normal socks, invest in some of the thicker socks of the sort used by mountain walkers, or buy a merino wool blend. Remember, don't go for pure wool (unless it's merino) for the reasons I've explained before.

Wet feet are unpleasant enough in the summer, but feel particularly horrible in the winter. For this reason, I carry a spare pair of socks with me. I've rarely needed them, but just knowing I have the option to change out of damp footwear makes me feel better.

Skin Protection

Remember that cold can be damaging to the skin, particularly in the wind, and the sun can be deceptively strong in March and April, even when the air is cool. After a dull winter, your skin may be pale and more prone to burning.

I wear moisturising cream and, if the sun is shining, will apply a light sunblock too.

Cold Weather and Mobile Phones

Your mobile phone may stop working in very cold weather. I discuss this problem in more detail in the chapter, *Staying in Contact*.

Top Tips for Winter Walking

- Check the weather forecast and daylight hours before you set off.
- Invest in a good fleece.
- Wear a jacket that is both waterproof and windproof.
- Carry a torch with you, just in case you get caught in the dark.
- If you anticipate road walking in the dusk, make sure you either wear reflective clothing, or take reflective armbands with you.

Chapter Twenty-Three

Personal Safety

There is a famous long-distance trail running for 2,200 miles down the east side of the United States called the Appalachian Trail. It's not a coastal walk. Much of the route is through dense forests and mountainous terrain, and in places, a walker will be many miles away from the nearest road, surrounded by a true wilderness.[199]

On the Appalachian Trail, hikers are in danger from a variety of hazards, such as falling trees, steep slopes, snowstorms, and from wildlife such as wild bears and poisonous snakes. Despite all these dangers, and with over a million visitors annually, rangers estimate that only two to three people die every year while out on the Trail. Although there have been a handful of murders over the years, most of the deaths are due to physical illness, such as heart attacks and hypothermia.[200]

The English coast, on the other hand, offers a much tamer environment. You will never be more than a few miles from a village and there is usually a farm building somewhere on the horizon. We don't have bears in our woods, although you may encounter three potentially lethal animals (I'll come to these later.)

In fact, the most important risk you will face while walking the coast paths of Britain comes from one source. I'll mention that source in a moment, but first I want to talk about the single most immediate fear that people cite when telling me how brave I am to walk alone.

Stranger Danger

When I told my aunt I was walking the coast, she immediately asked if I was worried about being followed and attacked by 'bad boys'. My aunt, in her coy way, was asking not just about the danger of robbery, but about the possibility of rape. Many women have expressed similar fears about lone walking.

Statistically, you are more likely to be raped by someone you know rather than a stranger.[201] And I don't believe many would-be rapists would waste time hanging around the coast path on the odd chance that a lone female might pass, since they are far more likely to find potential victims near their homes or in a busy town centre. But this is no reassurance to those women who have been unfortunate enough to be sexually assaulted, nor to those who have been violently mugged. The same types of fears can apply to men too.

It's not unreasonable for people to be anxious about the thought of walking on their own, and you don't have to walk alone. You can take a friend, or a group of friends. Or a large dog.

Footpaths do, certainly, lead you through some of the seedier sides of towns and villages. Even if the countryside looks scenic and the village is chocolate-box pretty, you should never forget that there is widespread rural deprivation out there.[202,203] Jobs are scarce in small villages, and the cost of food and fuel is higher than in a metropolitan area. It's not that rural deprivation turns people into criminals, but poverty and envy can be powerful, motivating factors for robbery.

Once, walking through Bideford in Devon, I realised my path would take me close to a group of scruffy young lads sitting on a bench, clearly drinking from bottles half-heartedly hidden in paper bags. Never a good sign. I looked around but there was no alternative route. I quickly stowed my camera away at the bottom of my rucksack and tucked my phone into my bra. (Of all the things I couldn't bear to lose, my phone was number one on the list and my camera a close second place.)

At times like this, it's best to avoid seeming nervous and I remembered some good advice. **Don't look like a victim. Walk like an exclamation mark, not a question mark.** I stood up straight, pulled my shoulders back, and marched towards the group on the bench, hoping my body language would make me look confident and assertive.

My own rule when approaching a person who looks menacing is to give them a big smile and a warm hello. My rational is that I believe it would be difficult to mug a casual friend and much easier to mug a complete stranger. Saying 'hello' turns me into a casual friend. Or, maybe, into an irritating and clearly mad old woman. But definitely not into a victim, or so I hope.

I walked towards the young men, marching like a sergeant major and smiling like a lunatic. I didn't quite manage to say 'hello'. But I got past without any bother.

I only mention this incident to show that I am not immune from fear of strangers, particularly those who look as if they might need my money more than I do. But, as yet, all my fear has been without foundation. Statistically, there are far more dangerous creatures to worry about on the coast.

A Double Murder

As far as I can discover, there has only been a single case of murder on a coast path in Britain. In fact, it was a double murder, and this horrible incident didn't happen in England, but in Wales.

In 1989, a husband and wife, Peter and Gwenda Dixon, were on a camping holiday near Little Haven in St Bride's Bay. On the last day of their stay, they went for a stroll along the Pembrokeshire coast path and were attacked by a local man, John Cooper. Cooper's motives seem to be partly robbery and partly sexual. He tied up Peter, assaulted Gwenda, and shot them both dead. After this, he carefully hid their bodies and it was some days before they were discovered.[204]

For a long time, Peter and Gwenda's murder remained unsolved. John Cooper was arrested for other crimes and sent to prison for robbery and assault, but there was nothing to link him to the couple.

Then, 20 years after the Dixon's murder, developments in forensic evidence allowed the police to re-examine the case and they identified traces of Peter's blood, both on Cooper's clothing and on his shotgun. Cooper was also linked to a previous unsolved murder of a brother and sister, who were shot in their remote farmhouse in 1985, and to a sexual assault on a couple of teenage girls in 1996.[205]

In 2011, John Cooper was convicted of both the double murders, and the sexual assaults, and is currently serving four life sentences. He will never be released.[206]

I've given a brief account of this murder because it is the only one I know of that has taken place on a coastal path in Britain. I use it to illustrate that even walking with a companion will not protect you against a determined assailant. I also use it as an example of how unusual this sort of crime really is. The case received widespread publicity, generated many columns of newsprint, and even spawned a book,[207] and it did all this precisely because it was an exception – a highly unusual and bizarre occurrence.

The fact is that the most dangerous person you are likely to come across on a coastal walk in the UK is not a menacing stranger, it's... YOU!

Cliffs

The commonest causes of death on the coast are accidents.[208] And perhaps the commonest accident on the coast is falling from a cliff. And the commonest reason people fall off cliffs is because they want to.

Perhaps I shouldn't use the word 'fall'. Jump is the correct word. People jump off cliffs.

I remember walking across Beachy Head. It was a beautiful, sunny day and, as I followed a well-trodden path over the top of the high cliffs, I noticed how little protection there was from the sheer drop. In some places, there was a rudimentary wire fence. In other places, there was no barrier at all. At first, I was pleased the beautiful scenery wasn't spoilt by health and safety considerations, and then I noticed a poignant sight, one that sent shivers up and down my spine. There, scattered at intervals along the crumbling cliff edge, were withered bunches of flowers, some with a smattering of little crosses, some with messages and faded photographs. Memorials.

For a brief moment, I thought, Perhaps this is where people scatter the ashes of loved ones. What a nice idea. And, for another brief moment, I hoped this might be true. But it didn't take me long to realise I was completely wrong.

On my arrival at Eastbourne station, one of the things that struck me was the sign at the station exit with an advert for The Samaritans and a signpost. Usually, access to the Samaritans is via a phone line, but here they have an actual physical office for people to visit. Up on Beachy Head cliffs, there were more Samaritan signs.

The penny dropped.

On a beautiful day, with the sea a milky blue and the sun blazing, it's hard to imagine anyone wishing to end their lives. But it happens.

Beachy Head – with its iconic white cliffs, which tower 530 feet above a shallow sea – turns out to be one of the most popular places in the world for suicides. There are, on average, 20 successful attempts a year.[209,210,211,212]

For example, in 2012, Laraine Goodwin was strolling along the top of Beachy Head with her husband. She asked him to put their dog on its lead, and then she calmly walked off the cliff. Bystanders rushed to comfort her stunned husband and initial reports suggested she had been blown off the headland by the wind, but an inquest established that she had deliberately chosen to take her own life, and the coroner recorded her death as a suicide.[213,214]

Deliberate deaths are one thing, but cliffs are dangerous places, and some of the deaths that occur are entirely accidental.

It was the Friday of the Bank Holiday weekend in early May 2012. On the rugged coast of Cornwall's Lizard Peninsula, Harry McCabe was enjoying the first day of his holiday and taking an early-evening walk along the cliffs above Mullion Cove. Accompanying him was his wife, Samantha, their 12-year-old daughter, Faye, and another young girl, a friend of Faye's. Harry apparently wanted to take a better photograph of the scenery. He walked past a viewing point and headed closer to the cliff edge. The girls screamed as he suddenly disappeared from view.[215]

Harry's body was later recovered from the rocks, and an inquest confirmed he had died from the fall, sustaining multiple injuries and a broken neck.[216]

What happened? Did the edge of the cliff give way? Was Harry tired after travelling down to Cornwall and did this make him careless? Did the fading light of the afternoon affect his judgement? We'll never know for certain why he lost his footing and fell.

In July 2015, near Brighton and just a little further along the coast from Beachy Head, a teenage boy was experimenting with LSD on the cliff top. Disorientated and confused, he ran towards the edge and either jumped or fell, landing far below on a popular walkway that runs along the bottom of the cliffs. Passers-by tried to help, but the boy's injuries were too severe and he died shortly afterwards in hospital.

This wasn't the first death from a cliff fall in the area, but the dead boy was Arthur Cave, and he happened to be the son of Nick Cave, the musician. As a result, the tragedy was widely reported both nationally and internationally. Although that stretch of cliffs is another favourite suicide spot, there is nothing to suggest that Arthur's death was anything other than an awful accident, but an accident in which drugs played a major part.[217]

Cliffs can kill in other ways. A month before Arthur's death, in June 2015, a young woman called Georgie Le Fyord was celebrating the end of her A-level maths exam with a friend. They walked down to the pretty beach at Llantwit Major in Wales. Signs warned them the cliff above was unstable, so they chose a picnic spot some distance away from the rocks, sat down, and began tucking into bread and cheese, and sparkling wine. Suddenly, a shower of stones fell from the cliff, and one of them hit Georgie on the head, killing her instantly. Her friend was unharmed.[218]

We can't escape the conclusion that the coast is a place where accidents happen. And yet, given the millions of people who visit the coast every year, the risks are small – certainly much smaller than the gamble you take with your life every time you get into a car.[219] And the risks can be minimised further if you are mindful of the dangers and always pay attention to your surroundings.

Tips for Keeping Safe on Cliffs:

- Look out for hazards such as loose rocks, tree roots, and slippery scree.
- Wear sensible footwear.
- If you're down on the shore, don't linger under unstable cliffs.
- If you are up on the cliff top, don't get too close to the edge.
- Avoid excess alcohol and drugs as these can impair your judgement.

Illness and Injury

There might be good reasons why you are nervous of walking alone, and the fear of possible injury, or the recurrence of a pre-existing illness, may seem a real deterrence to walking, even with company.

What if you fall and twist your ankle, or break an arm or a leg? What happens if you're struck by an unexpected heart attack? Maybe you suffer from epilepsy, or have had several mini strokes, and are afraid you might have an attack while out walking.

Nobody is guaranteed a risk-free walk, but here are some suggestions that might help you feel more confident during your expeditions.

Things You Can Do To Keep Yourself Safe

Carry a charged phone and enter an ICE number in your contact list or address book (ICE stands for 'In Case of Emergency'). I will talk about ICE numbers in more detail in the *Staying in Contact* chapter.

Take at least one walking pole with you. This can act as a makeshift splint or walking stick if you twist an ankle or, even worse, break something.

If you have a longstanding medical condition, such as asthma, diabetes or epilepsy, I assume you will take any necessary intervention medication with you. And you may like to wear a bracelet or necklace with important medical information printed on it. For example, a MedicAlert bracelet can be ordered from www.medicalert.org.uk and there are many other suppliers. I list a selection in *Helpful Resources*.

You can, however, construct an entirely free medical alert for yourself on your own computer. Write a short summary of your medical conditions and print this off. Put the paper in a waterproof container or bag, and carry it in a pocket.

If you take an assortment of prescribed medication, you might consider carrying your repeat prescription slip with you too, with details of your drugs printed out. Again, make sure you keep this in a waterproof container.

TOP TIP: A standard NHS urine sample bottle makes an excellent and lightweight, waterproof container – but don't tell anyone I told you this.

First-Aid Equipment

It seems sensible to carry some first-aid equipment on your walks, but only take items you think you really might need and know how to use. I've seen some people recommending an extensive first-aid kit, containing such things as arm slings and eye pads. Unless you know how to put on a sling (and most people don't), or can think of a good reason why you might need an eye pad, I suggest you keep it simple and lightweight.

Here is a basic first-aid kit, which you can slip into a pocket:

- A single blister strip of painkillers
- A few blister plasters
- Selection of self-adhesive dressings of various sizes
- A supply of clean tissues

In addition, I carry sunblock, lip screen, and insect spray.

Remember, you're not spending a week in the wilderness. On the English coast, you will rarely be more than a couple of hours away from medical help.

I seldom use anything from my first-aid kit, apart from tissues. In fact, my blister plasters are usually given away to fellow walkers! This makes me a popular walking companion.

You could carry antiseptic gel, but I don't bother. In fact, antiseptic gels and lotions are of little value in protecting from infection and can harm healing tissues. The best way to clean a cut or a graze is to hold it under running tap water, although this isn't possible when out in the field. Wet wipes may be useful for getting rid of surface dirt.[220,221]

Common Injuries

The commonest medical problems a walker is likely to encounter, in my experience, are blisters, aching joints and sore muscles. Oh, and I'd better mention sausage fingers.

Sausage Fingers

This non-medical term describes the finger swelling many walkers experience if they walk for long distances with their hands held down by their sides. It might occasionally be caused by hyponatraemia, from drinking too much water, but it's usually due to the simple effects of gravity causing fluid to accumulate in your lower arms.[222] Although not serious in itself, swollen hands can be uncomfortable, particularly if you are wearing rings.

To avoid sausage fingers, don't walk for prolonged periods with your hands by your sides. You can bend your elbows at right angles as you walk, as joggers do, or keep your hands raised by hooking your thumbs under your backpack shoulder straps, as you see many walkers do. Or use poles, which force you to keep your elbows bent and your hands raised.

Foot Blisters

You will get blisters. Almost every walker gets blisters, but beginner walkers are more at risk than experienced walkers. Just as it takes time to build up your walking muscles, it takes time for your feet to become used to walking long distances.

I once read that it takes 1,000 miles before your feet become conditioned to hard walking, and was thrilled as I approached my first 1,000-mile mark – thinking that would mean an end to blisters. But I still got them. The reason? The man who said it took 1,000 miles to condition your feet was John Merrill, and he meant 1,000 miles of continuous walking.[223] For those of us who walk in stages and intermittently, we may never achieve the bliss of blister-free feet.

Because this is such an important topic, I'm writing a useful booklet *(How to Treat Blisters: a Handbook for Walkers)* where I cover the prevention, anatomy and treatment of blisters in greater detail, and where you can find additional information if you are interested in digging deeper, but I'll just cover the basics here.

Foot Care

Preventing blisters is easier, and less painful, than dealing with the wretched things after they've appeared. So it's worth thinking about foot care.[224,225,226]

Your key aims are to keep your feet supple and your toenails short.

We often talk about our feet toughening up, but that doesn't mean developing a thick layer of skin on our heels or soles. In fact, thick and toughened skin can contribute to blisters, so it's best to get rid of hard skin on your heels and other areas by using a foot scrubber or an emery board.

I usually use foot cream too. You can buy expensive foot care products, but any cheap brand of moisturiser will do. I use E45, aqueous cream or Nivea. It's best to avoid greasy ointments, such as Vaseline or similar products. They linger in your socks and can make for unpleasant walking.

Footwear

I've talked about choosing footwear in a previous section. Comfort is your key aim. If you are badly troubled by blisters, it might be worth re-reading the chapters on *Shoes and Boots* and *Socks Matter Too*. If what you're using isn't working, you might need to buy some different equipment.

Plasters Before Blisters

Another trick is to apply a blister plaster to the vulnerable areas of your feet *before* a blister has actually formed. You can base this on your training walks, or assess your feet at lunchtime after your first half-day of walking, when you will soon discover which areas of your feet are feeling sore.

I can predict, with each pair of boots I own, where I will get a blister. My favourite pair gives me blisters on the outside of my big toes. Another pair, a heavy set I use on muddy walks, gives me a blister on the back of my heel.

What to Do When You Have a Blister

The conventional advice is to stop walking immediately, never burst the blister, and just leave it to heal naturally.[227] Most long-distance walkers know this advice is pretty useless because nobody wants to abandon their trek on account of a blister and, if you continue walking, the blister will probably burst spontaneously inside your boots anyway.

If you develop a painful blister with an obvious fluid-filled pocket, my strong advice is to burst the blister with a clean needle at the first convenient opportunity. This will immediately relieve the discomfort and allow you to continue your walk without any pain.

You don't need fancy equipment. (Some people seem determined to turn a simple bursting-a-blister procedure into a major surgical operation.) In fact, an ordinary sewing needle will do. Ideally, both the needle and your skin should be cleaned first by washing in tap water and then dried thoroughly. There is really no need to use antiseptics or disinfectants as any method you can use is unlikely to be effective and will just give you a false sense of reassurance.[228,229]

If you are badly troubled by a blister while out walking, you can stick a blister plaster over the top. Or you can pop it in the field, literally, as long as you have a safe way of carrying a clean needle with you, and as long as your feet aren't too grubby. Wipe away any obvious dirt using a tissue and water from your bottle. Wait for your skin to dry before inserting the needle.

> The key to avoiding infection is to always use a clean, *dry* needle on clean, *dry* skin, and to cover the drained blister afterwards with a blister dressing.

Blister Plasters

There are various makes on the market and all of them work on the same principle. They provide a cushion barrier between your skin and your footwear. In addition, most blister plasters are absorbent and will soak up any leaking fluid if your blister has popped.

The gold-standard blister plaster is the Compeed range, which can be bought from any high-street pharmacist, or a supermarket with a pharmacy section. Compeed make other products too, such as corn plasters and cold-sore patches, so make sure you are choosing a blister plaster and not something else.

Personally, I find Compeed rather overpriced, and usually buy Superdrug's own brand of blister plasters. They aren't as padded as Compeed but seem to stick to my skin better. Other pharmacists make similar products. Boots make an own-brand blister plaster that feels very similar to Compeed, but isn't much cheaper.

One problem with Compeed is that it tends to peel off when you pull your socks on. I've found Compeed will stick better when warmed up. Put the plaster on your skin and wait 20 minutes or so before pulling your socks over it.

TOP TIP: Buy a number of different types of blister plaster and experiment to see which suits you the best.

Aches and Pains

There are numerous aches and pains that can beset a walker. These range from minor muscle aches to serious joint problems. In general, most aches and pains are trivial and will settle in a few days if you rest or reduce your walking distances. If you continue to suffer pain and discomfort, you may need to seek medical advice.

Joint Pain

Older walkers are more prone to joint pains than younger ones. This might be because you have some pre-existing arthritis. Or it may simply be your body reacting to unfamiliar exercise. After an energetic few days on the north Cornish coast – which is similar to walking up and down a rollercoaster ride over and over again – my knees became painful and swollen. They settled down after a few days of rest back home.

Funnily enough, going downhill may be more difficult than going uphill. This is where a walking pole will really help because it takes the pressure off your legs and gives you a built-in 'bannister' to take your weight.

If you have a pain in your groin, coupled with a weird ache in your knee, it could be coming from your hip joint. Pain on the *outside* of your hip is probably coming from muscles or tendons around your thigh, not from the hip joint itself.

Tips for Joint Pain

To avoid stressing your joints, build up your walking distances gradually and remember, a hilly walk will have a greater impact than a flat walk.

After a particularly long or tiring walk, why not go for a shorter walk the next day?

If your joints are painful and swollen at the end of the day:

- Take some paracetamol or other suitable painkiller (as long as this is allowed and won't interfere with any other medical condition or medication).
- Cover the joint in either a warm flannel or an icepack. Which to choose? Be guided by what your body seems to need and choose the one that feels most soothing.

Minor pains are unlikely to be a sign of a serious problem, but if the pain doesn't subside after a week or two of rest, you might like to make a non-urgent appointment with your GP to check it out. Please remember, your doctor is unlikely to be very sympathetic if you continue walking on a painful joint, so be prepared to rest up for a week or two.

I must confess to taking the odd paracetamol in advance of a strenuous walk. I don't recommend this. It's better to build up your walking muscles properly than to rely on painkillers.

Muscle Pain and Stiffness

Muscle aches and pains are common, particularly after an energetic day out walking. Stiffness is usually noticeable after a few hours of rest.

The muscles you use when walking are located along the back of your leg, mainly in your buttocks and the back of your upper thigh. After climbing hills, you may feel the muscles of your calf protesting too. You are unlikely to put much stress on the muscles at the front of your thigh – unless you have been climbing long flights of steps or very steep slopes.

Looking at the evidence from other sports, such as running and field sports, there is no evidence that pre-sport stretching helps. But there is some evidence that stretching at *the end* of an exercise session can help reduce muscle stiffness and pain.[230,231] When I first started walking, I used to stretch out before I got into my car at the end of the walk. I still do this sometimes if a walk has been particularly long or strenuous.

Post-Walk Stretching Exercise:

- Stand close to and facing a wall. Place your hands flat on the wall for balance.
- Bend both knees slightly.
- Stretch one leg out behind you – not too far – and put your toes on the floor.
- Slowly straighten out your back leg while pushing your heel down towards the ground.

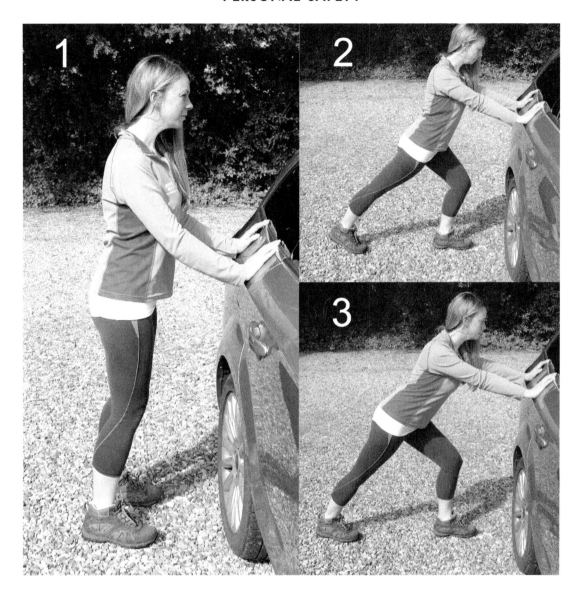

As you do this, you should feel a gentle stretch in the muscles at the back of your leg. If the stretch is too much, or too little, change the distance of your foot from the wall.

If there is no wall handy, you can do this exercise against a gate, a fence, or by leaning on the boot of your car.

A warm bath at the end of the day really helps my muscle pains. Unfortunately, many B&Bs only provide showers. A hot shower is better than nothing, but you can't beat a good wallow in a warm bath.

Other areas of your body can be stressed by walking. Back pain, for example, can be caused by poor posture or by carrying a heavy backpack. Over-striding can put a strain on your lower back and on your pelvic muscles and, if you are troubled by low back pain while walking, try reducing the length of your stride.

There are numerous other conditions I could mention here, including shoulder strains from swinging your backpack on, and a stress fracture in one of the small bones in your foot, which can come on after repetitive walking for mile after mile and day after day. Some people develop painful heels due to a mysterious condition called plantar fasciitis. Others can develop iliotibial tract strain along the outside of the thigh. (As a doctor, I am a terrible hypochondriac, and have been convinced I've had each and every one of these conditions several times!)

TOP TIP: Listen to your body. A mild pain can usually be ignored. A severe pain should be listened to. A pain that doesn't settle with rest probably needs checking out.

Chapter Twenty-Four

Dangerous Animals

In this chapter, I will talk about the three most dangerous animals you are likely to meet along the English coast. And none of them are human beings.

Cows

When people think of dangerous cattle, they think of bulls. But bulls are rare, whereas cows are common.

In most circumstances, of course, cows are perfectly safe. But in other circumstances, cows can turn into killing machines.[232] They don't attack with teeth or claws, but kill you in the same way that a motorcar will kill a pedestrian, by knocking you down and running you over, in other words, by their sheer, crushing weight. A fully-grown cow weighs half a ton; some heavier breeds weigh nearly a ton.[233]

In fact, cows kill an average of five to six people every year in the UK. Most of these deaths are farm workers. But around a quarter are walkers.[234]

You can find the official mortality statistics for the year 2014/2015 on the Health and Safety Executive's website at http://www.hse.gov.uk/foi/fatalities/2014-15.htm. This records eight deaths from 'coming into contact with cattle', seven of which were farm workers, but one was a walker called Peter Jakeman.

Peter Jakeman was a respected 62-year-old magistrate who lived in Cornwall. In May 2014, Peter and his wife decided to take a holiday in Derbyshire. They were walking their dogs through the Okeover Estate near Ashbourne, when a herd of cattle charged at them. Peter was knocked down and trampled. Despite being airlifted to hospital by the air-ambulance helicopter, he died shortly afterwards from his injuries.[235]

The statistics simply give us figures for deaths, but there are numerous other cases where walkers have been threatened by cattle and injured, or simply badly scared. How many? We'll never know. Minor injuries go unreported, and most scary encounters are not recorded.

On the same day as Peter Jakeman was killed, another walker, 68-year-old Robert Tatler, was walking with dogs in a nearby field in the same area. He describes how a ring of cattle surrounded him and one black cow 'went for me'. He was knocked to the ground, but managed to pick himself up. As he stumbled towards the edge of the field and safety, the same black cow knocked him down again. Luckily, a nearby farm worker saw what was happening and rushed over in a vehicle to rescue him.[236]

Robert was lucky. He escaped with minor injuries, although he spent some time in hospital for observation. It was while he was in hospital, recovering, that he learnt of Peter Jakeman's death.

It is unlikely that Robert's story would have appeared in newspapers if it hadn't been for Peter Jakeman's death.

None of these tragedies happened near the coast, but I use them to illustrate the dangers that cows can pose to walkers, even if you follow all the rules, which I will describe shortly.

Bullocks and Bulls

Bullocks are immature male bulls, and, if less than 10 months old, are legally allowed to be in a field crossed by a footpath. A group of bullocks running towards you is a fearsome sight, but you are unlikely to be harmed if you stand your ground.

A solitary bull may be dangerous and it is illegal to put a bull on his own in a field with a footpath. But a non-dairy bull is allowed near a footpath, as long as he is accompanied by a herd of cows.[237] I guess the bull is too busy – or too tired – performing his masculine duties to feel aggressive towards walkers.

Advice on Dealing With Cows

I have received a lot of advice on dealing with cows, some of which is contradictory, but I will share the best tips with you now. To understand these tips and why they might work, it is important to understand two facts about cattle.

First of all, as my husband constantly reminds me, cows and bullocks are curious about new things that appear in their field. If you see a procession of cattle heading towards you, it is usually only because they want to check you out. Cattle are very short-sighted, so in order to see you clearly, they need to come fairly close.[238]

Most normal cows won't come any nearer than around three metres (ten feet), but some may be happy to sneak up close behind you when they think you aren't looking.

Have you ever played 'Grandmother's Footsteps'? It's a game where children try and creep up on a 'grandmother', who stands some distance away with her back towards them. From time to time, the 'grandmother' will turn around and look at the children, who must all freeze and stand as still as statues. Well, I've played the 'grandmother' while groups of young bullocks tried to sneak up behind me!

On another occasion, after being surrounded by a group of bullocks in a field, the ones behind me began licking my bare arms. I think they were after the salt. It was a strange experience, but not a threatening one.

However, even a friendly bullock could cause a serious injury if he accidentally knocked you down and then trampled on you.

So, to avoid contact with cattle, you want to appear large and slightly scary (but not *too* threatening – for reasons I'll explain shortly).

The best advice is to stay calm. Don't run, because cattle will chase after you to see what you're up to, and can easily outrun you anyway. Stand still, or keep walking slowly in the direction you want to go. Let the animals approach and take a good look at you.

I've also read the suggestion that you should stay calm because your increased rate of breathing, pounding heart, and the adrenaline in your sweat will make the cattle think you are a predator. Telling somebody else to stay calm is easy enough; actually staying calm yourself when faced with a rampaging group of cattle... well, that's more difficult

This brings me on to my second fact about cattle.

Secondly, cattle are *prey* animals, not predators. Their natural instincts are designed around defence, not attack. This doesn't mean a cow won't attack you if they think you pose an immediate threat to them, or if they think you are threatening their young calves, particularly if you have a dog with you. I will deal with dogs in a moment, but for now, I suggest you think of it from a cow's point of view.

How does a cow know whether you are a predator, or not?

A predator will check out its prey, keeping its eyes directly focused on its target. It will move towards its potential victim in a purposeful manner, and it will try to separate that one animal from the herd in order to bring it down.

So, if you want to appear harmless to cattle:

1. Don't look directly at them.
2. Don't walk straight towards them.
3. Don't take a route that will isolate one animal from the rest of the herd.
4. Don't get between a cow and her calves.

Of course, depending on the circumstances, you may be forced to break one of these rules. The cows, for example, may be lying directly in front of the only exit route from the field. There may be so many beasts crammed into a small area that you can't avoid walking between one or more animals and the rest of the herd. And you may not spot the calf lying in the long grass until you stumble across it.

The rule I find hardest to keep is the first one. 'Don't look directly at them.' That's really difficult to do when you are feeling nervous and unsure of the best route to take. But I think it is good advice. I recently watched a *Countryfile* programme (on the BBC), which featured Britain's only truly wild cattle, the Chillingham herd. New warden, Ellie Crossley, explained how you should avoid eye contact with the bulls as they could interpret this as a challenge.[239]

Whether cattle perceive a direct gaze as a threat or a challenge is unclear. Maybe it depends on the nature of the animal. But I think it is good advice to avoid prolonged staring – until you are on the other side of the fence, of course.

Dogs

Dangers Created by Your Dog

A cow may or may not consider a human to be a predator, but it will certainly regard your dog as a possible threat. This is particularly the case if a cow has young calves. Most, but not all, of the walkers injured by cattle have been in the company of a dog. This is true of both Peter Jakeman and Robert Tatler, mentioned above. And in 2009, the blind politician, David Blunkett, was seriously injured while out walking with his guide dog.[240]

The following advice is given by the National Union of Farmers:

'When walking with dogs in fields with cattle, the advice is to avoid getting between cows and their calves; to keep your dog under close and effective control on a lead around cows and sheep, but not to hang onto your dog if you are threatened by cattle – let it go and allow the dog to run to safety.'[241]

The Ramblers Association gives similar advice in bullet format, and add that incidents with cattle should be reported to the landowner, the highway authority, the Health and Safety Executive and, if serious, to the police.[242] This is excellent advice, because the farmer really does need to know if his or her cattle are behaving in a manner that could be putting walkers or farm workers at risk. But discovering the name of the landowner may not be easy, so reporting it to the local authority may be the best option. (At the end the chapter, *Understanding Rights of Way*, I explained how to track down the responsible authority.)

Dangers Created by Other People's Dogs

When not creating a nuisance to cattle, dogs may create a problem for other walkers.

There is the matter of dog mess on the path itself, which is all too common in areas where you are walking close to a public car park or access road. I've grown to realise that most dog 'walkers' rarely venture more than a couple of hundred metres from their vehicles. In fact, you will be able to tell when you are approaching civilisation by the number of doggy deposits you discover underfoot.

But dog problems can be more serious than smelly mess.

I've had my trousers seized by a ferocious terrier, who left teeth marks in the material. And I have had to walk backwards down a lane when two farm dogs decided I was an intruder who needed driving away.

Once, on the green downs near Dover, a pack of dogs appeared over the horizon and galloped towards me, led by an enormous German Shepherd with a terrifying bark. The pack was under the control, supposedly, of a young woman, who was, I think, a paid dog walker. I don't know how much she charged per animal, but she must have been making a fortune. Luckily, she finally realised what was happening and began calling out. The pack came to a halt about 20 feet away from me. This incident left me shaking and anxious for the rest of the day.

As a general rule, small dogs make more noise and can seem more aggressive than larger dogs. Terriers are the worst for snapping at your ankles but are unlikely to do much harm if they do bite. Labradors and retrievers are usually very friendly, although it was a golden retriever that gave me my frightening experience on the lane outside a farm, as I described above.

Dogs kept outside and in isolated areas are less likely to be socialised and are more likely to react strongly to your presence. This includes working dogs such as English collies and large dogs kept as guard dogs.

Tips for Dealing with Other People's Dogs

If the owner has the animal under control and on a lead, don't stop to make a fuss of the dog. Walk on by.

If a dog bounds up to you, whether looking friendly or unfriendly, stoop down a little way and offer the backs of your hands for the dog to sniff. While doing this, speak to the dog in a friendly voice, saying 'Hello' or 'What's all this fuss about, then?'

Why stoop? It prevents the dog from jumping up and covering you in mud. But don't bend right down or stoop very low. The dog might intercept this as a doggy bow and a signal you want to play, causing it to leap up at you.[243]

Why let the dog sniff you? Because that is how the dog introduces himself and establishes who you are. A good sniff is the equivalent of a doggy handshake.

Why offer the backs of your hands? You may want to reserve your palms and fingers for handling any snacks and food! And a curled fist creates less of a tempting target then an open palm and fingers, if the dog decides to take a nibble.

After a quick sniff, and maybe a lick or two, the dog will usually run back to its owner.

Dogs are territorial. If you see a dog standing at a gate and barking ferociously, read its body language. Like cows, barking dogs should be given a wide berth but – as long as the tail is waving – are unlikely to attack.

When not guarding their front gates, dogs may be guarding other members of their pack and, in most cases, dogs regard their owners as their pack. So, even when on a lead, some dogs may strain aggressively towards you while barking and growling a warning. Stopping to talk to the owner might seem counterintuitive, but may take some of the heat out of the situation. If the owner seems to recognise you as a friend, the dog will follow their human's example.

Some dogs may resent you following behind their owner because you appear to pose a possible threat. They'll keep pulling back and turning round to bark at you. In this case, it is best to try to overtake, perhaps explaining to the owner why you want to do this so that he or she can step aside and let you pass.

A dog might regard a walker's stick as a weapon – or, sometimes, as a possible plaything. If a dog takes a strong dislike – or a strong liking – to your walking pole, try making it less obvious by tucking it under your arm.

Other dogs will take umbrage at the sight of your backpack. I think this is because it alters your shape and makes you look like something other than a human being. I've never had to resort to removing my backpack to pacify a dog, but it is a possible strategy.

If a dog runs up in an aggressive way, and won't be placated by your friendly voice and your offer of your hands for a quick sniff, it's time to worry. First, look around for the owner. They should come to your rescue. If the dog is alone and unsupervised, continue talking to it gently and begin to back off slowly. Don't turn around and don't run. Continue backing away until you are a safe distance away from dog, at least 20 yards. You can judge the distance because the dog will begin to lose interest in you.

I've never been bitten in anger by a dog. But I know it can and does happen to some unlucky walkers. If all else fails, a walking pole can be used as a weapon to fend off an attack. Use it only as a last resort, when all else has failed, because waving a stick may actually provoke an attack.

Later, when you are safe, you really should consider reporting aggressive dogs to the local authorities. Dog owners do have a responsibility for keeping their animals under control. Even if you are walking on private land, if you are on a public footpath, the owners must make sure your passage in unhampered by aggressive animals, and that includes dogs. (See the chapter, *Understanding Rights of Way*, where the final section tells you how to report a problem.)

In general, of course, most dogs you come across are entirely friendly. I enjoy meeting dogs on my walks and they make excellent walking companions.

Snakes

I include snakes on my list of dangerous animals because they are something many walkers worry about. Certainly I do. In fact, when walking through long grass, I often resort to wearing my gaiters in order to protect my ankles from possible snake attacks, although I know I'm being paranoid; I have never been bitten by a snake.

In fact, there are only three species of snakes in the UK,[244] and only one of these is venomous. The adder. I will spend some time talking about the adder shortly.

Grass Snakes

The commonest type of snake in the UK is the harmless grass snake. These can bite, but they don't inject venom, and so their bite will only cause a transient feeling of discomfort. You can usually tell if a snake has bitten you because you are likely to see the creature wriggling away and, if you look at the site of the bite, you will see two small puncture wounds.

Adders

The second type of snake is the one we all worry about, because it's venomous. The adder.

It is worth looking at some photographs of adders. The most distinctive thing about the snake is the zigzag markings along its back. In a male adder, these are dark and dramatic. In a female adder, the colours might be a more subdued shade of brown. Just to confuse matters, there is a rare variety of adder that is completely black, although, I gather, if you look closely, you can still make out its zigzag markings.

Why do you need to be able to recognise an adder? So that you can take the right action if you are bitten.

There is a good collection of adder photographs on the Wildscreen Arkive site at http://www.arkive.org/adder/vipera-berus/.

Smooth Snakes

The third type of snake is harmless and very rare. You are unlikely to come across one because the smooth snake can only be found in a few places along the south coast. Its markings may be mistaken for an adder, but the pattern on a smooth snake's back is more fragmented than the adder's clear zigzags.

Slow Worms (Not Actually a Snake)

The slow worm is a strange creature that looks like a little snake at first glance, but it's not a snake. In fact, the slow worm isn't even a worm. It's a legless lizard and is completely harmless.

On my travels around the coast, I've been lucky enough to see three adders, two slow worms and numerous grass snakes. They are all shy creatures, and you are unlikely to meet one on a well-trodden path or if you are walking with a group of companions. The only time I met a fully-grown male adder was on a sea bank when I had inadvertently left the proper footpath. It was both a terrifying and exhilarating experience.

Please remember that all British reptiles are legally protected. It is an offence to harm or kill one. That includes all three types of snakes and the slow worm. It is also illegal to sell or trade one of these creatures.[245]

Now, let's get back to adders.

Adder Bite Statistics

Here are the most widely quoted statistics on adder bites:[246]

1. Around 100 people report adder bites in the UK every year. Most of these are bitten while trying to catch or handle a snake.
2. 70% of adder bites produce nothing but a little redness and swelling. In some cases, the bite is a 'dry bite', meaning the snake has not injected any venom, while in other cases, only small amounts of venom have been injected.
3. 30% of cases aren't so lucky and the bite produces serious symptoms. Because you won't know immediately if you are in the unlucky 30%, **it's always best to go to A&E if you are bitten by an adder.**
4. There have been 10 deaths in the UK due to adder bites in the past 130 years, and the last fatality was a child who was bitten in Scotland in 1975. For this reason, adder bites should never be taken lightly, especially in children.[247]

What to Do if an Adder Bites You:

If you are unlucky enough to be bitten by a snake, try to snatch a quick photograph of the creature on your phone or camera. This will help confirm identification later on.

Don't do what you might have seen in films and try to tie off the affected area or suck out the poison.

Here is the latest advice on treating adder bites:

1. Remove any tight clothing and jewellery from affected area.
2. Leave the bite alone, don't use a ligature, and don't try to suck out the poison.
3. Try to move around as little as possible.
4. Seek medical help, and this means a visit your nearest A&E department.[248,249]

In practice, if you are bitten by an adder, you may need to limp to the nearest road and either get a friend to pick you up in a car and take you to A&E, or call an ambulance.

Symptoms may take several hours to develop and can continue to worsen over the course of a few days, so don't be fobbed off by false reassurance in the early stages. Look for increasing swelling and redness at the site of the bite, general itchiness, feeling faint, and diarrhoea.

Some people develop a severe reaction to adder venom. If you develop tingling around the lips, begin to feel faint, or have difficulty breathing, you must seek help **as an emergency**. Call 999 immediately.

Chapter Twenty-Five

Staying in Contact

When Vera Andrews walked the coast in 1984, she ran up a personal debt of £1,800, and £300 of that was the cost of phone calls.[250] Vera didn't have the luxury of a modern mobile phone. She had to find and use public phone boxes.

Today, our lives have been revolutionised by our mobile devices and, depending on the type of contract you have, calls and texts are either free or virtually free. We are used to being in constant contact with friends and family.

But let me introduce you to four problems faced by coastal walkers with mobile phones. The first two are common, the second two less so, but it's useful to know about them.

1. Lack of signal
2. Phone battery problems
3. Very cold weather
4. Running out of phone credit

As we discuss these problems, I'll suggest some simple solutions.

Lack of Mobile Signal

Losing your phone signal for prolonged periods can leave you feeling vulnerable, exposed and lonely, especially if you are a city dweller and not used to extensive phone black spots.

It will happen. Many remote areas of our coast are badly served by phone masts.[251] I've encountered problems along the Norfolk coast, in patches throughout Lincolnshire, on the Dengie Peninsula in Essex, and along substantial stretches of the South West Coast Path in Dorset, Devon and Cornwall. Those are just a few examples.

The good news is that your GPS system will be unaffected by phone black spots, because it relies on direct satellite communication, not on the mobile signal. But beware. A difficulty arises if you are using a GPS smartphone app that requires an Internet connection to display a map. For this reason, I suggest you always check if the GPS app you intend to use will store maps, and make sure you download the ones you need in advance.

When you enter a phone black spot, your mobile phone goes into a frantic panic. It will search, desperately, to find a connection, automatically sending out signals at very regular intervals to start with. These signals gradually decrease in frequency until your phone eventually stops trying to connect and goes into the mobile equivalent of a sulk. If this has happened, even if you move back into a signal area, your phone will continue to show no connection.

Tips to Try When You Have no Mobile Signal:

- Your phone might be sulking. Go into settings and switch to airplane mode for a few moments, and switch back again. If that doesn't work, try powering down your phone completely and restarting it.
- If there is the barest flicker of a signal, a text message might just get through. Even if it doesn't transmit immediately, your phone will keep trying to send the text for a short period, during which time you might have moved into a better signal area.
- If you need to make a 999 call, there may be a mobile signal available, just not one from your own service provider. A 999 call is recognised as an emergency, and if there is any mast within signal distance, it should pick it up. It's worth trying to make the call.[252]

Note: Some people advocate calling 112, which is the European emergency help number. In the UK, 999 and 112 calls are treated in exactly the same way and there is no difference and no advantage to calling one or the other.[253]

Phone Battery Problems

Our smartphones are busy little things. When we aren't using them to make phone calls, they may still be connecting to all types of services and downloading data. This includes things like Facebook updates, Twitter notifications, game app reminders, email downloads, etc.

If you're using a GPS app, your phone will be using up charge at regular intervals, whenever it checks-in with the GPS satellites.

Remember, when you enter a signal black spot, your phone will make frenetic attempts to find and connect to a telecoms mast, including boosting the signals it sends out to maximum power. The worst situation is when you keep drifting in and out of connectivity because your phone never gets a chance to calm down.

Tips to Try if Your Battery is Running Out of Juice:

- **Two simple things to do:** Go into Settings to reduce the brightness of your screen and switch off any vibration modes.
- Consider **turning off your GPS app**, if you're using one, and rely on your paper map instead.
- You can quickly **close down unnecessary apps**. On an Apple phone, double-tap the large button to make all your open apps appear (with an Android phone, tap the multitasking button), and then swipe each app upwards and off the screen. (You can find detailed information on turning off specific app notifications on various websites. I list a few in the *Helpful Resources* chapter at the end of this book.)
- If you want to stop your phone sending and receiving all signals, **switch to airplane or flight mode**. Remember, this will cause you to lose both phone signals and GPS tracking too.
- The most important tip of all is to **carry a phone charger**. You can buy a small one that fits into your pocket or rucksack. Just remember to keep it charged!

There are numerous other tips and tricks to reduce battery drain. I list a few websites that provide advice in the *Helpful Resources* chapter at the end of this book.

Very Cold Weather

When I walked into Plymouth on Good Friday, 2013, it was bitterly cold with a cruel wind. I was well wrapped up and warm enough, but I realised my iPhone was losing charge at an alarming rate. I kept checking it but, somewhere around the 20% battery mark, my phone turned itself off and refused to turn back on.

Disaster! I was relying on a phone call to fix a rendezvous point with my husband when I reached Plymouth. In such a big city, how would we find each other?

I realised the phone's case felt like a block of ice in my hands. If I warmed it up, could I coax it back to life and make that important phone call? It was worth a try. The warmest place I could think of was inside my bra and, by the time I reached Plymouth, my phone had warmed up nicely and was working again. Problem solved.

Later, I checked the web for iPhone information and discovered that the recommended temperature operating range is between 0° and 35° Celsius (that's 32° and 95° Fahrenheit). The reason? The phone's lithium-ion (li-ion) batteries can become permanently damaged in extremes of heat or cold, and for this reason, your phone is programmed to shut down to protect itself.[254] The vast majority of smartphones use the same li-ion batteries and have similar failsafe mechanisms.

TOP TIP: On a cold day, carry your mobile in an inner pocket, close to your body.

No Phone Credit?

In an emergency, even if you have no credit left on your Pay-as-you-go phone, you can ring 999 or 112 and still get through. (Remember, this will only work if there is a mobile phone mast somewhere in the vicinity.) It's important to give the 999 service as much detail as you can on that first phone call, or ring them back if you remember something important to tell them. Why? Because although you can contact them with no credit, they can't contact you.

For lesser medical emergencies, you can ring 111, the number for urgent but non-emergency healthcare across England. This will work if you have at least 1p of credit left, but you may not be able to get through if you have run out completely.

For non-emergency police help, you can phone 101 from anywhere in England, Wales or Scotland. This requires at least 15p (at the time of writing) of credit on your phone.[255]

Meeting Places and Route Cards

The above advice covers some of the common mobile phone problems you might run across on your walking expeditions.

There are other things that could happen, of course. You could fall over and damage your phone. Or lose it. Or drop it in water. Or get it drenched in an unexpected rainstorm. Our phones are wonderful, but we can't rely on them 100% of the time.

For this reason, it makes sense to take the following precautions:

- Arrange a designated meeting place in advance if you are planning on meeting up with a friend who is either supplying you with hospitality or transport back home.
- Let your nearest and dearest have an itinerary, so that they know roughly where you should be at any given time.
- If staying away from home, leave information with your B&B or hotel, just in case something happens. They should know what time you are expecting to return and, importantly, what to do and who to contact if you don't reappear.

The simplest way to inform people of your walking plans is to use a special form known as a route card.

Route Cards

Ideally, any walker planning a long hike should fill out a walking itinerary form or route card. The Walkhighlands website promotes safe walking in Scotland and provides a couple of template forms you can use.

1. The **Clive Form**. This is named after an experienced hill-walker and journalist, Clive Dennier, who disappeared and died while walking in the Highlands.[256]
2. The **Going to the Hills Form**. The Scottish mountain rescue organisations promote this form, which is similar to the Clive Form but requires a little more information.

Both these forms can be downloaded from www.walkhighlands.co.uk/safety/.

There are many other, and far more complicated, route cards you can fill out, designed primarily for mountain and wilderness walking, and containing much unnecessary information as far as coastal walking is concerned. These two forms (the Clive Form and Going to the Hills Form) contain the essentials and are all you need for most coastal walks in England.

Location Tracker Apps

For additional safety, you can have a location tracker app running on your smartphone. This is an app that shares your location with designated friends or family members, who can track your movements by using the same app on their smartphone.

Examples of the tracker apps are Glympse,[257] Life360 Family Locator,[258] and Phone Tracker.[259] Find My Friends is an Apple app that comes preinstalled on the iPhone.[260] There is an alternative Android version available.[261]

The ViewRanger app has an in-built BuddyBeacon, which allows someone to track you via the ViewRanger website, as long as you supply your buddy with your PIN number.[262]

It's also possible to use Google+ to display your location. To do this, you need to have a Google+ account and set up location sharing in the 'Personal Info and Privacy' section of your account.[263]

I don't use one of these apps, so can't pick one to recommend, but suggest the following steps.

1. Choose an app that doesn't broadcast your whereabouts to the world, only to your chosen contacts.
2. Agree in advance with your contacts which app to use.
3. Make sure you have *all* downloaded the app *and* know how to use it, before you set off.

Don't forget, if you have a tracker app switched on, it will eat up your battery power in the same way as Winnie the Pooh gets through honey. Quickly!

Distress Signals: Whistling and Flashing

I don't carry a whistle, but many walkers do. Why? You can use a whistle as a distress signal if you run into trouble and can't get through to 999 on the phone.

I do carry a torch and this can be used for signalling too, but will only work when it's dark.

According to the England and Wales Mountain Rescue website (http://www.mountain. rescue.org.uk/mountain-advice), this is the recognised distress signal:

Six long blasts. Pause for one minute. Repeat.

They advise you to carry on the whistle blasts or torch flashes until someone reaches you, and don't stop just because you know you've been heard or seen. Rescuers may need to use your signals to locate you.

The problem with this system is that most ordinary people don't know anything about the six-blast distress signal. Even if they hear your whistles, or see your torch flash, they may not realise you're in trouble. An alternative is to use the SOS pattern (dot dot dot, dash dash dash, dot dot dot), which is now officially obsolete, but still recognised by most people.[264]

TOP TIP: Which distress signal should you use? If I was in trouble, I would alternate six long blasts with the SOS signal.

Don't Forget the Ice

ICE stands for In Case of Emergency and is recognised across the country by the emergency services as being the contact person to call if you are in trouble.[265]

Who should be your ICE? Usually, it's your nearest and dearest: your partner, parent, adult child, best friend, etc. If this person is also the person you are walking with, you might like to have an ICE-2 as a backup. Or even an ICE-3.

Where do you put your ICE contact details?

- On your phone in your contacts list.
- On a piece of paper in your top pocket.
- On the bedside table of your hotel or B&B.
- On the dashboard of your car.
- In the information included in your route card.

Hopefully, nobody will ever need to find your ICE number, but it's a useful and easy precaution to take.

Personal Locator Beacons

Personal Locator Beacons (or PLBs) are another option. When activated, the Beacon transmits a radio signal to the UK Mission Control Centre at RAF Kinloss in Scotland, which then alerts the appropriate UK search and rescue services. Originally designed to be used on the ocean in a maritime emergency, the rescue facility has recently been extended to cover the countryside too.

If you buy a PLB unit, you must register it with the Maritime Coastguard Agency and you must also nominate and register an Emergency Point of Contact (EPOC) with the agency. The EPOC is similar to your ICE – it must be somebody who knows you and can confirm you are out walking, and that the beacon activation is likely to be a genuine emergency.

There are no subscription fees for this service.

A PLB is the most advanced safety system you can use, and it works even if you are outside of the mobile phone network coverage. It doesn't provide two-way communication with the rescue service, but will ensure an effective rescue effort is launched. The battery in a Beacon, as long as it is unused, should last for five years. Once activated, the Beacon continues transmitting until the battery runs flat. This will give you at least 24-48 hours of signalling time.[266]

I don't carry a Personal Locator Beacon. It would be just another thing to rattle around in my rucksack, and yet another electronic device to worry about. But that doesn't mean *you* shouldn't use one.

In remote situations, especially if you walk alone over hills, a beacon might be a lifesaver.

Chapter Twenty-Six

How to Keep Going

In his book, *Turn Right at Land's End*, John Merrill says, 'I firmly believe that marathon walking as I practise it is principally a mental exercise.'[267] I agree. Some of my most difficult moments have been, literally, all in my mind.

Hills

One of the joys of walking is the knowledge that over the top of every steep hill, there will be a downward slope and the possibility of a great view. But that doesn't make the climb any easier, and many of us will have experienced the phenomena where you think you are coming to the top of a massive hill, only to find you've simply reached the crest of one of its lower slopes. Ahead the hill continues, up and up, on and on.

I do think there is a golden moment when you suddenly realise you are near the top of a climb. There is a subtle change in the breeze – it feels stronger, cooler, and fresher. And then your heart quickens and your pace picks up, your muscles find a new energy. Nearly there, you're nearly there!

So keeping a positive attitude when climbing hills really helps. No hill goes on forever.

Pacing is important. I remember climbing up Golden Cap, the tallest hill on the south coast of Britain.[268] It was steep and I was tired after a long morning of walking. Near the top, a father and son overtook me. They charged past, full of energy, leaving me feeling deflated and somewhat humiliated. They were wearing sandals and trainers, both slightly overweight, and clearly not experienced walkers. How could they climb so quickly?

When I reached the top, I found the duo lying on their backs, gasping for breath. Meanwhile, I walked around, took photographs, and admired the views. Then I sat down for a quick drink and a snack and, just as I was setting off down the other side of the hill, I saw the son struggling to his feet and calling to his dad to get up.

Yes, they had climbed the hill quickly, and far quicker than me. But they paid the price.

A long-distance walker has to learn to pace himself or herself. We can't wear ourselves out with a burst of energy and spend the rest of the day recovering. As the tortoise said to the hare, 'Slowly, slowly catchee monkey.' Or something similar!

Tips for climbing a steep slope:

- Shorten your stride, while keeping a steady pace.
- Resist the urge to hurry in order to get the climb over with.
- Avoid stopping and starting. If you feel you must stop for a rest, try bargaining with your body. For example, if you climb another 20 steps, you can rest for 20 seconds. Or focus on a near goal, such as the next bend in the path or a bush on the slope ahead, before you stop.
- Think of something else, anything else, to take your mind off your aching calves and panting lungs. (Here, the tips for dealing with boring bits might come in handy...)

Boring Bits

Hills can make us pant and puff, long distances can make our feet ache, but boredom will turn our muscles to lead.

In my opinion, boredom is the single biggest cause of fatigue while out walking. An interesting 20-mile walk will seem... well, interesting and worthwhile. But a five-mile slog on a boring route will feel like an eternity.

The Dengie Peninsula is in Essex, a county I imagined to be crowded and overpopulated. But the stretch of coastal path between Bradwell-on-Sea and Burnham-on-Crouch was one of the loneliest walks I ever undertook. Lonely and boring. 17 miles (27 km) of pretty much nothingness.

You walk along a seawall covered in short and featureless grass. On one side is marshland, stretching almost to the horizon, with the sea just visible as a grey strip of water in the far distance. On the landward side is a water-filled ditch, and then, slowly rising farmland, but you won't see any farm buildings because they're tucked away on the other side of a low ridge. In fact, the only buildings you'll come across are Bradwell Power Station, currently decommissioned, and St Peter's Chapel. After St Peter's Chapel, heading south, you won't find a public road or access track until you reach Burnham-on-Crouch.

In the absence of stimuli, your brain amuses itself by inventing things, and on the day I walked this section, I was bothered by optical illusions.

Behind me, the sea level appeared to have risen and was flooding across the fields. Pulling out my binoculars, I could see submerged hedges and trees with their trunks surrounded by water. This was most alarming, until I realised it was a mirage caused by heat shimmer.

Ahead, a mile or two away, I saw a man crouching on the seawall. He appeared unnaturally motionless and I wondered what he was doing. Fishing? In the mud-filled marsh? Surely not. When I got closer, I realised it wasn't a man at all, just a solitary blackberry bush.

Later on, I saw another bush that looked, again, like a crouching figure. But, oh no, I wasn't going to be fooled by another optical illusion. It wasn't until I was a few paces away that I realised this time it really was a crouching figure or, more precisely, a young hiker sitting on the bank, staring out across the marsh while eating his picnic lunch. I don't know who was more surprised by our encounter, me or him.

He was the only person I met during that long and tedious day.

Of course, what is boring to me might be wildly interesting to you. And vice versa. For example, I like industrial landscapes. And I enjoy walking through the edge lands; those hinterlands between rural and urban landscapes, where you come across weird mechanical constructions, chemical plants, sewage works, chimneys spewing strange-smelling gases, storage facilities where jumbles of portable cabins look like giant Lego bricks, and scrap-metal yards full of enigmatic and rusting objects. Oh, and I love power stations – especially those with huge, curving chimneys.

I remember stopping near Ramsgate to take a photograph of Richborough Power Station, whose curvaceous cooling towers rose majestically above the shallow expanse of Pegwell Bay. The view took my breath away.

'Don't tell me you're taking a photo of *that*,' said a passing stroller, who clearly disapproved of my choice of subject matter. But I thought the structures were beautiful.

I once read a walking blog where somebody said there was no such thing as a boring walk. Maybe. But there are boring *bits* to any walks. That's a fact.

In her book, *The Sea on our Left*, Shally Hunt writes this about a particularly monotonous stretch of road walking: 'I had to switch on my cerebral video, write this book in my head, or make up verse and worse, just to pass the monstrous miles.'[269]

Shally was right. When the external world is boring us to tears, we have to turn inwards.

Tips for Dealing With Boring Sections:

- Listen to music on your smartphone. I don't do this myself, but David Cotton says he wouldn't have survived some sections of his round-the-coast walk without music.
- Listen to podcasts, or streamed radio programmes.
- Sing to yourself – either out loud or silently.
- Construct amazing stories in your head.
- Continue that unfinished argument with that very annoying person who has been irritating you for years.
- Write an imaginary letter to your boss/mother/mother-in-law/ex, telling them exactly what you think of them.
- Recite a poem or compose a new one of your own.
- Compose a hit tune.
- Make a bucket list in your head.
- Imagine what would happen if you won a million in the lottery, and plan how you would spend it.
- Think of what you're going to eat and drink at the end of the day.

Loneliness

If you walk alone, one of the factors you will have to contend with is loneliness. I enjoy my own company, and am quite happy seeing nobody all day. In fact, the best sort of walking – as far as I'm concerned – is where you don't meet another human being for mile after mile after mile. I'm not a total hermit. I do like meeting the occasional walker, from time to time. And sometimes, in really isolated areas, I find myself talking to the sheep.

The loneliest time for a solitary walker is not during the walk itself, but afterwards. An evening alone is much less enjoyable than an evening with companionship, especially when it comes to eating a meal. Nowadays, I'm reasonably happy sitting in a pub on my own with a bar snack, although at first, I felt terribly self-conscious. Sometimes, like Bill Bryson, I take a book to read between courses. Unlike Bill Bryson, I don't read while I'm actually eating. The evening meal is one of the best parts of the day!

I think it is easier for men, who often find a ready set of mates at a pub bar, while a woman on her own seems to be viewed with some suspicion. It must be even harder for younger women, who can attract the wrong type of attention.

For me, the best of all worlds is to walk alone but meet up with a companion in the evening (in my case, my long-suffering husband).

If travelling alone, bed and breakfast places may be more hospitable than hotels and motels. You won't find much company in the evening, because most B&Bs don't provide an evening meal and some don't provide a sitting room, but you will at least have company in the morning – either in the shape of other guests, who are usually very friendly, or the host or hostess. Hosts are often a great source of local information, although they will often insist of telling you about walks you really must do, rather than trying to help you get on with the walk you have actually got planned.

In my experience, maintaining social media connections is the key to relieving loneliness. At the very minimum, a phone helps you stay in touch via voice or text messages, but if you have a smartphone and can read and send emails, all the better. And you can't beat being able to access your friends and family via Facebook, Snapchat, Twitter, Instagram, or whatever platform you prefer using.

If you want to keep in touch with other walkers, you can do so via various Twitter hashtags and Facebook groups. Both Garmin and Satmap provide Internet forums for users to share their experiences, and plenty of other community forums exist on the Internet, including Strava, along with a host of walking blogs.

I provide links to various walking sites in the *Finding Fellow Walkers* section within the *Helpful Resources* chapter.

Overwhelmed?

John Westley, who walked 9,500 miles around the coast of mainland Britain and Ireland, said the key to facing this onerous mileage was to break it into 'manageable daily portions'. In John's case, this was 22 miles a day. 'Don't look beyond your immediate target – that's the secret,' he said.[270]

Helen Krasner saw her walk as a 'long stroll'. When she completed the Scottish coast, she writes, 'It had not been difficult on a day to day basis, but looking back, it was hard to believe it had been possible.'[271]

Bill Bryson, writing about his trek along the Appalachian Trail, noted, 'All that is required of you is the willingness to trudge.'[272]

I believe there's much truth in all three of the quotes above.

TOP TIP: If you're planning a long walk, don't look too far ahead. Keep your attention focused on the day and on the moment. Remember, walking is simply a matter of putting one foot in front of the other, and repeating this again and again until you reach your destination.

Chin Up

You've almost finished this book, and I wonder how you're feeling, because I realise I've spent the last few sections talking about the hazards of walking. I've covered some of the dangers you'll encounter, the injuries you might suffer from, and I've finished with a section on how you can cope when the going gets tough.

I really hope none of this has put you off your walking adventures. Walking is an extremely safe activity compared to most, and is certainly safer than driving a car.

Please remember, the most dangerous person you are likely to come across on your coastal walks is yourself. This book should equip you with the knowledge and skills to minimise risks and to walk safely.

As you make progress, you will find you can walk longer and further. Regular walking will improve not just your fitness, but also your sense of wellbeing. Notice how often you meet a hiker, and notice how often that hiker is smiling.

Walkers are a happy bunch of people, and I know your walking will bring you tremendous joy.

In the next section, *Additional Information*, I suggest some places you might like to start your walking adventures. Of course, you may already have a firm idea of where you're going to begin, and you may even have completed many miles by this stage. Whether you are a complete beginner, or an improving enthusiast, I wish you many happy months – and years – of coastal walking.

Section 6

Additional Information

'I dived into the library to find any books I could about the coast of Britain.'
(*Shally Hunt*, while preparing for her coastal walk with her husband Richard)[273]

Sometimes, the best way to tackle a project is just to get out there and *do* it. So, in the next chapter, *Places to Start Walking*, I suggest three areas where you might like to begin your adventure.

Although I've tried to make this book as comprehensive as possible, there is always more to learn about coastal walking and about long-distance walking in general. In the final chapter, *Helpful Resources*, I provide a list of useful sources of information, including the many organisations and websites I've mentioned earlier. In addition, I suggest a number of inspirational books written by fellow walkers.

Chapter Twenty-Seven
Places to Start Walking

When I first started walking, I drove to the coastal town closest to my home, parked the car, pulled on my boots, and set off.[274] My first walk was self-designed, using an Ordnance Survey map and following a route described by David Cotton on his website.[275] It involved a degree of trespassing, multiple blisters, and a frantic scramble to catch the last bus back.

For your first foray into the world of serious long-distance walking, I suggest you don't copy my mistakes. The English Coast Path is not yet completed, but sections of the coast do have well-developed coastal paths already mapped out for you. If you start with a recognised coastal path, your experience will be much easier than mine.

Suggested Starting Points

Here is a list of existing, official, long-distance coastal routes

- Norfolk Coast Path: 63 miles (101 km) from Hunstanton to Sea Palling[276]

- Suffolk Coast Path: 50 miles (80 km) between Lowestoft and Felixstowe[277]
- South West Coast Path: 630 miles (1,014 Km) around Dorset, Devon, Cornwall[278]
- West Somerset Coast Path: 25 miles (40 km) from Minehead to River Parrett[279]
- Cleveland Way (coastal part): 50 miles (80 km) Saltburn to Filey Brigg[280]

Below, I've made three suggestions for the start of your coastal walk. The first two are taster sessions; the third one is good place to start a serious trek. These are all places with good public transport links, and places I am familiar with, and, for this reason only, they are all located in the southern half of England. There is magnificent scenery in the north as well and you can start wherever you like. These are just some suggestions to get you going.

Isle of Portland, Weymouth (13 Miles, 1 day)

I've chosen this particular walk as a 'taster' walk, because it provides a convenient, circular route of 13 miles. The scenery is wonderfully varied and you get to experience a bit of everything the coast can offer in terms of terrain, except for sand. Shingle, yes. You'll see plenty of shingle, but no sand.

Technically an island, Portland is linked to the mainland by a causeway and the 13-mile hike around the Isle forms part of the wonderful South West Coast Path. Although the Isle feels reasonably remote, the nearby town of Weymouth is easily accessible by rail and road. Bus services connect Portland to Weymouth, or you can drive and park in Portland.

The Isle has a bit of everything. It starts with an easy march along the causeway and ends with a challenging stretch of shingle beach – which you can attempt if you want to. On the way, you will see the site of the 2012 Olympic Village, built for the sailing races, and have a view of the tremendous reach of the deep harbour, Portland Port. You will walk past both new quarries and old quarry workings, from where the gleaming Portland

Stone was transported to build many London buildings, including Buckingham Palace. You will pass close to a young offenders' prison, follow the path over high cliffs, and enjoy the magnificent lighthouse. If you wish, you can take a short detour and explore the Tout Quarry Sculpture Park.

Portland has a special feel to it. If feels a little odd, a little weird, a little different.

From Weymouth, you can walk in the opposite direction to reach Lulworth Cove, which is one of the most striking beauty spots in the UK. But, for the purposes of a one-day 'taster' walk, I don't think you can beat the Isle of Portland.

Eastbourne to Brighton (27 Miles, 2 days)

This is a challenging section of the south coast, which takes you across the iconic white cliffs of Beachy Head and the Seven Sisters. When people think of white cliffs on the south coast of England, they usually think of Dover, but these ones are far more magnificent.

In addition, you will enjoy two wonderful – but very different – English seaside resorts. Eastbourne is sedate and stately. Brighton is flamboyant and raucous. In between, there is the beautiful estuary of Cuckmere Haven, the sleepy town of Seaford, the ferry port of Newhaven, and you will cross the Greenwich Meridian at a strange place called Peacehaven.

During this section of coastline, you will need to take two inland detours to cross both the meandering River Cuckmere near the Seven Sisters, and the deep River Ouse at Newhaven. You will come across evidence of erosion and crumbling cliffs, as the limestone is gradually eroded by a milky sea. All this provides a wonderful introduction to the variety of scenery, and the different challenges, involved in coastal walking.

The total distance of the walking route between the two seaside resorts is 27 miles (43 km), which is too far for a beginner, but you can tackle it in two stages. I suggest breaking your hike at Seaford.

Brighton, Seaford and Eastbourne are all linked by rail, but the best way of travelling between these towns is by the Coaster Bus (http://www.buses.co.uk/travel/coaster12.aspx), which runs every 10 to 15 minutes and continues into the late evening.

The Norfolk Coast Path (50 Miles, 3-5 days)

Norfolk is a great place to begin your walking adventure. The route is mostly flat, with no challenging climbs, and so provides a gentle introduction to long-distance walking for people unused to hiking.

The Norfolk Coast Path forms one-half of a National Trail. (The inland Peddars Way route forms the second half.) Because the coastal section is part of a designated National Trail, the route is well maintained and signposted. You can follow the official route of the coast path, which in some places takes you on inland diversions along higher ground with good views. Or you can plot your own course and stick closer to the coast following beaches, footpaths and quiet lanes.

The other reason for recommending the Norfolk Coast Path is because the route is well served by an excellent bus service, the little Coasthopper. This bus runs along the coast road, parallel to the entire 50-mile route between Hunstanton and Cromer. This means you are never more than a few minutes' walk away from a ride back to your starting point, giving you tremendous flexibility. You can choose short walks or longer ones, heading inland to pick up the bus whenever you feel you've had enough. The service runs, roughly, every half hour in the summer, and hourly during the winter. Don't forget to check the time of the last bus before you set out.

As part of the plan to create the England Coast Path, the Norfolk coastal path has recently been extended eastwards beyond the end of the official National Trail. This new section connects Cromer to Sea Palling and beyond. But, be warned: the Coasthopper service ends at Cromer and the public transport links become far more challenging as you travel further east.

Norfolk takes a little effort to get to by car. There is no motorway link and the roads are slow, but there is a regular train service to Kings Lynn, with a bus connection onwards to Hunstanton, and another rail service runs connects with the bus at Sheringham.

The area is known for its wide skies and has some lovely, unspoilt beaches. You will come across soft sand and challenging shingle beaches, which will test your endurance if you choose to walk along them. In many places, the sea is encroaching, and you will come across a variety of coastal defences in various stages of decay, giving you renewed respect for the power of the waves.

You may meet seals on some of the more deserted beaches, and you are certain to see plenty of bird life, so don't forget to pack your binoculars.

To help plan your walking, you will find information about the Norfolk Coast Path on the National Trails website at http://www.nationaltrail.co.uk/peddars-way-and-norfolk-coast-path. You can find information about the Coasthopper bus on its site: http://www.coasthopper.co.uk.

Chapter Twenty-Eight
Helpful Resources

In this chapter, I list the resources I've mentioned previously and present them in the same order, roughly, in which I've covered the relevant topics within this book. At the end, you will find a list of fellow bloggers and a selection of walking books.

I would love to hear how you are getting on with your own coastal treks. If you have any questions to ask me, or additional advice you can add for other walkers, please feel free to leave comments on my blog: www.coastalwalker.co.uk.

Walking Organisations

Ramblers: the national walking charity: http://www.ramblers.org.uk/
Long Distance Walkers Association: https://www.ldwa.org.uk/

Other Organisations That Support Walking and Hiking

Open Spaces Society: http://www.oss.org.uk/
Sustrans: promoting cycling and walking routes: http://www.sustrans.org.uk/
The National Trust: providing some access land: http://www.nationaltrust.org.uk/
Woodland Trust: http://www.woodlandtrust.org.uk/
Natural England: https://www.gov.uk/government/organisations/natural-england
The UK's 15 National Parks: http://www.nationalparks.gov.uk
Areas of Outstanding Natural Beauty: http://www.landscapesforlife.org.uk/

Trails and Paths

National Trails official site: http://www.nationaltrail.co.uk/
South West Coast Path: https://www.southwestcoastpath.org.uk/
Wales Coast Path: http://www.walescoastpath.gov.uk/
Somerset Coast Path: search for the PDF file on http://www.somerset.gov.uk/
Sustrans and the National Cycle Network: http://www.sustrans.org.uk/
Current state of the England Coast Path:
https://www.gov.uk/government/collections/england-coast-path-improving-public-access-to-the-coast

Countryside Code

https://www.gov.uk/government/publications/the-countryside-code

Planning Your Day's Walk

Transport

Plan a train journey: http://www.nationalrail.co.uk/
Plan a bus journey: http://www.traveline.info/

Weather and Tides

Tides: https://www.tidetimes.org.uk/
Weather forecast: http://www.bbc.co.uk/weather/
Information on wind strengths: https://en.wikipedia.org/wiki/Beaufort_scale

Ordnance Survey (OS) Maps

Main website: www.ordnancesurvey.co.uk
Free and subscription OS maps:
https://www.ordnancesurvey.co.uk/osmaps/
http://footpathmaps.com/
http://www.bing.com/

OS map symbols for the *Explorer* and *Landranger* series:
https://www.ordnancesurvey.co.uk/education-research/resources/map-symbol-sheets.html

Other Maps

Google Maps: https://www.google.co.uk/maps/
Talkytoaster: http://talkytoaster.co.uk/
OpenStreetMaps: https://www.openstreetmap.org/

Guidebooks

Cicerone: http://www.cicerone.co.uk/

Access Information

Available Open Access Land: http://www.openaccess.naturalengland.org.uk/wps/portal/oasys/maps/MapSearch
National Cycle Network: http://www.sustrans.org.uk/ncn/map/national-cycle-network

Reporting a Blocked Public Right of Way (PROW)

Find your local council: https://www.gov.uk/find-your-local-council
Fix My Street, one-stop reporting: https://www.fixmystreet.com/
Report through The Ramblers: http://www.ramblers.org.uk/go-walking/report-a-path-or-access-problem.aspx

Apps to Log Your Trips

Map My Tracks http://www.mapmytracks.com/
Runkeeper https://runkeeper.com/
Map My Hike http://www.mapmyhike.com/
Map My Walk: http://www.mapmywalk.com/

Walk Jog Run http://www.walkjogrun.net/
ViewRanger http://www.viewranger.com/

Tracker Apps

Overview: http://www.cnet.com/news/location-tracking-apps/
Glympse: https://www.glympse.com/
Life360: https://www.life360.com/family-locator/
Google Friend Locator:
https://play.google.com/store/apps/details?id=com.fsp.android.friendlocator

Advice on Mobile Phone Battery Drainage

PC Advisor: http://www.pcadvisor.co.uk/how-to/mobile-phone/how-improve-smartphone-battery-life-facebook-3284240/
Tom's Guide: http://www.tomsguide.com/us/improve-android-battery,news-21193.html
App Instructor: http://appinstructor.com/blog/2014/the-ultimate-guide-to-solving-ios-battery-drain
Apple temperature advice: https://support.apple.com/en-gb/HT201678

Crowdfunding and Charity Sites

Kickstarter: https://www.kickstarter.com/
Crowdfunder: http://www.crowdfunder.co.uk/
Indiegogo: https://www.indiegogo.com
GoGetFunding: http://gogetfunding.com/
Just Giving: https://home.justgiving.com/
FundRazr: https://fundrazr.com/

Accommodation

Hotels & B&Bs

Booking.com: http://www.booking.com
Budget Hotels: http://www.budgethotels.com/
Lastminute.com: http://www.lastminute.com/hotels/
Late Rooms: http://www.laterooms.com

Specific Hotel Chains

Ibis: http://www.ibis.com/
Premier Inn: http://www.premierinn.com
Travel Lodge: https://www.travelodge.co.uk

Campsites

Camping and Caravanning Club: http://www.campingandcaravanningclub.co.uk/
Pitch Up: https://www.pitchup.com/
Campsites.co.uk: http://www.campsites.co.uk/

Hostels

YHA: http://www.yha.org.uk/
Hostel World: http://www.hostelworld.com/

Reviews

TripAdvisor: http://www.tripadvisor.co.uk/

Clothing and Equipment Stockists

Berghaus: http://www.berghaus.com/
Blacks: http://www.blacks.co.uk
Cotswold Outdoors: http://www.cotswoldoutdoor.com/
Craghoppers: http://www.craghoppers.com/
Go Outdoors: http://www.gooutdoors.co.uk
John Lewis: http://www.johnlewis.com/
Millets: http://www.millets.co.uk
Mountain Warehouse: http://www.mountainwarehouse.com
Trespass: http://www.trespass.com

For Waterproof Socks

Dexshell: http://dexshell.co.uk
Sealskinz: http://www.sealskinz.com/UK

Walking Safety Advice

General advice: http://www.mountain.rescue.org.uk/mountain-advice

Both the Clive Form and the Going to the Hills form can be downloaded from this Scottish site: www.walkhighlands.co.uk/safety

NFU advice re: cattle and dogs: http://www.nfuonline.com/science-environment/access-issues/cattle-and-rights-of-way--reducing-the-risk/

Ramblers' advice on livestock: http://www.ramblers.org.uk/advice/safety/walking-near-livestock.aspx

NHS Choices: What to do about snakebites: http://www.nhs.uk/Conditions/Bites-snake/Pages/Symptoms.aspx

Medical Information Bracelets and Jewellery

www.medicalert.org.uk
www.medi-tag.co.uk
www.universalmedicalid.co.uk
www.theidbandco.com
www.medicaltags.co.uk
www.onelifeid.com
www.iceid.co.uk

Finding Fellow Walkers

Ramblers Groups: http://www.ramblers.org.uk/go-walking/group-finder.aspx
Long Distance Walkers Association: https://www.ldwa.org.uk
Walking Forum: http://www.walkingforum.co.uk
Walkers Forum: http://walkersforum.com
Twitter tags: #walking #amwalking #walk1000miles #UKCoastalWalk
Garmin users: https://connect.garmin.com
Strava: https://www.strava.com
David Cotton maintains a list of coastal walkers:
http://www.britishwalks.org/walks/Named/CoastWalk/Links.php

Coastal walking blogs

My blog: http://coastalwalker.co.uk
Alan Palin: http://walkingthecoastofgreatbritain.com/
Babs and Nancy: https://babsandnancy.wordpress.com/
David Cotton: http://www.britishwalks.org
David Higgins: http://www.coastinground britain.co.uk
Helpful Mammal: http://helpful-mammal.livejournal.com
Jon Combe: https://britishcoast.wordpress.com/about

John Gale: http://jgacs.co.uk/personal/Welcome.html
Martyn West: http://walkaroundbritainscoast.blogspot.co.uk
Nic and family: https://thecoastalpath.net
Patricia: https://joiningthedotsblogdotcom.wordpress.com
Pete Hill: http://gbcoastwalk.com/
Philip Williams: http://philipwilliams.uk.com
Quintin Lake: https://theperimeter.uk/
Ted Richards: http://walesenglandcoastalwalk.blogspot.co.uk/

Books About Walking

Coast Walking

I've Seen Granny Vera by Vera Andrews
The Sea on Our Left by Shally Hunt
Shake Well Before Use by Tom Isaacs
Midges, Maps and Muesli by Helen Krasner
Turn Right at Land's End by John Merrill
Two Feet, Four Paws by Spud Talbot-Ponsonby
A Bit Far for You Dear by Jannina Treadwell
And the Road Below by John Westley

Specific Sections of Coast

Essex Coast Walk by Peter Caton
Exmouth and Plymouth by Gary Holpin

Walking in General

Rambling The Beginner's Bible by John Bainbridge
A Walk in the Woods by Bill Bryson
Clear Waters Rising by Nicholas Crane
Strolling with John by John Merrill
On Walking by Phil Smith
Wanderlust: A History of Walking by Rebecca Solnit
Wild: A Journey from Lost to Found by Cheryl Strayed

Acknowledgements

Any book requires input from a variety of sources, and this book is no different.

I would like to thank my wonderful husband, John Fields, for his love, support and commitment over the years. Without him to make my life easier, I would never have achieved so much. And thanks go to my daughters, who have tolerated their mother's mad escapades with great patience and mild amusement.

My coastal walking would have been far more difficult without the help and guidance of many other walkers, too numerous to mention, who have supplied both practical help and encouragement. Special thanks go to John Merrill, Helen Krasner, David Cotton, Andy Philips, Alan Palin, and Jon Combe, who walked ahead, and whose experiences have guided my own steps. In reality, every commentator on my blog has helped through their continual support and wise advice. Although I walk alone, I've never been without virtual companionship.

Also, I owe much gratitude to the walking community of women who have inspired me, with special thanks to Marie Keates, who also walks alone, and her Facebook community.

Finally, I'm grateful for the support of my editor, Leila Dewji, without whose enthusiastic encouragement, and ability to slip deadlines, this book would never have been published.

About the Author

At this point, it is normal for the author to write about his or herself in the third person.

For example: 'Ruth is a staggeringly brilliant writer whose prose is dripping with poignant beauty.'

This is a peculiar convention, since everyone knows that an author's bio is written by the author. So, I will discard the traditional approach and just tell you about myself.

I had been a family GP for 25 years and a senior manager in the NHS for 10 years, before returning to my first career choice – writing. I've recently completed a degree in Creative Writing at Birkbeck, University of London, and have been lucky enough to have a few short pieces published in various journals and magazines.

My main supporter is my wonderful husband, with whom I've produced three beautiful girls, who have grown up to be reasonably well-balanced adults.

I live in the historic Lincolnshire town of Stamford, a place that is about as far removed from the sea as you can get in the United Kingdom. But I love the coast, and in April 2010, I began walking the Norfolk Coast Path and found I couldn't stop. Since then, I've been making my way (very slowly) around the coastline of Britain. I've completed over 2,000 miles of the UK coastline, and am still walking.

You can find me in various places on the Internet:
http://ruthlivingstone.net is my writing blog.
http://coastalwalker.co.uk is where I blog about my walk.
Or you can contact me on Twitter: @RuthlessTweets.

Other walking publications:
Soggy Socks: A Rainy Day Walk to Porthallow. Published 2015
How to Treat Blisters: A Handbook for Walkers. Publication 2016
Walking in England: A Guide for Americans. Publication 2016

Index

References and endnotes

Section 1

1   'Health Benefits' page on The Ramblers website: http://www.ramblers.org.uk/advice/facts-and-stats-about-walking/health-benefits-of-walking.aspx

Chapter One

2   Steve Wright quote: http://www.brainyquote.com/quotes/quotes/s/stevenwrig128152.html

3   Helen Krasner, *Midges, Maps & Muesli* (Ashbourne: Garth, 1998) pp 9-10

4   'Country stroll tops list out (of) 40 favourite pastimes', *Newslite*, 2012: http://newslite.tv/2012/08/29/country-stroll-tops-list-out-4.html

5   'How do you bag your Munros?' by FionaOutdoors, *Scotland Outdoors* website: http://www.scotoutdoors.com/features/how-do-you-bag-your-munros

6   Haran, Brady, 'The Farm Furthest From the Sea', *BBC online East Midlands*, 2003: http://news.bbc.co.uk/1/hi/england/derbyshire/3090539.stm

7   'Overview' section on *Wikipedia* page for Mount Everest: https://en.wikipedia.org/wiki/Mount_Everest#Overview

8   'Coastal Walkers (or how they walked the coast of Britain)' page on David Cotton's *British Walks* website: http://www.britishwalks.org/walks/Named/CoastWalk/Links.php

Chapter Two

9   Poirier, P., Després, J. P., 'Exercise in weight management of obesity', *Cardio Clin.* 2001 Aug;19(3):459-70: http://www.ncbi.nlm.nih.gov/pubmed/11570117

10   'Physical Activity Guidelines for Adults' (*Factsheet 4*), Department of Health, 2011: https://www.gov.uk/government/uploads/system/uploads/attachment_data/file/213740/dh_128145.pdf

11   'Physical Activity Guidelines for Children and Young People' (*Factsheet 3*), Department of Health, 2011: https://www.gov.uk/government/uploads/system/uploads/attachment_data/file/213739/dh_128144.pdf

12   Lordan, G., Pakrashi, D., 'Do all activities "weigh" equally?' *Risk Analysis*, Vol 35(11), Nov 2015, pp 2069-2086

13   'Is a brisk walk better for losing weight than going to the gym?' *NHS Choices*, Nov 2015: http://www.nhs.uk/news/2015/11November/Pages/Is-a-brisk-walk-better-for-losing-weight-than-going-to-the-gym.aspx

14   The Ramblers Association, 'Health Benefits of Walking' factsheet, 2010: http://www.ramblers.org.uk/advice/facts-and-stats-about-walking/health-benefits-of-walking.aspx

15   Morris, J. N., Hardman, A. E., 'Walking to health', *Sports Med*, 1997 Aug;24(2):96: http://www.ncbi.nlm.nih.gov/pubmed/9181668

16   Macmillan Cancer Research and Ramblers, *Walking Works*, 2013: https://www.walkingforhealth.org.uk/sites/default/files/Walking%20works_LONG_AW_Web.pdf

17   Walking for Health leaflet, 'Walking with health conditions': https://www.walkingforhealth.org.uk/get-walking/walking-health-conditions

18   'Cancer Statistics for the UK' on the *Cancer Research UK* website: http://www.cancerresearchuk.org/health-professional/cancer-statistics

19   'Physical Activity', *World Cancer Research Fund International*, 2015: http://wcrf.org/int/cancer-facts-figures/link-between-lifestyle-cancer-risk/physical-activity

20   'How physical activity prevents cancer', on *Cancer Research UK* website: http://www.cancerresearchuk.org/about-cancer/causes-of-cancer/physical-activity-and-cancer/how-physical-activity-prevents-cancer

21   'Commuting by walking or cycling can boost mental wellbeing', *National Institute for Health and Care Excellence*, Sept 2014: https://www.nice.org.uk/news/article/commuting-by-walking-or-cycling-can-boost-mental-wellbeing

22   *Mental Health Foundation*, 'Look after your mental health using exercise', January 2016: https://www.mentalhealth.org.uk/publications/how-to-using-exercise

Chapter Three

23   Helen Krasner, *Midges, Maps & Muesli* (Ashbourne: Garth, 1998)

24   Bird Identifier facility, RSPB website: http://www.rspb.org.uk/discoverandenjoynature/discoverandlearn/birdidentifier/

25   Elizabeth's Tilbury speech, July 1588, on the *British Library* website: http://www.bl.uk/learning/timeline/item102878.html

26   'Beating the Bounds' page on *Wikipedia*: https://en.wikipedia.org/wiki/Beating_the_bounds

27   Shally Hunt, *The Sea on our Left* (Chichester: Summersdale, 1997). p 162

Section 2

28   Helen Krasner, *Midges, Maps & Muesli* (Ashbourne: Garth, 1998) p 157

Chapter Four

29   John N. Merrill, *Turn Right at Land's End* (Matlock: JNM Publications, 1988)

30   Vera Andrews, *I've Seen Granny Vera* (Clacton-on-Sea: Patrick Lawrence Publishing, 1985)

31   Helen Krasner, *Midges, Maps & Muesli* (Ashbourne: Garth, 1998)

32   David Cotton, 'Coast Walks' section of his website: http://www.britishwalks.org/walks/Named/CoastWalk/index.php

33   Shally Hunt, *The Sea on our Left* (Chichester, Summersdale Publishers, 1997)

34   *Around the Coast* website: http://www.alison-and-martyn.org.uk/

35   Spud Talbot-Ponsonby, *Two Feet, Four Paws: Walking the Coastline of Britain* (Chichester: Summersdale Publishers, 1996)

36   Jannina Tredwell, *A Bit Far for You Dear* (self-published, 2009)

37   Andy Phillips, Twitter stream: https://twitter.com/apcafc/

38   Alan Palin's website: http://walkingthecoastofgreatbritain.com/

39   Patricia Richards-Skensved's website: https://joiningthedotsblogdotcom.wordpress.com/

REFERENCES AND ENDNOTES

Chapter Five

40   'How long is the UK coastline?', The British Cartographic Society: http://www.cartography.org.uk/ default.asp?contentID=749

41   'England Coast Path' page on National Trails website: http://www.nationaltrail.co.uk/england-coast-path/

42   John N. Merrill, *Turn Right at Land's End* (Matlock: JNM Publications, 1988) p 3

43   Calculated from the 'Coastwalk' section on David Cotton's *British Walks* website: http://www. britishwalks.org/walks/Named/CoastWalk/index.php

44   Calculated from the mileages recorded in the book: Helen Krasner, *Midges, Maps & Muesli* (Ashbourne: Garth, reprint. 2007) pp. 158-171

45   Tom Isaacs, *Shake Well Before Use* (London: Cure Parkinsons Press, 2007) p 332

46   'How long is the UK coastline?', The British Cartographic Society: http://www.cartography.org.uk/ default.asp?contentID=749

47   John N. Merrill, *Turn Right at Land's End* (Matlock: JNM Publications, 1988) p 3

48   'Coastwalk' page on David Cotton's *British Walks* website: http://britishwalks.org/walks/Named/ CoastWalk/index.php Around the Coast website: http://www.alison-and-martyn.org.uk/

49   Alison and Martyn King's website, *Around the Coast*: http://www.alison-and-martyn.org.uk/

50   Helen Krasner, *Midges, Maps & Muesli* (Ashbourne: Garth, reprint. 2007) p 171

51   Jannina Tredwell, *A Bit Far for You Dear* (self-published, 2009)

52   Pete Hill, 'Pointless Stats' on *GB Coast Walk* website: https://gbcoastwalk.com/pointless-statistics/

53   Vera Andrews, *I've Seen Granny Vera* (Clacton-on-Sea: Patrick Lawrence Publishing, 1985)

Chapter Six

54   Ted Richards' blog, *Wales & England Coastal Walk*: http://walesenglandcoastalwalk.blogspot. co.uk/

Chapter Seven

55   John Merrill, *Walking My Way* (London: Chatto & Windus - The Hogarth Press, 1984) p xi

56   'The Countryside Code', on GOV.UK website: https://www.gov.uk/government/publications/the-countryside-code/

57   John N. Merrill, *Turn Right at Land's End* (Matlock: JNM Publications, 1988) p 2

58   'My Rules' page, by Pete Hill, on *GB Coast Walk* website: http://gbcoastwalk.com/my-rules/

59   Nat Severs, 'About' page on *Nomad's Land* website, 2010: https://natsevs.wordpress.com/

60   Ted Richards, 'Background' page, *Wales & England Coastal Walk* website: http:// walesenglandcoastalwalk.blogspot.co.uk/p/background.html

61   'The very loose rules' page, *B & N's Ridiculous Journey* blog: https://babsandnancy.wordpress. com/the-very-loose-rules/

Chapter Eight

62   'England Coast Path' on the National Trails website: http://www.nationaltrail.co.uk/england-coast-path

63   Wales Coast Path website: http://www.walescoastpath.gov.uk/

64   Scotland's Coastal Path, FAQ page: http://www.nationalcoastalpath.co.uk/faqs.html

65   'Scotland's Great Trails' on the Walk Highlands website: http://www.walkhighlands.co.uk/long-distance-routes.shtml

66   'England Coast Path: improving public access to the coast' on the Official GOV.UK website: https://www.gov.uk/government/collections/england-coast-path-improving-public-access-to-the-coast

67   Norfolk Coast Path on Norfolk County Council website: http://www.norfolk.gov.uk/leisure_and_culture/norfolk_trails/long_distance_trails/norfolk_coast_path_including_england_coast_path/index.htm

68   'Long-Distance Walks Guide', page on the *Suffolk Coast and Heaths* website: http://www.suffolkcoastandheaths.org/publications/walking-and-cycling-guides/long-distance-walks-guide/

69   South West Coast Path website: https://www.southwestcoastpath.org.uk/

70   'West Somerset Coast Path' PDF leaflet from Somerset County Council website: www.somerset.gov.uk/EasySiteWeb/GatewayLink.aspx?alId=41825

71   'Cleveland Way' on the National Trails website: http://www.nationaltrail.co.uk/cleveland-way

72   'Coastal Access Completion by 2020 – Provisional Timings and Stretches,' map by Natural England, Feb 2016: GOV.UK website: https://www.gov.uk/government/uploads/system/uploads/attachment_data/file/500418/coastal-access-england-map.pdf

73   'Wales' new coast path still makes walkers tread 170 miles of roads' on *WalesOnline* website: http://www.walesonline.co.uk/news/wales-news/wales-new-coast-path-still-1837225

74   'Saxon Shore Way' page on the Kent Ramblers website: http://www.kentramblers.org.uk/KentWalks/Saxon_Shore/

75   Ordnance Survey website: https://www.ordnancesurvey.co.uk/

76   'Coastal Walkers (or how they walked the coast of Britain)' page on David Cotton's *British Walks* website: http://www.britishwalks.org/walks/Named/CoastWalk/Links.php

77   Twitter conversation with Guinness Book of Records: https://twitter.com/GWR/status/530691748524462080

78   John N. Merrill, *Turn Right at Land's End* (Matlock: JNM Publications, 1988) p 199

79   Vera Andrews, *I've Seen Granny Vera* (Clacton-on-Sea: Patrick Lawrence Publishing, 1985) p 4

80   River Thames entry in online *Encyclopaedia Britannica*: http://www.britannica.com/place/River-Thames

81   Helen Krasner, *Midges, Maps & Muesli* (Ashbourne: Garth, reprint. 2007) pp. 39-43

82   'Butley Ferry' page on *Orford and Orford Ness* website: http://www.orford.org.uk/visit-explore-stay/what-to-do/butley-ferry/

83   'The A228 and why it needs SPECS', Medway County Council leaflet, 2007: http://www.medway.gov.uk/pdf/the_a228_and_why_it_needs_specs-2.pdf

84   '15-Allhallows to Grain', blog post on Nic's website, *The Coastal Path*, 2012: https://thecoastalpath.net/2012/04/14/15-allhallows-to-grain/

Section 3

85   John N. Merrill, *Turn Right at Land's End* (Matlock: JNM Publications, 1988) p 2

Chapter Nine

86   John N. Merrill, *Turn Right at Land's End* (Matlock: JNM Publications, 1988) p 1

87   'Offa's Dyke Path' on National Trails website: http://www.nationaltrail.co.uk/offas-dyke-path/

88   'Hadrian's Wall Path' on National Trails website: http://www.nationaltrail.co.uk/hadrians-wall-path/

89   Henry David Thoreau, Walden, *The Duty of Civil Disobedience*, first published 1854: http://www.gutenberg.org/

90   Shally Hunt, *The Sea on our Left* (Chichester, Summersdale Publishers, 1997)

91   John N. Merrill, *Strolling with John* (Matlock: JNM Publications, 2nd edition 1987) p 3

92   'National Railcard' page on the National Rail website: http://www.nationalrail.co.uk/times_fares/46540.aspx

93   'Apply for an older person's bus pass' page on the GOV.UK website: https://www.gov.uk/apply-for-elderly-person-bus-pass

94   Helen Krasner, *Midges, Maps & Muesli* (Ashbourne: Garth, 1998)

95   Vera Andrews, *I've Seen Granny Vera* (Clacton-on-Sea: Patrick Lawrence Publishing, 1985)

96   Vera Andrews, *I've Seen Granny Vera* (Clacton-on-Sea: Patrick Lawrence Publishing, 1985) p 145

97   Vera Andrews, *I've Seen Granny Vera* (Clacton-on-Sea: Patrick Lawrence Publishing, 1985) p 145

98   Just Giving website: https://home.justgiving.com/

99   'One Woman Walks Wales' on KickStarter: https://www.kickstarter.com/projects/onewomanwalkswales/one-woman-walks-wales/

Chapter Ten

100   'Walk #253: Kings Lynn to Hunstanton' on David Cotton's *British Walks* website (posted 2002): http://www.britishwalks.org/walks/2002/253.php

101   Map My Walk website: http://www.mapmywalk.com/

102   Google Maps: https://www.google.com/maps/

103   John N. Merrill, *Strolling with John* (Matlock: JNM Publications, 2nd edition 1987) p 17

104   John N. Merrill, *Turn Right at Land's End* (Matlock: JNM Publications, 1988) p 3

105   'Naismith's Rule' *Wikipedia* page: https://en.wikipedia.org/wiki/Naismith%27s_rule

106   'Eric Langmuir', Obituaries, *The Guardian*, by Ed Douglas, 2005: http://www.theguardian.com/news/2005/sep/27/guardianobituaries.mainsection

107   Langmuir's correction to Naismith's Rule: https://en.wikipedia.org/wiki/Naismith%27s_rule

108   'How to Train for a Marathon', *Runner's World* website: http://www.runnersworld.com/tag/marathon-training

109   'Beginner Marathon Program', *Cool Running* website: http://www.coolrunning.com/engine/2/2_4/130.shtml

110   'Training Plan: your first marathon', Training Schedule, *Women's Running*: http://cdn.womensrunning.competitor.com/wp-content/uploads/2012/11/First-Marathon-Training-Plan-2.pdf

111   'In The Long Run', by Hal Higdon and Bud Baldaro, *Runners World* (2002): http://www.runnersworld.co.uk/general/in-the-long-run/163.html

112 'Marathon long runs' on *Runners Connect* website: https://runnersconnect.net/running-training-articles/marathon-long-runs/

Chapter Eleven

113 'Overview. Rights of way and accessing land' on the GOV.UK website: https://www.gov.uk/right-of-way-open-access-land/overview

114 'Use public rights of way. Rights of way and accessing land' on the GOV.UK website: https://www.gov.uk/right-of-way-open-access-land/use-public-rights-of-way

115 'Rules for Pedestrians. General Guidance.' in The Highway Code on the GOV.UK website: https://www.gov.uk/guidance/the-highway-code/rules-for-pedestrians-1-to-35

116 'About the National Cycle Network' on the Sustrans website: http://www.sustrans.org.uk/ncn/map/national-cycle-network/about-network

117 'Countryside and Rights of Way Act 2000', on legislation.gov.uk website: http://www.legislation.gov.uk/ukpga/2000/37/contents

118 National Parks website: http://www.nationalparks.gov.uk/

119 Areas of Outstanding Natural Beauty: http://www.landscapesforlife.org.uk/

120 'National Nature Reserves in England' on the GOV.UK website: https://www.gov.uk/government/collections/t/heritage-coasts-definition-purpose-and-natural-englands-role

121 'Sites of Special Scientific Interest' on the GOV.UK website: https://www.gov.uk/guidance/protected-areas-sites-of-special-scientific-interest

122 'Heritage Coasts' on the GOV.UK website: https://www.gov.uk/government/publications/heritage-coasts-protecting-undeveloped-coast

123 'Environmentally Sensitive Area', on *Nature Net*: http://naturenet.net/status/esa.html

124 Marine Conservation Zones, page on Wildlife Trusts website: http://www.wildlifetrusts.org/mcz

125 'National Scenic Areas' on Scottish Natural Heritage website: http://www.snh.gov.uk/protecting-scotlands-nature/protected-areas/national-designations/nsa/

126 Ramsar website: http://www.ramsar.org/

127 'Heritage Coasts' by David Ross, on *Britain Express* site: http://www.britainexpress.com/countryside/coast/index.htm

128 'The Lizard' page on *Wikipedia*: https://en.wikipedia.org/wiki/The_Lizard

129 'The Lizard Heritage Coast' by David Ross, on *Britain Express* website: http://www.britainexpress.com/countryside/coast/lizard.htm

130 'Our Coastal Portfolio' on The Crown Estate's website: http://www.thecrownestate.co.uk/coastal/

131 Duchy of Cornwall: http://duchyofcornwall.org/

132 Duchy of Lancaster website: http://www.duchyoflancaster.co.uk/

133 'Public Rights of Way: local highway authority responsibilities' on GOV.UK site: https://www.gov.uk/guidance/public-rights-of-way-local-authority-responsibilities

Chapter Twelve

134 Shally Hunt, *The Sea on our Left* (Chichester, Summersdale Publishers, 1999 edition) p 10

135 John N. Merrill, *Strolling with John* (Matlock: JNM Publications, 2nd edition 1987) p 16

136 Bill Bryson, *A Walk in the Woods* (London, Doubleday, 1997)

137 'We're all about location' on the Ordnance Survey website: https://www.ordnancesurvey.co.uk/about/overview/what-we-do.html

138 'Our History' on the Ordnance Survey website: https://www.ordnancesurvey.co.uk/about/overview/history.html

139 'Minecrafting with OS OpenData' on the Ordnance Survey website: https://www.ordnancesurvey.co.uk/innovate/developers/minecraft-map-britain.html

140 'Custom Made Maps', Ordnance Survey website: https://www.ordnancesurvey.co.uk/shop/custom-made-maps.html

141 Shally Hunt, *The Sea on our Left* (Chichester, Summersdale Publishers, 1999 edition) p 10

142 Cicerone guidebooks website: http://www.cicerone.co.uk/

143 Garmin's UK website: http://www.garmin.com/en-GB

144 Satmap website: https://satmap.com/

145 Map My Tracks website: http://www.mapmytracks.com/

146 Runkeeper app website: https://runkeeper.com/running-app

147 Map My Walk website: http://www.mapmywalk.com

148 WalkJogRun app: http://www.walkjogrunapp.com/

149 ViewRanger website: http://www.viewranger.com/en-gb

150 OS Maps iTunes app: https://itunes.apple.com/gb/app/os-maps/id978307846

151 OS Maps Android app: https://play.google.com/store/apps/details?id=uk.co.ordnancesurvey.osmaps

152 OS MapFinder app: https://www.ordnancesurvey.co.uk/shop/mapfinder/

Chapter Thirteen
153 BBC Weather 'Apps FAQ': http://www.bbc.co.uk/weather/about/24085989

154 Google Maps: https://www.google.com/maps/

155 Bing Maps: http://www.bing.com/mapspreview

Section 4
156 John Bainbridge, *Rambling The Beginner's Bible* (Fellside Books, 2014) opening of Chapter Two

Chapter Fourteen
157 John N. Merrill, *Turn Right at Land's End* (Matlock: JNM Publications, 1988) p 199

158 John Westley, *And the Road Below* (Oldbury: Meridian Books, 1994) pp 198-201

Chapter Fifteen
159 'Foot Facts' on *Foot.com*: http://www.foot.com/site/professional/foot-facts

160 'Hyperhidrosis' on *NHS Choices*: http://www.nhs.uk/conditions/Hyperhidrosis/Pages/Introduction.aspx

161 'How to stop smelly feet' on *NHS Choices*: http://www.nhs.uk/Livewell/foothealth/Pages/smellyfeet.aspx

162 'Merino' page on *Wikipedia*: https://en.wikipedia.org/wiki/Merino

163 John N. Merrill, *Turn Right at Land's End* (Matlock: JNM Publications, 1988) p 199

Chapter Sixteen

164 'How volcano chaos unfolded: in graphics', *BBC News*: http://news.bbc.co.uk/1/hi/world/europe/8634944.stm

165 'Air travel disruption after the 2010 Eyjafjallajokull eruption' on *Wikipedia*: https://en.wikipedia.org/wiki/Air_travel_disruption_after_the_2010_Eyjafjallaj%C3%B6kull_eruption

166 John N. Merrill, *Turn Right at Land's End* (Matlock: JNM Publications, 1988) p 8

167 'How to choose a waterproof jacket', Mountain Warehouse guide: http://www.mountainwarehouse.com/expert-advice/waterproof-jacket-guide/

168 Nicholas Crane, *Clear Waters Rising: A Mountain Walk across Europe* (London: Penguin, 1997)

169 'Nicholas Crane Interview', *Wanderlust Travel Magazine*, Issue 74, Oct 2005: http://www.wanderlust.co.uk/magazine/articles/interviews/nicholas-crane-interview

Chapter Seventeen

170 John N. Merrill, *Turn Right at Land's End* (Matlock: JNM Publications, 1988)

171 Helen Krasner, *Midges, Maps & Muesli* (Ashbourne: Garth, reprint. 2007) pp 20-21

172 Bill Bryson, *A Walk in the Woods* (London, Doubleday, 1997)

173 Cheryl Strayed, *Wild: A Journey from Lost to Found* (London: Atlantic Books 2012)

Chapter Eighteen

174 'Dehydration – Symptoms', *NHS Choices*: http://www.nhs.uk/Conditions/Dehydration/Pages/Symptoms.aspx

175 Hyponatraemia Symptoms, *Mayo Clinic*: http://www.mayoclinic.org/diseases-conditions/hyponatremia/basics/symptoms/con-20031445

176 Almond CD et al, 'Hyponatraemia among Runners in the Boston Marathon', *The New England Journal of Medicine*, 352:1550-1556 April 14, 2005: http://www.nejm.org/doi/full/10.1056/NEJMoa043901

177 'IMMDA (International Marathon Medical Directors Association) advisory statement on guidelines for fluid replacement during marathon running' written by Tom Noakes. 2001: https://www.usatf.org/groups/Coaches/library/2007/hydration/IMMDAAdvisoryStatement.pdf

178 'Dealing with a Hangover', Drinkaware: https://www.drinkaware.co.uk/check-the-facts/health-effects-of-alcohol/hangovers/dealing-with-a-hangover

179 John N. Merrill, *Strolling with John* (Matlock: JNM Publications, 2nd edition 1987) p 18

180 'IMMDA's Revised Fluid Recommendations for Runners & Walkers', *AIMS (Association of International Marathons and Distance Races)* approved 2006: http://www.aims-association.org/guidelines_fluid_replacement.htm

181 Google Maps: https://www.google.co.uk/maps/

182 Bing Maps: http://www.bing.com/mapspreview/

183 John Merrill's chocolate consumption was calculated from 1,511 bars he claimed to have eaten over 269 walking days during his 311-day trek around the coast (he rested for 6 weeks following a stress fracture). John N. Merrill, *Turn Right at Land's End* (Matlock: JNM Publications, 1988)

REFERENCES AND ENDNOTES

Chapter Nineteen

184   'Where to "Go" in the Great Outdoors', leaflet produced by The Mountaineering Council of Scotland: http://www.mcofs.org.uk/assets/access/where-to-go-leaflet.asp.pdf

Chapter Twenty

185   Peter Caton, *Essex Coast Walk*, (Leicester: Matador, 2009)

Chapter Twenty-One

186   'Camping', Dartmoor National Park website: http://www.dartmoor.gov.uk/visiting/vi-enjoyingdartmoor/camping/

187   'The do's and don'ts of wild camping' by Phoebe Smith, *Wanderlust Travel Magazine*: http://www.wanderlust.co.uk/magazine/articles/advice/the-dos-and-donts-of-wild-camping/

188   Camping and Backpacking on Dartmoor, booklet by the Dartmoor National Park Authority: http://www.dartmoor.gov.uk/__data/assets/pdf_file/0017/43910/vi-camping_booklet_309.pdf

189   YHA website: http://www.yha.org.uk/

190   TripAdvisor website: https://www.tripadvisor.co.uk/

191   YHA Membership information: https://www.yha.org.uk/membership

192   LateRooms.com hotel booking website: http://www.laterooms.com/

193   Lastminute.com hotel booking website: http://www.lastminute.com/

Section 5

194   Jannina Tredwell, *A Bit Far for You Dear* (self-published, 2009) p 43

Chapter Twenty-Two

195   Wind speed information from 'Beaufort Scale' page on *Wikipedia*: https://en.wikipedia.org/wiki/Beaufort_scale

196   'Lapse Rate' page on *Wikipedia*: https://en.wikipedia.org/wiki/Lapse_rate

197   'Temperature' on *MountainSafety.co.uk* website: http://www.mountainsafety.co.uk/Weather-Temperature.aspx

198   'Walk – The Hangman Hills' on South West Coast Path website: https://www.southwestcoastpath.org.uk/walksdb/259/

Chapter Twenty-Three

199   Appalachian Trail Conservancy website: http://www.appalachiantrail.org/

200   'In wake of death, Appalachian Trail experts highlight need for safety' by Karen Chávez, March 2015 in *Citizen-Times*: http://www.citizen-times.com/story/sports/outdoors/2015/03/24/hiking-deaths-rare-heavily-traveled-appalachian-trail/70394614/

201   'Myths vs Realities' page on *Rape Crisis England & Wales* website: http://rapecrisis.org.uk/mythsvsrealities.php

202   'A Profile of Deprivation' on Office for National Statistics Archive website: http://www.ons.gov.uk/ons/rel/regional-trends/area-based-analysis/a-profile-of-deprivation-in-larger-english-seaside-destinations--2007-10/art-a-profile-of-deprivation-in-larger-english-seaside-destinations--2007-and-2010.html

203 'Rural and urban areas: comparing lives using rural/urban classifications' by Tim Pateman, *Regional Trends*, 2011: http://www.palgrave-journals.com/rt/journal/v43/n1/full/rt20112a.html

204 'Pembrokeshire murders background: The Peter and Gwenda Dixon murders', *Wales Online*, May 2011:   http://www.walesonline.co.uk/news/wales-news/pembrokeshire-murders-background-peter-gwenda-1835454

205 'Four brutal murders that took two decades to solve' by Steven Morris, *The Guardian*, 26th May, 2011: http://www.theguardian.com/uk/2011/may/26/john-cooper-murders-finally-solved

206 'John Cooper guilty of two Pembrokeshire double murders' on *BBC News, South West Wales*: http://www.bbc.co.uk/news/uk-wales-south-west-wales-13538545

207 Steve Wilkins and Jonathan Hill, *The Pembrokeshire Murders: Catching the Bullseye Killer* (Bridgend: Seren Books, 2013)

208 'RNLI reveal South West coastal fatality figures', *The Cornishman*, July 9th 2015: http://www.cornishman.co.uk/RNLI-reveal-South-West-coastal-fatality-figures/story-26860471-detail/story.html

209 'I've picked up 250 bodies from the bottom of Beachy Head...' *Daily Mirror*, 23 June 2009: http://www.mirror.co.uk/news/uk-news/ive-picked-up-250-bodies-401824

210 Crisis Intervention, Search and Rescue, the Beachy Head Chaplaincy team website: http://www.bhct.org.uk/wp/

211 Surtees SJ, 'Suicide and Accidental Death at Beachy Head', *British Medical Journal* (Clin Res Ed) 1982;284:321: http://www.bmj.com/content/284/6312/321.abstract

212 'Beachy Head' page on *Wikipedia*: https://en.wikipedia.org/wiki/Beachy_Head

213 'Woman killed in Eastbourne cliffs accident', *BBC News Sussex*, 15th July 2012: http://www.bbc.co.uk/news/uk-england-sussex-18847244

214 'Sundridge mother had tried to take her life before, inquest hears', *Sevenoaks Chronicle*, December 29, 2012: http://www.sevenoakschronicle.co.uk/Sundridge-mother-tried-life-inquest-hears/story-17691925-detail/story.html

215 'Cornwall cliff plunge tourist died "trying to take pictures"' *Telegraph Travel*: http://www.telegraph.co.uk/travel/travelnews/9249509/Cornwall-cliff-plunge-tourist-died-trying-to-take-pictures.html

216 'Family of Mullion cliff death holidaymaker call for better safety', *The Packet*, 30th January 2013:   http://www.falmouthpacket.co.uk/news/10192719.Family_of_Mullion_cliff_death_holidaymaker_call_for_better_safety/

217 'Nick Cave's son took LSD before cliff fall death, inquest hears' by Damien Gayle, *The Guardian*, 10th November 2015: http://www.theguardian.com/music/2015/nov/10/nick-caves-son-died-from-fall-after-taking-lsd-inquest-hears

218 'Woman describes horror as friend is killed by falling rock right next to her on beach' *South Wales Evening Post*, September 7th 2015: http://www.southwales-eveningpost.co.uk/Woman-describes-horror-friend-killed-falling-rock/story-27751717-detail/story.html

219 'Annual road fatalities' page on GOV.UK website: https://www.gov.uk/government/publications/annual-road-fatalities

220 'Cuts and grazes' page, *NHS Choices* website: http://www.nhs.uk/conditions/cuts-and-grazes/Pages/Introduction.aspx

221 'Cuts and grazes' page, St John Ambulance website: https://www.sja.org.uk/sja/first-aid-advice/bleeding/cuts-and-grazes.aspx

222 'Why Do You Get Swollen Hands and Fat Fingers When You Walk' by Wendy Bumgardner, *About Health*, June 2015: http://walking.about.com/cs/med/a/swollenhands.htm

223 'John Merrill (marathon walker)' on *Wikipedia*: https://en.wikipedia.org/wiki/John_Merrill_ (marathon_walker)

224 'How to Prevent Foot Blisters' on *Blister Prevention* website: http://www.blisterprevention.com.au/how-to-prevent-blisters

225 'Preventing Blisters' page on *NHS Choices*: http://www.nhs.uk/Conditions/Blisters/Pages/Prevention.aspx

226 'Tips for dealing with Blisters' on The Ramblers website: http://www.ramblers.org.uk/go-walking/group-finder/areas/dorset/groups/dorset-4050-walkers/tips-for-dealing-with-blisters.aspx

227 'Treating blisters' on the *NHS Choices* website: http://www.nhs.uk/Conditions/Blisters/Pages/Treatment.aspx

228 'Skin disinfection review: Review of Literature' by Health Protection Scotland: http://www.documents.hps.scot.nhs.uk/hai/infection-control/publications/skin-disinfection-review.pdf

229 'Immunisation against infectious disease (The Green Book)', Public Health England, 11th Sept 2013, p 29: https://www.gov.uk/government/collections/immunisation-against-infectious-disease-the-green-book

230 'Do I need to stretch before exercising?' by *NHS Choices*: http://www.nhs.uk/Livewell/fitness/Pages/Do-I-need-to-stretch-before-or-after-a-run-or-sports-and-exercise.aspx

231 'Does Stretching Matter?' by Elizabeth Quinn, 20th February, 2015, *About Health* website: http://sportsmedicine.about.com/cs/flexibility/a/aa022102a.htm

Chapter Twenty-Four

232 'Cows officially the most deadly large animals in Britain', by Jess Staufenberg, *The Independent*: http://www.independent.co.uk/news/uk/home-news/cows-officially-the-most-deadly-large-animals-in-britain-a6727266.html

233 'How much do cows weigh?' Aug 18th 2013 on *Dairy Moos* website: http://www.dairymoos.com/how-much-do-cows-weight/

234 'Overview of fatal incidents involving cattle' (between April 2000 and March 2015) by the Agriculture Industry Advisory Committee of the Health and Safety Executive, 2015: http://www.hse.gov.uk/aboutus/meetings/iacs/aiac/090615/aiac-paper-150601.pdf

235 'Tributes paid to former councillor, Peter Jakeman, trampled to death by cows in Ashbourne', by Joey Severn, May 16th 2014, *Derby Telegraph*: http://www.derbytelegraph.co.uk/Tributes-paid-councillor-Peter-Jakeman-trampled/story-21105328-detail/story.html

236 'Walker injured by cows on same day holidaymaker was killed near Ashbourne', May 20th, 2014, *Derby Telegraph*: http://www.derbytelegraph.co.uk/Derbyshire-man-trampled-cows-killed-man-day/story-21115215-detail/story.html

237 'Animals and rights of way', The Ramblers website: http://www.ramblers.org.uk/advice/rights-of-way-law-in-england-and-wales/animals-and-rights-of-way.aspx

238 'Cattle: vision and other special senses' on *Animal Behaviour* website: http://www.animalbehaviour.net/cattle/

239   'Ellie Crossley, the cowgirl taking on our last wild herd', by Tom Rowley, 28th March 2015, *Daily Telegraph*: http://www.telegraph.co.uk/news/earth/agriculture/farming/11502245/Ellie-Crossley-the-cowgirl-taking-on-our-last-wild-herd.html

240   'MP Blunkett injured in cow attack', 8th June 2009, *BBC News*: http://news.bbc.co.uk/1/hi/8089498.stm

241   'Livestock and rights of way – reducing the risk', National Farmers Union (NFU) website: http://www.nfuonline.com/science-environment/access-issues/cattle-and-rights-of-way--reducing-the-risk/

242   'Walking near Livestock', The Ramblers website: http://www.ramblers.org.uk/advice/safety/walking-near-livestock.aspx

243   'Dog Body Language: Play Bow', by Amy Bender, 25th November, 2014, *About Home* website: http://dogs.about.com/od/dogtraining/a/play-bow-dog-body-language.htm

244   'How to identify UK animals: Reptiles', 16th May 2013, *BBC Nature Features*: http://www.bbc.co.uk/nature/22062931

245   'Amphibians and reptiles and the law' on *Naturenet*: http://naturenet.net/law/herps.html

246   'Snake bites' on *NHS Choices* website: http://www.nhs.uk/Conditions/Bites-snake/Pages/Introduction.aspx

247   Reid HA, 'Adder bites in Britain', *British Medical Journal*, 1976 Jul 17; 2(6028): 153-156: http://www.ncbi.nlm.nih.gov/pmc/articles/PMC1687390/

248   'Snake bites – Treatment' on *NHS Choices* website: http://www.nhs.uk/Conditions/Bites-snake/Pages/Treatment.aspx

249   'Clinical Review: Treatment of Bites by Adders and Exotic Venomous Snakes', by David A. Warrell, *British Medical Journal*, 2005; 331:1244: http://dx.doi.org/10.1136/bmj.331.7527.1244

Chapter Twenty-Five

250   Vera Andrews, *I've Seen Granny Vera* (Clacton-on-Sea: Patrick Lawrence Publishing, 1985) p 145

251   'Mobile Services Map' on Ofcom website: http://maps.ofcom.org.uk/mobile-services/

252   'Mobile Phone' page on *MountainSafety.co.uk*: http://www.mountainsafety.co.uk/EP-Mobile-Phone-Voice-aspx

253   '999 or 112 – Which is Best?' on *MountainSafety.co.uk*: http://www.mountainsafety.co.uk/EP-999-or-112-Which-is-Best-aspx

254   'Keeping iPhone, iPad, and iPod Touch within acceptable operating temperatures', Apple support information: https://support.apple.com/en-gb/HT201678

255   'Telephone numbers in the United Kingdom' page on *Wikipedia*: https://en.wikipedia.org/wiki/Telephone_numbers_in_the_United_Kingdom

256   'Clive Dennier climbing safety campaign launched', Alistair Munro, 4th October 2013, *The Scotsman*: http://www.scotsman.com/news/clive-dennier-climbing-safety-campaign-launched-1-3126997

257   Glympse: https://www.glympse.com/

258   Life360: https://www.life360.com/

259   GPS Phone Tracker: http://www.gpsphonetracker.org/

260   Find My Friends, Apple app: https://itunes.apple.com/gb/app/find-my-friends/id466122094?mt=8

261   Find My Friends! Android app: https://play.google.com/store/apps/details?id=com.fsp.android. friendlocator

262   ViewRanger BuddyBeacon: http://www.viewranger.com/buddybeacon/v2/

263   Google+ location sharing: https://myaccount.google.com/locationsharing

264   'SOS' page on *Wikipedia*: https://en.wikipedia.org/wiki/SOS

265   'ICE – In case of emergency campaign' on *Smart Driving* website: http://smartdriving.co.uk/Driving/Driving_emergencies/ICE.html

266   'Personal Locator Beacons' on *MountainSafety.co.uk* website: http://www.mountainsafety.co.uk/EP-PLB.aspx

Chapter Twenty-Six

267   John N. Merrill, *Turn Right at Land's End* (Matlock: JNM Publications, 1988) p 1

268   'Golden Cap' on the Dorset official tourism website: http://m.visit-dorset.com/things-to-do/golden-cap-p1296663

269   Shally Hunt, *The Sea on our Left* (Chichester: Summersdale, 1997)

270   John Westley, *And the Road Below* (Oldbury: Meridian Books, 1994) p 197

271   Helen Krasner, *Midges, Maps & Muesli* (Ashbourne: Garth, reprint. 2007) p 120

272   Bill Bryson, *A Walk in the Woods* (London, Doubleday, 1997)

Section 6

273   Shally Hunt, *The Sea on Our Left* (Chichester: Summersdale, 2nd ed 1999) p 11

Chapter Twenty-Seven

274   'Stage 1: King's Lynn to Hunstanton' on *Ruth's Coastal Walk (UK)*, 2010, my walking blog: http://coastalwalker.co.uk/2010/04/18/stage-1-kings-lynn-to-hunstanton/

275   'Walk #253: Kings Lynn to Hunstanton' on David Cotton's *British Walks* website (posted 2002): http://www.britishwalks.org/walks/2002/253.php

276   Norfolk Coast Path information on the National Trails website: http://www.nationaltrail.co.uk/peddars-way-and-norfolk-coast-path

277   'Suffolk Coast Path' on the Long Distance Walker's Association website: https://www.ldwa.org.uk/ldp/members/show_path.php?path_name=Suffolk+Coast+Path

278   Official site, South West Coast Path: http://www.southwestcoastpath.org.uk/

279   'West Somerset Coast Path' on the Long Distance Walker's Association website: https://www.ldwa.org.uk/ldp/members/show_path.php?path_name=West+Somerset+Coast+Path

280   Coastal section of 'The Cleveland Way' on the National Trails website: http://www.nationaltrail.co.uk/cleveland-way

Lightning Source UK Ltd.
Milton Keynes UK
UKOW07f1144301017
311873UK00003B/26/P